VENTANA

THE SQL

Programmer's
Reference

Windows 95/NT & UNIX

Wayne S. Freeze

Library of Congress Catalog Card Number: 97-80785

First Edition 9 8 7 6 5 4 3 2 1

Printed in the United States of America

Ventana Communications Group
P.O. Box 13964
Research Triangle Park, NC 27709-3964
919.544.9404
FAX 919.544.9472
http://www.vmedia.com

Ventana Communications Group is a division of International Thomson Publishing.

President
Michael E. Moran

Associate Publisher
Robert Kern

Editorial Operations Manager
Kerry L. B. Foster

Production Manager
Jaimie Livingston

Brand Manager
Jamie Jaeger Fiocco

Art Director
Marcia Webb

Creative Services Manager
Diane Lennox

Acquisitions Editor
Neweleen A. Trebnik

Project Editor
Julia Higdon

Development Editor
Michelle Corbin Nichols
Julia Higdon

Copy Editor
Suzanne Rose

CD-ROM Specialist
Shadrack C. Frazier

Technical Reviewer
Russ Mullen

Desktop Publisher
Jaimie Livingston

Proofreader
Jill Greeson

Interior Designer
Jaimie Livingston

Cover Illustrator
Lisa Gill

About the Author

Born and raised in Baltimore, Maryland, **Wayne S. Freeze** currently spends his time writing computer books and developing computer software. He has written three other computer books, including *The Visual Basic 5 Programmer's Reference*, published by Ventana.

His experience with personal computers began twenty years ago when he built one of the original personal computer systems, the Altair 8800, from a kit. With a 4K BASIC in ROM and 1K of RAM, it wasn't very practical, but it was a lot of fun. Since then, he has used nearly every major type of personal computer built and currently has five different machines scattered around the house.

Wayne worked for the University of Maryland for seventeen years holding a number of positions, including Technical Support Manager for the University of Maryland at College Park's Administrative Computer Center. In that position, he was responsible for the systems programming staff who installed and maintained the MVS/ESA operating system on the IBM mainframe and advising the university's management on computer technology.

His hobbies include collecting cars ranging in size from a 1:144 scale stock car driven by Terry Labonte to a 1:1 Porsche Turbo driven only when there is no rain in sight. He can also be found at air shows photographing World War II fighters and someday hopes to get his pilot's license. In his spare time, he enjoys reading science fiction, watching stock car races, and going for long drives in the country. Now that he has started writing computer books, his spare time is mainly limited to his favorite activity: playing with his two children.

Wayne currently resides in Beltsville, Maryland, with his lovely wife, Jill, who helps him with his writing by deleting all those unnecessary commas and making sure that everything he writes makes sense. Her third computer book is expected out shortly. Wayne's son, Christopher, is four and has figured out how to crash Windows 95 on demand and is working on learning how to install his own software. Wayne's three year old daughter, Samantha, specializes in being cute and making sure his lap is never empty.

Acknowledgments

To Bill Adler, Jr. and Laura Belt, thanks for helping me to go from an overworked Technical Support Manager to an overworked writer in less than a year and a half. Just keep the new projects coming and send the contracts via TempEx.

To my friends at Ventana, especially Julia, Paulette, Neweleen, Michelle, and Jennifer. Thanks for all your help and patience in writing this book.

To Shaun, Kyle, Ian, Michelle, Wanda, Walter, Bob, Bob, Veronica, Scott, Elwyn, Rick, Walter, Joan, and the rest of my friends, thanks for your support. It means more than you know.

To Bucky and Goose, see you in March.

To Mom and Dad, here's another book. Surprise, surprise. I know that you'll enjoy reading this book just as much as my previous books.

To Chris and Sam, I love it when you scream, "Daddy's book! Mommy's book! Daddy's book! Mommy's book!" in the bookstore. Here's another one for you to find.

To Jill, six down and ninety-four more to go before we can retire (assuming that Bill and Laura will let us). Life sure is interesting around here. Take a few moments now and then to remember why we're doing this. And take time to remember this: I will always love you.

—W.S.F.

Dedication

To the memory of Tribble, my good friend and companion. I'll miss you.

Contents

Jump Tables

Alphabetical Listing of SQL Elements
(Data Types, Operators, Functions, Variables & Statements)

SQL Element	Type	Environment							Page
%found	Variable						Oracle		50
%isopen	Variable						Oracle		51
%rowcount	Variable						Oracle		51
%rowtype	Variable						Oracle		52
%type	Variable						Oracle		52
( )	Operator	ANSI	IBM	Informix	MS Access	MS SQL Server	Oracle	Sybase	50
*	Operator	ANSI	IBM	Informix	MS Access	MS SQL Server	Oracle	Sybase	46
+	Operator	ANSI	IBM	Informix	MS Access	MS SQL Server	Oracle	Sybase	45
/	Operator	ANSI	IBM	Informix	MS Access	MS SQL Server	Oracle	Sybase	46
<=	Operator	ANSI	IBM	Informix	MS Access	MS SQL Server	Oracle	Sybase	48
<>	Operator	ANSI	IBM	Informix	MS Access	MS SQL Server	Oracle	Sybase	49
<	Operator	ANSI	IBM	Informix	MS Access	MS SQL Server	Oracle	Sybase	47
=	Operator	ANSI	IBM	Informix	MS Access	MS SQL Server	Oracle	Sybase	47
>=	Operator	ANSI	IBM	Informix	MS Access	MS SQL Server	Oracle	Sybase	49
>	Operator	ANSI	IBM	Informix	MS Access	MS SQL Server	Oracle	Sybase	48

SQL Element	Type	Environment							Page
Alter Cluster	Statement						Oracle		162
Alter Database	Statement					MS SQL Server	Oracle		164
Alter Function	Statement						Oracle		166
Alter Index	Statement			Informix			Oracle		167
Alter Nodegroup	Statement		IBM						171
Alter Procedure	Statement						Oracle		171
Alter Tablespace	Statement		IBM				Oracle		181
Alter Table	Statement		IBM						172
Alter Trigger	Statement						Oracle		184
Alter View	Statement						Oracle		185
And	Operator	ANSI	IBM	Informix	MS Access	MS SQL Server	Oracle	Sybase	54
Ascii	Function		IBM	Informix		MS SQL Server	Oracle	Sybase	55
Asin	Function		IBM	Informix		MS SQL Server	Oracle	Sybase	55
Atan2	Function		IBM	Informix		MS SQL Server	Oracle	Sybase	56
Atan	Function		IBM	Informix		MS SQL Server	Oracle	Sybase	56
Avg	Function	ANSI	IBM	Informix		MS SQL Server	Oracle	Sybase	57
Begin Declare Section	Statement	ANSI	IBM						185
Begin Work	Statement			Informix					185
Between	Operator	ANSI	IBM	Informix	MS Access	MS SQL Server	Oracle	Sybase	58
Bfile	Data Type						Oracle		3
Binary	Data Type				MS Access	MS SQL Server		Sybase	3
Bit_Length	Function	ANSI							60
Bit	Data Type	ANSI				MS SQL Server		Sybase	4
Blob	Data Type		IBM				Oracle		5
Blob	Function		IBM						60
Byte	Data Type			Informix	MS Access				6
Call	Statement		IBM						186
Case	Operator	ANSI	IBM			MS SQL Server		Sybase	60
Cast	Operator	ANSI							62
Ceiling	Function		IBM	Informix		MS SQL Server	Oracle	Sybase	62
Character_length	Function	ANSI							65
Character	Data Type	ANSI	IBM	Informix		MS SQL Server	Oracle	Sybase	6
Char	Function		IBM			MS SQL Server		Sybase	63
Chr	Function		IBM	Oracle					64
Clob	Data Type		IBM				Oracle		8
Clob	Function		IBM						65

SQL Element	Type	Environment							Page
Close	Statement	ANSI	IBM	Informix		MS SQL Server	Oracle	Sybase	187
Coalesce	Function		IBM			MS SQL Server		Sybase	66
Collchar	Variable			Informix					66
Comment On	Statement		IBM				Oracle		187
Commit	Statement	ANSI	IBM	Informix		MS SQL Server	Oracle	Sybase	189
Concat	Function		IBM						67
Connect	Statement	ANSI	IBM	Informix			Oracle	Sybase	189
Convert	Function	ANSI							68
Cosh	Function						Oracle		69
Cos	Function		IBM	Informix		MS SQL Server	Oracle	Sybase	68
Cot	Function		IBM	Informix		MS SQL Server	Oracle	Sybase	69
Counter	Data Type				MS Access				8
Count	Function	ANSI	IBM	Informix		MS SQL Server	Oracle	Sybase	70
Create Bufferpool	Statement		IBM						191
Create Cluster	Statement						Oracle		192
Create Controlfile	Statement						Oracle		194
Create Database	Statement		IBM	Informix		MS SQL Server	Oracle		195
Create Default	Statement					MS SQL Server		Sybase	198
Create Distinct Type	Statement		IBM						199
Create Event Monitor	Statement		IBM						200
Create Function	Statement		IBM				Oracle		202
Create Index	Statement		IBM	Informix	MS Access	MS SQL Server	Oracle	Sybase	207
Create Nodegroup	Statement		IBM						212
Create Procedure	Statement		IBM	Informix		MS SQL Server	Oracle		212
Create Rule	Statement					MS SQL Server		Sybase	217
Create Schema	Statement		IBM	Informix			Oracle		218
Create Synonym	Statement		IBM	Informix			Oracle		219
Create Tablespace	Statement		IBM						227
Create Table	Statement		IBM						220
Create Trigger	Statement		IBM						232
Create View	Statement		IBM	Informix		MS SQL Server	Oracle	Sybase	236
Currency	Data Type				MS Access				9
Current Date	Variable		IBM						72
Current Degree	Variable		IBM						72
Current Explain Mode	Variable		IBM						73
Current Explain Snapshot	Variable		IBM						73

SQL Element	Type	Environment					Page
Current Function Path	Variable		IBM				74
Current Node	Variable		IBM				74
Current Query Optimization	Variable		IBM				75
Current Server	Variable		IBM				75
Current Timestamp	Variable		IBM				76
Current Timezone	Variable		IBM				77
Current Time	Variable		IBM				76
Current_date	Variable	ANSI					72
Current_timestamp	Variable	ANSI			MS SQL Server	Sybase	77
Current_time	Variable	ANSI					76
Current_user	Variable	ANSI			MS SQL Server	Sybase	77
Datetime	Data Type			Informix	MS Access	MS SQL Server	Sybase	10
Date	Data Type	ANSI	IBM	Informix		Oracle		9
Date	Function		IBM				78
Dayname	Function		IBM				80
Dayofweek	Function		IBM				80
Dayofyear	Function		IBM				81
Days	Function		IBM				81
Day	Function		IBM				79
Dbansiwarn	Variable			Informix			82
Dbapicode	Variable			Informix			82
Dbblobbuf	Variable			Informix			82
Dbclob	Data Type		IBM				11
Dbclob	Function		IBM				83
Dbdate	Variable			Informix			83
Dbdelimiter	Variable			Informix			84
Dbedit	Variable			Informix			84
Dblang	Variable			Informix			84
Dbmoney	Variable			Informix			85
Dbnls	Variable			Informix			85
Dbpath	Variable			Informix			86
Dbspacetemp	Variable			Informix			86
Dbtime	Variable			Informix			87
Dbupspace	Variable			Informix			88
Decimal	Data Type	ANSI	IBM	Informix	MS Access	MS SQL Server	Sybase	12
Decimal	Function		IBM				88

SQL Element	Type	Environment							Page
Declare Cursor	Statement	ANSI	IBM	Informix		MS SQL Server	Oracle	Sybase	237
Degrees	Function		IBM			MS SQL Server		Sybase	89
Delete	Statement		IBM	Informix	MS Access	MS SQL Server	Oracle	Sybase	238
Delimident	Variable			Informix					89
Describe	Statement		IBM				Oracle		238
Difference	Function		IBM			MS SQL Server			90
Digits	Function		IBM						90
Disconnect	Statement	ANSI	IBM	Informix		MS SQL Server	Oracle	Sybase	239
Double Precision	Data Type	ANSI	IBM	Informix	MS Access	MS SQL Server	Oracle	Sybase	13
Double	Function		IBM						91
Drop Bufferpool	Statement		IBM						240
Drop Cluster	Statement						Oracle		240
Drop Database	Statement		IBM	Informix		MS SQL Server	Oracle		241
Drop Default	Statement					MS SQL Server		Sybase	241
Drop Distinct Type	Statement		IBM						242
Drop Event Monitor	Statement		IBM						242
Drop Function	Statement		IBM				Oracle		243
Drop Index	Statement		IBM	Informix	MS Access	MS SQL Server	Oracle	Sybase	243
Drop Nodegroup	Statement		IBM						244
Drop Package	Statement						Oracle		244
Drop Procedure	Statement		IBM	Informix		MS SQL Server	Oracle	Sybase	245
Drop Rule	Statement					MS SQL Server		Sybase	245
Drop Schema	Statement		IBM	Informix			Oracle		246
Drop Synonym	Statement		IBM	Informix			Oracle		246
Drop Tablespace	Statement		IBM				Oracle		247
Drop Table	Statement		IBM	Informix	MS Access	MS SQL Server	Oracle	Sybase	247
Drop Trigger	Statement		IBM	Informix		MS SQL Server	Oracle	Sybase	248
Drop View	Statement		IBM	Informix		MS SQL Server	Oracle	Sybase	248
End Declare Section	Statement	ANSI	IBM						248
Event_mon_state	Function		IBM						92
Execute Procedure	Statement			Informix					250
Execute	Statement		IBM	Informix		MS SQL Server	Oracle	Sybase	249
Exists	Operator	ANSI	IBM	Informix	MS Access	MS SQL Server	Oracle	Sybase	92
Exp	Function		IBM	Informix		MS SQL Server	Oracle	Sybase	93
Extract	Function	ANSI							93
Fetch	Statement		IBM	Informix			Oracle	Sybase	250

SQL Element	Type	Environment							Page
Fet_buf_size	Variable			Informix					94
Float	Data Type	ANSI	IBM	Informix	MS Access	MS SQL Server	Oracle	Sybase	14
Float	Function		IBM						94
Floor	Function		IBM	Informix		MS SQL Server	Oracle	Sybase	95
Flush	Statement			Informix					251
Free Locator	Statement		IBM						252
Free	Statement			Informix					252
Generate_unique	Function		IBM						96
Grant	Statement		IBM	Informix		MS SQL Server	Oracle	Sybase	252
Graphic	Data Type		IBM						15
Graphic	Function		IBM						96
Guid	Data Type				MS Access				16
Hextoraw	Function						Oracle		97
Hex	Function		IBM						97
Hour	Function		IBM						98
Identity	Data Type							Sybase	16
Image	Data Type					MS SQL Server		Sybase	17
Include	Statement		IBM						255
Informixconretry	Variable			Informix					100
Informixcontime	Variable			Informix					100
Informixdir	Variable			Informix					100
Informixserver	Variable			Informix					101
Informixserver	Variable			Informix					101
Informixstacksize	Variable			Informix					101
Info	Statement			Informix					255
Insert	Function		IBM						102
Insert	Statement		IBM	Informix	MS Access	MS SQL Server	Oracle	Sybase	256
Integer	Data Type	ANSI	IBM	Informix	MS Access	MS SQL Server	Oracle	Sybase	17
Integer	Function		IBM						103
Interval	Data Type	ANSI		Informix					18
In	Operator	ANSI	IBM	Informix	MS Access	MS SQL Server	Oracle	Sybase	99
Julian_day	Function		IBM						104
Lang	Variable			Informix					104
Lcase	Function		IBM						108
Lc_collate	Variable			Informix					105
Lc_ctype	Variable			Informix					106

SQL Element	Type	Environment							Page
Lc_monetary	Variable		Informix						106
Lc_numeric	Variable		Informix						107
Lc_time	Variable		Informix						107
Left	Function		IBM						109
Length	Function		IBM	Informix			Oracle		110
Like	Operator	ANSI	IBM	Informix	MS Access	MS SQL Server	Oracle	Sybase	110
Load From	Statement			Informix					258
Locate	Function		IBM						111
Lock Table	Statement		IBM	Informix			Oracle		258
Log10	Function		IBM			MS SQL Server		Sybase	112
Log	Function		IBM	Informix	MS Access	MS SQL Server	Oracle	Sybase	112
Long Raw	Data Type		IBM						19
Long Varchar	Data Type		IBM						20
Long Vargraphic	Data Type		IBM						21
Longbinary	Data Type				MS Access				22
Long_varchar	Function		IBM						113
Long_vargraphic	Function		IBM						113
Long	Data Type				MS Access		Oracle		19
Lower	Function	ANSI				MS SQL Server	Oracle	Sybase	113
Ltrim	Function		IBM			MS SQL Server	Oracle	Sybase	114
Max	Function	ANSI	IBM	Informix		MS SQL Server	Oracle	Sybase	114
Memo	Data Type				MS Access				22
Microsecond	Function		IBM						116
Midnight_seconds	Function		IBM						116
Minute	Function		IBM						118
Min	Function	ANSI	IBM	Informix		MS SQL Server	Oracle	Sybase	117
Mlslabel	Data Type						Oracle		24
Mod	Function		IBM				Oracle		118
Money	Data Type			Informix		MS SQL Server		Sybase	23
Monthname	Function		IBM						119
Month	Function		IBM						119
Nchar	Data Type			Informix			Oracle		24
Nclob	Data Type						Oracle		25
Nodefdac	Variable			Informix					120
Nodenumber	Function		IBM						120
Not	Operator	ANSI	IBM	Informix	MS Access	MS SQL Server	Oracle	Sybase	121

SQL Element	Type	Environment							Page
		ANSI	IBM	Informix	MS Access	MS SQL Server	Oracle	Sybase	
Nullif	Function		IBM			MS SQL Server		Sybase	122
Null	Operator	ANSI	IBM	Informix	MS Access	MS SQL Server	Oracle	Sybase	121
Number	Data Type						Oracle		26
Numeric	Data Type	ANSI		Informix		MS SQL Server		Sybase	26
Nvarchar	Data Type			Informix			Oracle		28
Octet_length	Function	ANSI							123
Onconfig	Variable			Informix					123
Open	Statement		IBM	Informix			Oracle	Sybase	259
Or	Operator	ANSI	IBM	Informix	MS Access	MS SQL Server	Oracle	Sybase	123
Output	Statement			Informix					260
Partition	Function		IBM						125
Path	Variable			Informix					125
Pi	Function					MS SQL Server		Sybase	125
Position	Function	ANSI							126
Posstr	Function		IBM						126
Power	Function		IBM	Informix		MS SQL Server	Oracle	Sybase	127
Prepare	Statement		IBM	Informix			Oracle	Sybase	260
Put	Statement			Informix					261
Quarter	Function		IBM						128
Radians	Function		IBM			MS SQL Server		Sybase	128
Raiserror	Statement					MS SQL Server			261
Raise_error	Function		IBM						128
Rand	Function		IBM	Informix		MS SQL Server		Sybase	129
Raw	Data Type		IBM						29
Real	Data Type	ANSI	IBM	Informix	MS Access	MS SQL Server	Oracle	Sybase	30
Real	Function		IBM						129
Recover	Statement						Oracle		262
Release	Statement		IBM						263
Rename Column	Statement			Informix					263
Rename Database	Statement			Informix					264
Rename Table	Statement		IBM	Informix					264
Repeat	Function		IBM						130
Replace	Function		IBM						130
Revoke	Statement		IBM	Informix			Oracle	Sybase	265
Right	Function		IBM						131
Rollback	Statement	ANSI	IBM	Informix			Oracle	Sybase	267

SQL Element	Type	Environment						Page
Timestamp	Data Type	ANSI	IBM			MS SQL Server	Sybase	37
Timestamp	Function		IBM					143
Time	Data Type	ANSI	IBM					36
Time	Function		IBM					142
Tinyint	Data Type					MS SQL Server	Sybase	37
To_binary_integer	Function						Oracle	145
To_char	Function						Oracle	145
To_date	Function						Oracle	148
To_multi_byte	Function						Oracle	150
To_number	Function						Oracle	150
To_single_byte	Function						Oracle	150
Translate	Function	ANSI						151
Translate	Function		IBM					151
Trim	Function	ANSI						152
Truncate Table	Statement					MS SQL Server	Sybase	279
Truncate	Function		IBM					154
Ucase	Function		IBM					154
Unlock Table	Statement			Informix				280
Update Statistics	Statement			Informix		MS SQL Server	Sybase	282
Update	Statement		IBM	Informix	MS Access	MS SQL Server	Oracle	Sybase	280
Upper	Function	ANSI		Informix		MS SQL Server	Oracle	Sybase	155
Use	Statement					MS SQL Server	Sybase	283
User	Variable		IBM			MS SQL Server	Sybase	155
Values	Statement		IBM					284
Value	Function		IBM					155
Varbinary	Data Type				MS Access	MS SQL Server	Sybase	39
Varbit	Data Type	ANSI						38
Varchar	Data Type	ANSI	IBM	Informix		MS SQL Server	Oracle	Sybase	39
Varchar	Function		IBM					156
Vargraphic	Data Type		IBM					41
Vargraphic	Function		IBM					156
Week	Function		IBM					157
Whenever	Statement		IBM	Informix			Oracle	284
Year	Function		IBM					158

Alphabetical Listing of SQL Elements, Sorted by Type

Element	System						Page
Data Types *continued*							
Numeric	ANSI		Informix		MS SQL Server		Sybase	26
Nvarchar			Informix			Oracle		28
Raw		IBM						29
Real	ANSI	IBM	Informix	MS Access	MS SQL Server	Oracle	Sybase	30
Serial			Informix					31
Shortdatetime							Sybase	32
Short				MS Access				31
Single				MS Access				32
Smalldatetime					MS SQL Server			33
Smallint	ANSI	IBM	Informix		MS SQL Server	Oracle	Sybase	34
Smallmoney					MS SQL Server		Sybase	35
Text				MS Access	MS SQL Server		Sybase	35
Timestamp	ANSI	IBM			MS SQL Server		Sybase	37
Time	ANSI	IBM						36
Tinyint					MS SQL Server		Sybase	37
Varbinary				MS Access	MS SQL Server		Sybase	39
Varbit	ANSI							38
Varchar	ANSI	IBM	Informix		MS SQL Server	Oracle	Sybase	39
Vargraphic		IBM						41

Functions							
Element	System						Page
Abs		IBM	Informix		MS SQL Server	Oracle	Sybase	53
Acos		IBM	Informix		MS SQL Server	Oracle	Sybase	54
Ascii		IBM	Informix		MS SQL Server	Oracle	Sybase	55
Asin		IBM	Informix		MS SQL Server	Oracle	Sybase	55
Atan2		IBM	Informix		MS SQL Server	Oracle	Sybase	56
Atan		IBM	Informix		MS SQL Server	Oracle	Sybase	56
Avg	ANSI	IBM	Informix		MS SQL Server	Oracle	Sybase	57
Bit_Length	ANSI							60
Blob		IBM						60
Ceiling		IBM	Informix		MS SQL Server	Oracle	Sybase	62
Character_length	ANSI							65
Char		IBM			MS SQL Server		Sybase	63
Chr		IBM	Oracle					64

Element	System						Page
Functions *continued*							
Length		IBM	Informix			Oracle		110
Locate		IBM						111
Log10		IBM			MS SQL Server		Sybase	112
Log		IBM	Informix	MS Access	MS SQL Server	Oracle	Sybase	112
Long_varchar		IBM						113
Long_vargraphic		IBM						113
Lower	ANSI				MS SQL Server	Oracle	Sybase	113
Ltrim		IBM			MS SQL Server	Oracle	Sybase	114
Max	ANSI	IBM	Informix		MS SQL Server	Oracle	Sybase	114
Microsecond		IBM						116
Midnight_seconds		IBM						116
Minute		IBM						118
Min	ANSI	IBM	Informix		MS SQL Server	Oracle	Sybase	117
Mod		IBM				Oracle		118
Monthname		IBM						119
Month		IBM						119
Nodenumber		IBM						120
Nullif		IBM			MS SQL Server		Sybase	122
Octet_length	ANSI							123
Partition		IBM						125
Pi					MS SQL Server		Sybase	125
Position	ANSI							126
Posstr		IBM						126
Power		IBM	Informix		MS SQL Server	Oracle	Sybase	127
Quarter		IBM						128
Radians		IBM			MS SQL Server		Sybase	128
Raise_error		IBM						128
Rand		IBM	Informix		MS SQL Server		Sybase	129
Real		IBM						129
Repeat		IBM						130
Replace		IBM						130
Right		IBM						131
Round		IBM	Informix		MS SQL Server	Oracle	Sybase	132
Rtrim		IBM	Informix		MS SQL Server	Oracle	Sybase	132
Second		IBM						133

Operators

Element	System							Page
( )	ANSI	IBM	Informix	MS Access	MS SQL Server	Oracle	Sybase	50
*	ANSI	IBM	Informix	MS Access	MS SQL Server	Oracle	Sybase	46
+	ANSI	IBM	Informix	MS Access	MS SQL Server	Oracle	Sybase	45
/	ANSI	IBM	Informix	MS Access	MS SQL Server	Oracle	Sybase	46
<=	ANSI	IBM	Informix	MS Access	MS SQL Server	Oracle	Sybase	48
<>	ANSI	IBM	Informix	MS Access	MS SQL Server	Oracle	Sybase	49
<	ANSI	IBM	Informix	MS Access	MS SQL Server	Oracle	Sybase	47
=	ANSI	IBM	Informix	MS Access	MS SQL Server	Oracle	Sybase	47
>=	ANSI	IBM	Informix	MS Access	MS SQL Server	Oracle	Sybase	49
>	ANSI	IBM	Informix	MS Access	MS SQL Server	Oracle	Sybase	48
And	ANSI	IBM	Informix	MS Access	MS SQL Server	Oracle	Sybase	54
Between	ANSI	IBM	Informix	MS Access	MS SQL Server	Oracle	Sybase	58
Case	ANSI	IBM			MS SQL Server		Sybase	60
Cast	ANSI							62
Exists	ANSI	IBM	Informix	MS Access	MS SQL Server	Oracle	Sybase	92
In	ANSI	IBM	Informix	MS Access	MS SQL Server	Oracle	Sybase	99
Like	ANSI	IBM	Informix	MS Access	MS SQL Server	Oracle	Sybase	110
Not	ANSI	IBM	Informix	MS Access	MS SQL Server	Oracle	Sybase	121
Null	ANSI	IBM	Informix	MS Access	MS SQL Server	Oracle	Sybase	121
Or	ANSI	IBM	Informix	MS Access	MS SQL Server	Oracle	Sybase	123
||	ANSI							53
–	ANSI	IBM	Informix	MS Access	MS SQL Server	Oracle	Sybase	45

Statements

Element	System			Page
Alter Bufferpool		IBM		161
Alter Cluster				Oracle	162
Alter Database			MS SQL Server	Oracle	164
Alter Function				Oracle	166
Alter Index		Informix		Oracle	167
Alter Nodegroup		IBM		171
Alter Procedure				Oracle	171
Alter Tablespace		IBM		Oracle	181
Alter Table		IBM		172

Element	System		Page
Variables *continued*			
@@Io_busy		MS SQL Server	103
@@Langid		MS SQL Server	105
@@Language		MS SQL Server	105
@@Max_connections		MS SQL Server	115
@@Max_precision		MS SQL Server	115
@@Microsoftversion		MS SQL Server	116
@@Nestlevel		MS SQL Server	120
@@Packet_errors		MS SQL Server	124
@@Pack_received		MS SQL Server	124
@@Pack_sent		MS SQL Server	124
@@Procid		MS SQL Server	127
@@Remserver		MS SQL Server	130
@@Rowcount		MS SQL Server	132
@@Servername		MS SQL Server	133
@@Spid		MS SQL Server	137
@@Textsize		MS SQL Server	142
@@Timeticks		MS SQL Server	144
@@Total_errors		MS SQL Server	152
@@Total_read		MS SQL Server	153
@@Total_write		MS SQL Server	153
@@Trancount		MS SQL Server	153
@@Version		MS SQL Server	157
Collchar	Informix		66
Current Date	IBM		72
Current Degree	IBM		72
Current Explain Mode	IBM		73
Current Explain Snapshot	IBM		73
Current Function Path	IBM		74
Current Node	IBM		74
Current Query Optimization	IBM		75
Current Server	IBM		75
Current Timestamp	IBM		76
Current Timezone	IBM		77
Current Time	IBM		76
Current_date	ANSI		72

System Specific SQL Elements, Sorted by Type

ANSI SQL-92 Elements

Data Types

Element	Page	Element	Page
Bit	4	Numeric	26
Character	6	Real	30
Date	9	Smallint	34
Decimal	12	Timestamp	37
Double Precision	13	Time	36
Float	14	Varbit	38
Integer	17	Varchar	39
Interval	18		

Functions

Element	Page	Element	Page
Avg	57	Octet_length	123
Bit_Length	60	Position	126
Character_length	65	Substring	138
Convert	68	Sum	139
Count	70	Table_name	140
Extract	93	Table_schema	141
Lower	113	Translate	151
Max	114	Trim	152
Min	117	Upper	155

Operators

Element	Page	Element	Page
( )	50	=	47
*	46	>=	49
+	45	>	48
/	46	And	54
<=	48	Between	58
<>	49	Case	60
<	47	Cast	62

ANSI SQL-92 Elements *continued*

Operators *continued*

Element	Page	Element	Page
Exists	92	Null	121
In	99	Or	123
Like	110	||	53
Not	121	–	45

Statements

Element	Page	Element	Page
Begin Declare Section	185	Disconnect	239
Close	187	End Declare Section	248
Commit	189	Rollback	267
Connect	189	Select	268
Declare Cursor	237	Set Connection	276

Variables

Element	Page	Element	Page
Current_date	72	Current_user	77
Current_timestamp	77	Session_user	134
Current_time	76	System_user	140

IBM DB2 Version 5 Elements

Data Types

Element	Page	Element	Page
Blob	5	Long Raw	19
Character	6	Long Varchar	20
Clob	8	Long Vargraphic	21
Date	9	Raw	29
Dbclob	11	Real	30
Decimal	12	Smallint	34
Double Precision	13	Timestamp	37
Float	14	Time	36
Graphic	15	Varchar	39
Integer	17	Vargraphic	41

IBM DB2 Version 5 Elements *continued*

Functions			
Element	**Page**	**Element**	**Page**
Abs	53	Graphic	96
Acos	54	Hex	97
Ascii	55	Hour	98
Asin	55	Insert	102
Atan2	56	Integer	103
Atan	56	Julian_day	104
Avg	57	Lcase	108
Blob	60	Left	109
Ceiling	62	Length	110
Char	63	Locate	111
Chr	64	Log10	112
Clob	65	Log	112
Coalesce	66	Long_varchar	113
Concat	67	Long_vargraphic	113
Cos	68	Ltrim	114
Cot	69	Max	114
Count	70	Microsecond	116
Date	78	Midnight_seconds	116
Dayname	80	Minute	118
Dayofweek	80	Min	117
Dayofyear	81	Mod	118
Days	81	Monthname	119
Day	79	Month	119
Dbclob	83	Nodenumber	120
Decimal	88	Nullif	122
Degrees	89	Partition	125
Difference	90	Posstr	126
Digits	90	Power	127
Double	91	Quarter	128
Event_mon_state	92	Radians	128
Exp	93	Raise_error	128
Float	94	Rand	129
Floor	95	Real	129
Generate_unique	96	Repeat	130

IBM DB2 Version 5 Elements *continued*

Functions *continued*

Element	Page	Element	Page
Replace	130	Tan	141
Right	131	Timestampdiff	144
Round	132	Timestamp_iso	143
Rtrim	132	Timestamp	143
Second	133	Time	142
Sign	134	Translate	151
Sin	134	Truncate	154
Smallint	135	Ucase	154
Soundex	136	Value	155
Space	137	Varchar	156
Sqrt	137	Vargraphic	156
Substr	138	Week	157
Sum	139	Year	158

Operators

Element	Page	Element	Page
( )	50	And	54
*	46	Between	58
+	45	Case	60
/	46	Exists	92
<=	48	In	99
<>	49	Like	110
<	47	Not	121
=	47	Null	121
>=	49	Or	123
>	48	–	45

Statements

Element	Page	Element	Page
Alter Bufferpool	161	Close	187
Alter Nodegroup	171	Comment On	187
Alter Tablespace	181	Commit	189
Alter Table	172	Connect	189
Begin Declare Section	185	Create Bufferpool	191
Call	186	Create Database	195

IBM DB2 Version 5 Elements *continued*

Statements *continued*

Element	Page	Element	Page
Create Distinct Type	199	Drop Synonym	246
Create Event Monitor	200	Drop Tablespace	247
Create Function	202	Drop Table	247
Create Index	207	Drop Trigger	248
Create Nodegroup	212	Drop View	248
Create Procedure	212	End Declare Section	248
Create Schema	218	Execute	249
Create Synonym	219	Fetch	250
Create Tablespace	227	Free Locator	252
Create Table	220	Grant	252
Create Trigger	232	Include	255
Create View	236	Insert	256
Declare Cursor	237	Lock Table	258
Delete	238	Open	259
Describe	238	Prepare	260
Disconnect	239	Release	263
Drop Bufferpool	240	Rename Table	264
Drop Database	241	Revoke	265
Drop Distinct Type	242	Rollback	267
Drop Event Monitor	242	Select	268
Drop Function	243	Set Connection	276
Drop Index	243	Signal Sqlstate	278
Drop Nodegroup	244	Update	280
Drop Procedure	245	Values	284
Drop Schema	246	Whenever	285

Variables

Element	Page	Element	Page
Current Date	72	Current Query Optimization	75
Current Degree	72	Current Server	75
Current Explain Mode	73	Current Timestamp	76
Current Explain Snapshot	73	Current Timezone	77
Current Function Path	74	Current Time	76
Current Node	74	User	155

Informix Online Server Version 7.22 Elements

Data Types

Element	Page	Element	Page
Byte	6	Money	23
Character	6	Nchar	24
Datetime	10	Numeric	26
Date	9	Nvarchar	28
Decimal	12	Real	30
Double Precision	13	Serial	31
Float	14	Smallint	34
Integer	17	Varchar	39
Interval	18		

Functions

Element	Page	Element	Page
Abs	53	Log	112
Acos	54	Max	114
Ascii	55	Min	117
Asin	55	Power	127
Atan2	56	Rand	129
Atan	56	Round	132
Avg	57	Rtrim	132
Ceiling	62	Sin	134
Cos	68	Sqrt	137
Cot	69	Substr	138
Count	70	Sum	139
Exp	93	Tan	141
Floor	95	Upper	155
Length	110		

Informix Online Server Version 7.22 Elements *continued*

Operators

Element	Page	Element	Page
( )	50	And	54
*	46	Between	58
+	45	Exists	92
/	46	In	99
<=	48	Like	110
<>	49	Not	121
<	47	Null	121
=	47	Or	123
>=	49	–	45
>	48		

Statements

Element	Page	Element	Page
Alter Index	167	Drop Database	241
Begin Work	185	Drop Index	243
Close	187	Drop Procedure	245
Commit	189	Drop Schema	246
Connect	189	Drop Synonym	246
Create Database	195	Drop Table	247
Create Index	207	Drop Trigger	248
Create Procedure	212	Drop View	248
Create Schema	218	Execute Procedure	250
Create Synonym	219	Execute	249
Create View	236	Fetch	250
Declare Cursor	237	Flush	251
Delete	238	Free	252
Disconnect	239	Grant	252

Informix Online Server Version 7.22 Elements *continued*

Microsoft Access 97 Elements

Data Types

Element	Page	Element	Page
Binary	3	Integer	17
Byte	6	Longbinary	22
Counter	8	Long	19
Currency	9	Memo	22
Datetime	10	Real	30
Decimal	12	Short	31
Double Precision	13	Single	32
Float	14	Text	35
Guid	16	Varbinary	39

Function

Element	Page
Log	112

Operators

Element	Page	Element	Page
( )	50	And	54
*	46	Between	58
+	45	Exists	92
/	46	In	99
<=	48	Like	110
<>	49	Not	121
<	47	Null	121
=	47	Or	123
>=	49	–	45
>	48		

Statements

Element	Page	Element	Page
Create Index	207	Insert	256
Delete	238	Select	268
Drop Index	243	Update	280
Drop Table	247		

Microsoft SQL Server 6.5 Elements

Data Types

Element	Page	Element	Page
Binary	3	Numeric	26
Bit	4	Real	30
Character	6	Smalldatetime	33
Datetime	10	Smallint	34
Decimal	12	Smallmoney	35
Double Precision	13	Text	35
Float	14	Timestamp	37
Image	17	Tinyint	37
Integer	17	Varbinary	39
Money	23	Varchar	39

Functions

Element	Page	Element	Page
Abs	53	Lower	113
Acos	54	Ltrim	114
Ascii	55	Max	114
Asin	55	Min	117
Atan2	56	Nullif	122
Atan	56	Pi	125
Avg	57	Power	127
Ceiling	62	Radians	128
Char	63	Rand	129
Coalesce	66	Round	132
Cos	68	Rtrim	132
Cot	69	Sin	134
Count	70	Soundex	136
Degrees	89	Space	137
Difference	90	Sqrt	137
Exp	93	Substring	138
Floor	95	Sum	139
Log10	112	Tan	141
Log	112	Upper	155

Microsoft SQL Server 6.5 Elements *continued*

Operators

Element	Page	Element	Page
( )	50	And	54
*	46	Between	58
+	45	Case	60
/	46	Exists	92
<=	48	In	99
<>	49	Like	110
<	47	Not	121
=	47	Null	121
>=	49	Or	123
>	48	–	45

Statements

Element	Page	Element	Page
Alter Database	164	Drop Rule	245
Close	187	Drop Table	247
Commit	189	Drop Trigger	248
Create Database	195	Drop View	248
Create Default	198	Execute	249
Create Index	207	Grant	252
Create Procedure	212	Insert	256
Create Rule	217	Raiserror	261
Create View	236	Select	268
Declare Cursor	237	Setuser	277
Delete	238	Shutdown	277
Disconnect	239	Truncate Table	279
Drop Database	241	Update Statistics	282
Drop Default	241	Update	280
Drop Index	243	Use	283
Drop Procedure	245		

Microsoft SQL Server 6.5 Elements *continued*

Variables

Element	Page	Element	Page
@@Connections	67	@@Pack_sent	124
@@Cpu_busy	71	@@Procid	127
@@Cursor_rows	78	@@Remserver	130
@@Datefirst	79	@@Rowcount	132
@@Dbts	88	@@Servername	133
@@Error	91	@@Spid	137
@@Fetch_status	94	@@Textsize	142
@@Identity	98	@@Timeticks	144
@@Idle	98	@@Total_errors	152
@@Io_busy	103	@@Total_read	153
@@Langid	105	@@Total_write	153
@@Language	105	@@Trancount	153
@@Max_connections	115	@@Version	157
@@Max_precision	115	Current_timestamp	77
@@Microsoftversion	116	Current_user	77
@@Nestlevel	120	Session_user	134
@@Packet_errors	124	System_user	140
@@Pack_received	124	User	155

Oracle Version 8 Elements

Data Types

Element	Page	Element	Page
Bfile	3	Mlslabel	24
Blob	5	Nchar	24
Character	6	Nclob	25
Clob	8	Number	26
Date	9	Nvarchar	28
Double Precision	13	Real	30
Float	14	Smallint	34
Integer	17	Varchar	39
Long	19		

Oracle Version 8 Elements *continued*

Functions

Element	Page	Element	Page
Abs	53	Min	117
Acos	54	Mod	118
Ascii	55	Power	127
Asin	55	Round	132
Atan2	56	Rtrim	132
Atan	56	Sinh	135
Avg	57	Sin	134
Ceiling	62	Sqrt	137
Cosh	69	Substr	138
Cos	68	Sum	139
Cot	69	Tanh	142
Count	70	Tan	141
Exp	93	To_binary_integer	145
Floor	95	To_char	145
Hextoraw	97	To_date	148
Length	110	To_multi_byte	150
Log	112	To_number	150
Lower	113	To_single_byte	150
Ltrim	114	Upper	155
Max	114		

Operators

Element	Page	Element	Page
( )	50	And	54
*	46	Between	58
+	45	Exists	92
/	46	In	99
<=	48	Like	110
<>	49	Not	121
<	47	Null	121
=	47	Or	123
>=	49	–	45
>	48		

Oracle Version 8 Elements *continued*

Statements

Element	Page	Element	Page
Alter Cluster	162	Drop Cluster	240
Alter Database	164	Drop Database	241
Alter Function	166	Drop Function	243
Alter Index	167	Drop Index	243
Alter Procedure	171	Drop Package	244
Alter Tablespace	181	Drop Procedure	245
Alter Trigger	184	Drop Schema	246
Alter View	185	Drop Synonym	246
Close	187	Drop Tablespace	247
Comment On	187	Drop Table	247
Commit	189	Drop Trigger	248
Connect	189	Drop View	248
Create Cluster	192	Execute	249
Create Controlfile	194	Fetch	250
Create Database	195	Grant	252
Create Function	202	Insert	256
Create Index	207	Lock Table	258
Create Procedure	212	Open	259
Create Schema	218	Prepare	260
Create Synonym	219	Recover	262
Create View	236	Revoke	265
Declare Cursor	237	Rollback	267
Delete	238	Select	268
Describe	238	Update	280
Disconnect	239	Whenever	284

Variables

Element	Page	Element	Page
%found	50	%rowtype	52
%isopen	51	%type	52
%rowcount	51		

Sybase SQL Server Version 11.1 Elements

Data Types

Element	Page	Element	Page
Binary	3	Numeric	26
Bit	4	Real	30
Character	6	Shortdatetime	32
Datetime	10	Smallint	34
Decimal	12	Smallmoney	35
Double Precision	13	Text	35
Float	14	Timestamp	37
Identity	16	Tinyint	37
Image	17	Varbinary	39
Integer	17	Varchar	39
Money	23		

Functions

Element	Page	Element	Page
Abs	53	Lower	113
Acos	54	Ltrim	114
Ascii	55	Max	114
Asin	55	Min	117
Atan2	56	Nullif	122
Atan	56	Pi	125
Avg	57	Power	127
Ceiling	62	Radians	128
Char	63	Rand	129
Coalesce	66	Round	132
Cos	68	Rtrim	132
Cot	69	Sin	134
Count	70	Space	137
Degrees	89	Sqrt	137
Exp	93	Substring	138
Floor	95	Sum	139
Log10	112	Tan	141
Log	112	Upper	155

Sybase SQL Server Version 11.1 Elements *continued*

Operators

Element	Page	Element	Page
()	50	And	54
*	46	Between	58
+	45	Case	60
/	46	Exists	92
<=	48	In	99
<>	49	Like	110
<	47	Not	121
=	47	Null	121
>=	49	Or	123
>	48	–	45

Statements

Element	Page	Element	Page
Close	187	Drop View	248
Commit	189	Execute	249
Connect	189	Fetch	250
Create Default	198	Grant	252
Create Index	207	Insert	256
Create Rule	217	Open	259
Create View	236	Prepare	260
Declare Cursor	237	Revoke	265
Delete	238	Rollback	267
Disconnect	239	Select	268
Drop Default	241	Setuser	277
Drop Index	243	Shutdown	277
Drop Procedure	245	Truncate Table	279
Drop Rule	245	Update Statistics	282
Drop Table	247	Update	280
Drop Trigger	248	Use	283

Variables

Element	Page	Element	Page
Current_timestamp	77	System_user	140
Current_user	77	User	155
Session_user	134		

Introduction

After writing three books about Visual Basic, I wanted to write about a different subject. I was excited when Ventana offered me the opportunity to write about SQL. I have spent a lot of time over the years studying and maintaining database management systems and thought this would be a good opportunity to put that knowledge on paper.

I wanted to create the kind of reference that an experienced programmer would use. I got tired of flipping around through the help files and manuals and not finding the information I needed, or worse, finding too much information that wasn't useful. What you hold in your hands is the result of much time and effort to pull all of this information together. I didn't want a reference that would tell someone how to program, because they already *knew* how to program. I didn't want a book that contained a lot of fluff. I wanted a reference that would be comprehensive, informative, and concise. Something that would be a programmer's equivalent of a dictionary, thesaurus, and desk reference all rolled into one.

All examples in this book were executed on a Pentium 166 MMX system with 64 megabytes of memory and running Windows NT 4.0 Server service pack 3. While there are usually some differences between the NT implementation and the UNIX implementation of each database system, most of the differences relate to how the database is installed and tuned. This means that there are very few real differences to the SQL programmer. The differences are noted where appropriate.

Audience

This book covers the following SQL implementations: IBM DB2 Version 5, Informix Online Server 7.22, Microsoft Access 97, Microsoft SQL Server 6.5, Oracle8, and Sybase SQL Server 11.1. In order to better compare and contrast each implementation, I also included information about the ANSI-92 SQL standard. While the material in this book can be easily used by all levels of SQL programmers, beginning programmers might want to supplement this book with material that describes how to write SQL programs.

How This Book Is Organized

This book is organized into three main sections: Data Types; Operators, Functions & Variables; and Statements. Each section is arranged in alphabetical order by element. Each element contains some or all of the sections listed below:

- **Syntax**—contains an element's formal syntax (applies to statements and functions only).
- **Usage**—contains a short description of the element and how it is used.
- **Arguments**—contains a list of the arguments that are contained in the element with a short description of how they are used. If an element contains no arguments, then this section is omitted (applies to statements and functions only). This section might also include a list of constants associated with the argument.
- **Literals**—contains information about how literal values are formed in an SQL statement.
- **Implementation Notes**—contains information about the element that applies only to a specific database system.
- **Examples**—contains one or more examples that illustrate how to use the element.
- **See Also**—contains a list of elements that are similar to or related to the element.

I've added Tips throughout the book to provide useful tips or warnings about various features of SQL. Also present in this book is a series of Jump Tables. These tables are useful when you want to locate information in the book and you're not sure where to start or when you want to use a comprehensive cross-reference.

Conventions

To make the book easier to read, all SQL keywords are displayed in bold. If an element like a function contains a list of arguments, the argument names are listed in italics.

I also use three sets of symbols while describing the syntax of a function, statement, method, or event. The first set of symbols are the brackets "[" and "]". Anything inside brackets is optional.

Next are braces "{" and "}" and the vertical bar " | ". The braces are used to present a list of choices from which you may select exactly one item. Each item in the list is separated by a vertical bar.

The ellipsis "…" is used to indicate that the preceding syntax element may be repeated as many times as desired.

These conventions are used in the following example:

```
Execute
    { preparedstatement [ Using
        [ Descriptor :descriptor ] |
        :hostvar, [:hostvar ] . . .
        ] |
    Immediate :statement
    }
```

First **Execute** is in bold, because it is a SQL keyword. The arguments *preparedstatement*, *descriptor*, *hostvar*, and *statement* are in italics. The { *preparedstatement* [**Using** [**Descriptor** :*descriptor*] | :*hostvar*, [:*hostvar*] . . .] | **Immediate** :*statement* } means that you must select either the clause "*preparedstatement* [**Using** [**Descriptor** :*descriptor*] | :*hostvar*, [:*hostvar*] . . .]" or the clause "**Immediate** :*statement*". The expression [**Descriptor** :*descriptor*] means that you can include the clause "[**Descriptor** :*descriptor*" if you desire or simply skip it. The clause ":*hostvar*, [:*hostvar*] . . ." means that you can specify one or more values for ":*hostvar*" that are separated by commas.

Feedback

I love hearing from my readers, so you can visit my Web site at http://www.JustPC.com or send me e-mail at WFreeze@JustPC.com.

IBM DB2 Version 5

SQL was originally developed by IBM laboratories in the 1970s as one way to access a relational database. Since that time, SQL has been adopted as **the** standard for accessing relational databases. Unfortunately, IBM's database systems had lagged behind their competitors for the last few years. However, the latest implementation, DB2 version 5, has caught up with the competition and, in some areas, now surpasses them.

Informix Online Server Version 7.22

Informix Online Server is one of more advanced SQL database management systems on the market today. It contains such features as replication, support for SNMP, and global language support. It is available for Windows, UNIX, and Novell servers.

Microsoft Access 97

Microsoft Access is a lightweight application development system included with Microsoft Office 97 Professional. The core database engine (known as Microsoft Jet) is also included with both Visual Basic and Visual C++. While Access is somewhat limited in its SQL capabilities, both Visual Basic and Visual C++ provide full SQL support.

Microsoft SQL Server 6.5

Microsoft SQL Server is derived from an earlier version of Sybase's SQL Server. It is a high-performance database system designed to run on Windows NT Server systems. Microsoft has integrated SQL Server with the Internet Information Server (IIS) to help you build complex Web-based applications quickly and easily. While this database lags behind some of the other databases in terms of features, a new version of SQL Server is expected to be released shortly.

Oracle Version 8

Oracle sells one of the most popular database systems on the market today. It runs on nearly any computer system. Implementations are available for anything from PC systems running either Mac OS or Windows to the largest IBM mainframes running OS/390. Most users run their databases under UNIX or Windows NT. One of the key aspects of this database is its ability to isolate the client from the server. Thus, the client doesn't know if its database server is running on a PC or a mainframe. Version 8 shows that Oracle is not content to rest on its laurels and offers many new functions that puts it in the forefront of database vendors.

Sybase SQL Server Version 11.1

Probably the second most popular database system available today is Sybase SQL Server. This database offers a high degree of performance and scalability. As with most of the other database systems, it is fully supported on a variety of platforms, though most implementations reside on either a Windows NT or UNIX system.

ANSI SQL-92

The most current standard for SQL is the ANSI SQL-92. The standard is supposed to describe the features included in any SQL implementation. As is typical in this industry, the standard lags what the vendors actually implement. While each vendor's SQL implementation is generally compatible with the standard, each implementation includes so many unique extensions that it is difficult to choose which features to use. These differences make it difficult for a programmer to develop programs that run on multiple database systems. You have the choice of either using the extensions for a particular database and then writing different code to accommodate each database system, or using a subset of the SQL language that is common to all database systems. In general, using a common subset is probably best because it reduces your work, but in some cases you have to use the extensions in order to insure sufficient performance. A new version of the SQL standard is expected shortly; hopefully it will bring the various database systems a little bit closer to each other.

Data Types

1

Bfile

Oracle

Syntax   `Bfile`

Usage   The **Bfile** data type in Oracle8 represents the name of an external file containing a Binary Large Object (LOB) that is stored in a virtual directory created by the **Create Directory** command. This file is read-only and can't be modified through the DBMS.

See Also   **Alter Table** (statement), **Create Directory** (statement), **Create Table** (statement)

Binary

MS Access • MS SQL Server • Sybase

Syntax   `Binary` [(*length*)]

Usage   The **Binary** data type in MS Access, MS SQL Server, and Sybase SQL Server is used to provide an unstructured, fixed-length data type for storing binary data. This data type is similar to the ANSI **Bit** data type.

> **Tip**
>
> *While the Access database engine supports the **Binary** data type, there is no support for it in the Access programming environment. **Binary** data types must be maintained by other programming languages such as Visual Basic or Visual C++.*

Argument   ▪ *length*—the number of characters in the binary string. If omitted, this value will default to 1. The maximum size of *length* is 255.

See Also   **Alter Table** (statement), **Bit** (data type), **Create Table** (statement), **Varbinary** (data type)

Bit

Syntax	`Bit [ ( length ) ]`
Usage	The **Bit** data type represents an array of boolean values, each of which can contain either a 0 or 1 value. Any value other than 0 is treated as a 1.
Argument	▪ *length*—the number of bits in the bit array (see Table 1-1). If omitted, this value will default to 1.

Database	maximum length
ANSI	implementer defined
IBM DB2	not supported
Informix	not supported
MS Access	1
MS SQL Server	1
Oracle8	not supported
Sybase SQL Server	1

Table 1-1: Maximum length of a bit value.

> **Tip**
>
> *In order to save space, multiple **Bit** columns can be combined into a single byte of storage by MS SQL Server and Sybase SQL Server. Thus, up to 8 **Bit** columns can be saved into a single byte and 16 **Bit** columns will be stored in only two bytes.*

Literals	An ANSI **Bit** literal is constructed by enclosing the desired string of binary digits (0 or 1) inside a pair of single quotes ('') and preceded by a B. Hexadecimal values can be substituted for the binary digits if the string is preceded by an x. Thus, the binary string b'1010' and the hex string x'A' mean the same thing.
Implementation Notes MS Access	You can't specify the length of a **Bit** array. Also, a column defined as a **Bit** can't be assigned a **Null** value and can't be used as part of an index. Synonyms to **Bit** in Access include: **Boolean**, **Logical**, **Logical1**, and **Yesno**. In MS Access, the **Binary** data type is more like the ANSI **Bit** data type than the MS Access **Bit** data type.

MS SQL Server	You can't specify the length of a **Bit** array. Also, a column defined as a **Bit** can't be assigned a **Null** value and can't be used as part of an index. In MS SQL Server, the **Binary** data type is more like the ANSI **Bit** data type than the MS SQL Server **Bit** data type.
Sybase SQL Server	You can't specify the length of a **Bit** array. Also, a column defined as a **Bit** can't be assigned a **Null** value and can't be used as part of an index. In Sybase SQL Server, the **Binary** data type is more like the ANSI **Bit** data type than the Sybase SQL Server **Bit** data type.

See Also   **Alter Table** (statement), **Binary** (data type), **Create Table** (statement)

Blob

DATA TYPE

IBM • Oracle

Syntax   **Blob (*length* [K | M | G])**

Usage   The **Blob** data type represents a Binary Large Object that is stored in the database. A set of tools is provided to manipulate a **Blob** on the server or to transfer it to the client machine. Typically, a **Blob** is used to store an image, voice data, or some other large, unstructured block of data.

Argument   ▪ *length*—the number of bytes in the **Blob**.

Implementation Notes	IBM DB2	The maximum size of a **Blob** is 2,147,483,647 bytes. The size of the **Blob** is specified by *length*. If a **K**, **M** or **G** follows *length*, the size of the **Blob** is *length* multiplied by 1,024, 1,048,576, or 1,073,741,824, respectively. Also note that a Character string can be used to hold binary data when the For Bit Data clause is included.
	Oracle8	A **Blob** can contain up to 4 gigabytes of data.

See Also   **Alter Table** (statement), **Character** (data type), **Create Table** (statement), **Image** (data type)

Byte

DATA TYPE

MS Access • Informix

Syntax   **Byte**

Usage   The **Byte** data type in Microsoft Access represents a whole number that doesn't contain any fractional part. A **Byte** can only store values from 0 to 255. If you need to keep a larger number, see **Integer** (data type) or **Long** (data type). A **Byte** data type can also be referred to as **Integer1**.

The **Byte** data type in Informix represents a Binary Large Object, similar to a **Blob** data type in IBM DB2 or Oracle8 or a **Binary** data type in MS SQL Server or Sybase SQL Server. A **Byte** can range in length from 1 to about 2 gigabytes.

Literals   A **Byte** literal in Access consists of a series of numbers, such as 12 or 123. Note that commas (",") are not permitted in a **Byte** literal.

See Also   **Alter Table** (statement), **Binary** (data type), **Bit** (data type), **Blob** (data type), **Create Table** (statement), **Long** (data type), **Short** (data type)

Character

DATA TYPE

ANSI • IBM • Informix • MS SQL Server • Oracle • Sybase

Syntax   **Character** [(*length*)] [**For Bit Data**]

Char [(*length*)]

Usage   The **Character** data type represents a fixed-length string of characters. When one **Character** value is assigned to another **Character** value of a different size, it will be padded with spaces or truncated as needed.

The **For Bit Data** clause is an IBM extension that indicates that the value of the column should be treated as binary data. No code translations are performed when data is exchanged with other systems and binary comparisons are used instead of the system's normal collating sequence.

Argument   ▪ *length*—the number of characters in the character string (see Table 1-2). If omitted, this value will default to 1.

Database	maximum length
ANSI	implementer defined
IBM DB2	254
Informix	32,767
MS Access	see **Text** (data type)
MS SQL Server	255
Oracle8	2,000
Sybase SQL Server	255

*Table 1-2: Maximum length of a **character** value.*

Literals   A **Character** literal is constructed by enclosing the desired string of characters in single quotes ('). Two single quotes ('') together are used to indicate an empty string. When two single quotes appear inside a **Character** literal, they will be treated as a single quote.

An extended format **Character** literal is composed of multiple **Character** literals separated by zero or more spaces and a single newline marker. This provides an easy method to create a very large character string.

Implementation Notes   IBM DB2   **Character** refers to single byte characters. Double byte character strings are referred to as graphic and you should use the **Graphic** data type. Also note that a **Character** string can be used to hold binary data when the **For Bit Data** clause is included on the **Create Table** statement.

MS Access   Because the **Character** data type is not implemented, you should use the **Text** data type.

See Also   **Alter Table** (statement), **Clob** (data type), **Create Table** (statement), **Dbclob** (data type), **Graphic** (data type), **Long Varchar** (data type), **Long Vargraphic** (data type), **Nchar** (data type), **Nvarchar** (data type), **Text** (data type), **Varchar** (data type), **Vargraphic** (data type)

Clob

DATA TYPE

IBM • Oracle

Syntax   **Clob** (*length* [**K** | **M** | **G**])

Usage   The **Clob** data type represents a Character Large Object that is stored in the database.

Argument   ▪ *length*—the number of characters in the **Clob**.

Implementation Notes   IBM DB2   The maximum size of a **Clob** is 2,147,483,647 characters. The size of the **Clob** is specified by *length*. If a **K**, **M** or **G** follows *length*, the size of the **Clob** is *length* multiplied by 1,024, 1,048,576, or 1,073,741,824, respectively.

          Oracle8   A **Clob** can contain up to 4 gigabytes of data.

See Also   **Alter Table** (statement), **Blob** (data type), **Create Table** (statement), **Dbclob** (data type), **Nclob** (data type)

Counter

DATA TYPE

MS Access

Syntax   **Counter**

Usage   The **Counter** data type is an MS Access data type similar to a **Long,** but whose value is automatically incremented by 1 each time a record is inserted into a table.

See Also   **Alter Table** (statement), **Create Table** (statement), **Identity** (data type), **Long** (data type)

Currency

Syntax **Currency**

Usage The **Currency** data type is a MS Access data type containing a scaled integer value that ranges from –922,337,203,685,477.5808 to +922,337,203,685,477.5807. As its name suggests, it is ideal for carrying out monetary calculations because it contains an exact representation of the value.

See Also **Alter Table** (statement), **Create Table** (statement), **Long** (data type)

Date

Syntax **Date**

Usage The **Date** data type represents a year, month, and day value in the ANSI standard, an IBM DB2, or an Informix database and a year, month, day, hour, minute, and second value in an Oracle database.

Literals The ISO standard for a date is "yyyy-mm-dd" and for a time is "hh:mm:ss." The IBM USA standard for a date is "mm/dd/yyyy" and for time is "hh:mm AM" or "hh:mm PM." If a two-digit year is entered in an Informix database, the first two digits are assumed to be "19" to indicate a twentieth century date.

Implementation Notes IBM DB2 IBM implemented **Date** as a four-byte packed decimal number, where the first two bytes contain the year in the range of 0001 to 9999, the next byte contains the month in the range of 01 to 12, and the last byte contains the day of the month.

Informix Informix implemented **Date** as a four-byte packed decimal number, where the first two bytes contain the year in the range of 0001 to 9999, the next byte contains the month in the range of 01 to 12, and the last byte contains the day of the month.

Oracle8	A **Date** value can range from 1 January 4712 BC to 31 December 4712 AD. Use the **TO_Date** function to convert a value to a **Date** variable. If a value for time is not specified, it will default to 12:00:00 AM.

See Also   **Alter Table** (statement), **Create Table** (statement), **Datetime** (data type), **Shortdatetime** (data type), **Time** (data type), **Timestamp** (data type)

Datetime

DATA TYPE

Informix • MS Access • MS SQL Server • Sybase

Syntax   **Datetime** [*largequalifier* [**To** *smallqualifier* (*ssize*)]]

Usage   The **Datetime** data type represents a year, month, day, hour, minute, and second value. Sometimes a fractional part of a second is also included.

Only Informix allows you to include arguments to define the range of values stored in a **Datetime** column.

Arguments   ▪ *largequalifier*—one of the following: **Year**, **Month**, **Day**, **Hour**, **Minute**, **Second**, and **Fraction**.

▪ *smallqualifier*—one of the following: **Year**, **Month**, **Day**, **Hour**, **Minute**, **Second**, and **Fraction**. *Smallqualifier* must be a smaller unit of time than *largequalifier*.

▪ *ssize*—the number of digits of precision in *smallqualifier*. Applies only when **Fraction** is selected for *smallqualifier*.

Literals   Access uses number signs (#) to delimit a **Datetime** value. Most common formats are recognized, such as "#27-Jun-1965#," "#3/16/93 12:02 AM," and "August 13, 1994."

MS SQL Server and Sybase SQL Server both accept most common date and time formats enclosed in single quotes (' '). If a two-digit year is specified, then for values between 0 and 50, the twenty-first century is assumed (20xx) and for values between 51 and 99, the nineteenth century is assumed (19xx).

Implementation Notes   Informix

The arguments for a **Datetime** value allow you to include only the information you really need in the **Datetime** value.

MS Access	A **Datetime** value is really a **Double Precision** floating point number where the whole number part (left side of the decimal point) contains date values ranging from 1 January 100 to 31 December 9999. A negative number represents a date before 1900. Time information is encoded as the fractional part (right side of the decimal point), with a value of 0 meaning midnight and a value of .5 meaning noon.
MS SQL Server	A **Datetime** value can range from 1 January 1753 to 31 December 9999. Time values are accurate to within 3.33 milliseconds.
Sybase	A **Datetime** value can range from 1 January 1753 to 31 December 9999. Time values are accurate to within 3.33 milliseconds.

See Also   **Alter Table** (statement), **Create Table** (statement), **Date** (data type), **Interval** (data type), **Shortdatetime** (data type), **Time** (data type), **Timestamp** (data type)

Dbclob

DATA TYPE

IBM

Syntax   **Dbclob** (*length* [**K** | **M** | **G**])

Usage   The **Dbclob** data type represents a Double Byte Character Large Object that is stored in the database. A **Dbclob** can contain up to 1 gigabyte of data. This data type is intended to contain information encoded in a DBCS (Double Byte Character Set). The size of the **Dbclob** is specified by *length*. If a **K**, **M** or **G** follows *length*, the size of the **Dbclob** is *length* multiplied by 1,024, 1,048,576, or 1,073,741,824, respectively.

Argument   ▪ *length*—the number of characters in the **Dbclob**.

See Also   **Alter Table** (statement), **Blob** (data type), **Clob** (data type), **Create Table** (statement), **Graphic** (data type), **Vargraphic** (data type)

Decimal

ANSI • IBM • Informix • MS Access • MS SQL Server • Sybase

Syntax   **Decimal** [(*precision* [, *scale*])]

Usage   The **Decimal** data type represents a packed decimal number that contains the specified number of digits. A **Decimal** number contains an exact representation of the number, so no arithmetic errors can occur during calculations.

Arguments   ▪ *precision*—the total number of digits in the number, before and after the decimal point (see Table 1-3).

Database	maximum precision
ANSI	implementer defined
IBM DB2	31 digits
Informix	32 digits
MS Access	see **Money** (data type)
MS SQL Server	28 digits
Oracle8	see **Number** (data type)
Sybase SQL Server	38 digits

*Table 1-3: Maximum precision for a **Decimal** value.*

▪ *scale*—the number of digits after the decimal point (see Table 1-4).

Database	default scale
ANSI	implementer defined
IBM DB2	0
Informix	0
MS Access	see **Money** (data type)
MS SQL Server	0
Oracle8	see **Number** (data type)
Sybase SQL Server	0

*Table 1-4: Default scale for a **Decimal** value.*

Literals   The format of a **Decimal** literal is:

[+ | –] digits [. | . digits]

where *digits* is one or more numbers ("0", "1", . . . "9").

    Thus, one million can be expressed as 1000000 or +1000000. The number one hundredth (1/100) can be expressed as 0.01.

    Note that commas (",") are not permitted in a **Decimal** literal.

Implementation Notes   MS SQL Server   Microsoft SQL Server uses a 28-digit number for compatibility; however, you can specify any value from 1 to 38
as the default precision by using the /p option on the
SQLSERVR.EXE command line.

See Also   **Alter Table** (statement), **Create Table** (statement), **Double Precision** (data type), **Float**
(data type), **Money** (data type)

Double Precision

DATA TYPE

ANSI • IBM • Informix • MS Access • MS SQL Server • Oracle • Sybase

Syntax   `Double Precision`

`Double`

Usage   The **Double Precision** data type represents a floating point number that consists of a
leading digit followed by a fractional part that is raised to a power. Unlike an **Integer**
value, a **Double Precision** value is inexact. The specified number digits of precision
will be kept. While the exact size of a **Double Precision** varies from implementation to
implementation, the precision of a **Double Precision** will always be at least that of
Real. See Table 1-5.

> **Tip**
>
> *It is important to note that **Double Precision** numbers are not appropriate in many
> situations, especially where money values can be computed. While it is possible to represent
> money as a floating point value, performing calculations on these values can result in small
> errors. While these errors might not be important to most people, try explaining to your
> accountant how 2.00 plus 2.00 resulted in 3.99 instead of 4.00.*

Database	size
ANSI	implementer defined
IBM DB2	64 bits
Informix	64 bits
MS Access	64 bits
MS SQL Server	64 bits
Oracle8	see **Number** (data type)
Sybase SQL Server	64 bits

*Table 1-5: Size of a **Double Precision** value.*

Literals   The format of a **Double Precision** literal is:

[+ | –] digits [. | . digits] [E [+ | –] digits]

where *digits* is one or more numbers ("0", "1", ... "9").

Thus, one million can be expressed as 1000000, +1000000, 1E7, or 1.0E7. The number one-hundredth (1/100) can be expressed as 0.01 or 1E-2.

Note that commas (",") are not permitted in a **Double Precision** literal.

Implementation Notes   MS Access   Access only supports the name **Double** for a double precision floating point number. **Double Precision** is not recognized.

See Also   **Alter Table** (statement), **Create Table** (statement), **Decimal** (data type), **Float** (data type), **Number** (data type), **Numeric** (data type), **Real** (data type)

Float

DATA TYPE

ANSI • IBM • Informix • MS Access • MS SQL Server • Oracle • Sybase

Syntax   **Float** [(*precision*)]

Usage   The **Float** data type represents a floating point number that consists of a leading digit followed by a fractional part that is raised to a power. Unlike an **Integer** value, a **Float** value is inexact. The specified number digits of precision will be kept. While the exact size of a **Float** varies from implementation to implementation, the precision of a **Float** will always be at least that of **Precision.**

Tip

*It is important to note that **Float** numbers are not appropriate in many situations, especially where money values can be computed. While it is possible to represent money as a floating point value, performing calculations on these values can result in small errors. While these errors might not be important to most people, try explaining to your accountant how 2.00 plus 2.00 resulted in 3.99 instead of 4.00.*

Argument   ▪ *precision*—the number of digits in the number. If omitted, the default values will be selected from Table 1-6 below.

Database	size
ANSI	implementer defined
IBM DB2	64 bits
Informix	64 bits
MS Access	see **Single** (data type) or **Double Precision** (data type)
MS SQL Server	32 bits (*precision* <= 7), 64 bits (*precision* >= 8)
Oracle8	126 bits
Sybase SQL Server	64 bits

*Table 1-6: Size of a **Float** value.*

Literals   The format of a **Float** literal is:

[+ | –] digits [. | . digits] [E [+ | –] digits]

where *digits* is one or more numbers ("0", "1", . . . "9").

Thus, one million can be expressed as 1000000, +1000000, 1E7, or 1.0E7. The number one-hundredth (1/100) can be expressed as 0.01 or 1E-2.

Note that commas (",") are not permitted in a **Float** literal.

See Also   **Alter Table** (statement), **Create Table** (statement), **Decimal** (data type), **Double Precision** (data type), **Number** (data type), **Numeric** (data type), **Real** (data type)

Graphic

DATA TYPE

IBM

Syntax   **Graphic** [(*length*)]

Usage   The **Graphic** data type represents a fixed-length string of characters. When one **Character** value is assigned to another **Character** value of a different size, it will be padded with spaces or truncated as needed.

Literals   A **Graphic** literal is constructed by enclosing the desired string of characters in single quotes ('). Two single quotes ('') together are used to indicate an empty string. When two single quotes appear inside a **Graphic** literal, they will be treated as a single quote.

An extended format **Graphic** literal is composed of multiple **Graphic** literals separated by zero or more spaces and a single newline marker. This provides an easy method to create a very large character string.

Argument ▪ *length*—the number of characters in the character string, up to a maximum of 127. If omitted, this value will default to 1.

Implementation Notes   IBM DB2   **Graphic** refers to double byte characters. **Character,** **Varchar,** and **Long Varchar** refer to single byte character strings.
Note that the database must have MBCS enabled in order to use this data type.

See Also   **Alter Table** (statement), **Character** (data type), **Create Table** (statement), **Dbclob** (data type), **Vargraphic** (data type)

Guid

DATA TYPE

MS Access

Syntax   `Guid`

Usage   The **Guid** data type is an MS Access data type representing a 16-byte value that is used to support remote procedure calls.

See Also   **Alter Table** (statement), **Create Table** (statement)

Identity

DATA TYPE

Sybase

Syntax   `Identity`

Usage   The **Identity** data type is a Sybase data type whose value is a system-maintained sequence number.

See Also   **Alter Table** (statement), **Counter** (data type), **Create Table** (statement)

Image

MS SQL Server • Sybase

Syntax   `Image`

Usage   The **Image** data type represents a large variable-length binary value. This would typically be used to store picture or voice information in your database.

Implementation Notes   MS SQL Server   An **Image** can contain up to 2 gigabytes of data and can be converted into a **Binary** or **Varbinary** value using the **Convert** function.

       Sybase   An **Image** can contain up to 2 gigabytes of data.

See Also   **Alter Table** (statement), **Binary** (data type), **Blob** (data type), **Create Table** (statement), **Varbinary** (data type)

Integer

ANSI • IBM • Informix • MS Access • MS SQL Server • Oracle • Sybase

Syntax   `Integer`

          `Int`

Usage   The **Integer** data type represents a whole number that doesn't contain any fractional part. This value can be either a binary number or a decimal number, but in either case the value stored will always be exact. This is not true for values of type **Float**.

      While the exact size of an **Integer** varies from implementation to implementation (see Table 1-7), the precision of **Integer** will always be at least that of **Smallint**, though **Integer** will generally be larger.

Database	size
ANSI	implementer defined
IBM DB2	32 bits
Informix	32 bits
MS Access	16 bits
MS SQL Server	32 bits
Oracle8	32 bits
Sybase SQL Server	32 bits

*Table 1-7: Size and range of values for an **Integer** value.*

Literals   A **Integer** literal consists of a series of numbers, such as 123 or 12345. Note that commas (",") are not permitted in an **Integer** literal.

Implementation Notes   MS Access   Access contains two different types of integer numbers, **Integer** and **Long**.

                       Oracle   The exact size of an **Integer** depends on the host system running the database. Typically an **Integer** will be a 32-bit value with a range of -2147483648 to +2147483647.

See Also   **Alter Table** (statement), **Byte** (data type), **Create Table** (statement), **Decimal** (data type), **Integer** (data type), **Long** (data type), **Number** (data type), **Numeric** (data type), **Short** (data type), **Smallint** (data type), **Tinyint** (data type)

Interval

DATA TYPE

ANSI • Informix

Syntax   Interval [*largequalifier* (*lsize*) [**To** *smallqualifier* (*ssize*)]]

Usage   The **Interval** data type represents the difference in time between two **Datetime** values. For example, declaring a column as **Interval Year** (3) **To Month** will hold the number of years and months between two dates. This column can hold values up to 999 years and 11 months.

Arguments   ▪ *largequalifier*—one of the following: **Year, Month, Day, Hour, Minute, Second**, and **Fraction**.

         ▪ *lsize*—the number of digits of precision in *largequalifier*.

         ▪ *smallqualifier*—one of the following: **Year, Month, Day, Hour, Minute, Second**, and **Fraction**. *Smallqualifier* must be a smaller unit of time than *largequalifier*.

         ▪ *ssize*—the number of digits of precision in *smallqualifier*.

See Also   **Alter Table** (statement), **Create Table** (statement), **Datetime** (data type)

Long

Syntax Long

Usage The **Long** data type available in MS Access represents a whole number that doesn't contain any fractional part. This value can be either a binary number or a decimal number, but in either case, the value stored will always be exact. This is not true for values of type **Float**. The size of a **Long** is 32 bits.

The **Long** data type available in Oracle is totally different from the **Long** data type for Access. Oracle's **Long** data type is very similar to a **Clob** or **Varchar**. It is designed to hold large variable-length character strings, up to a maximum of 2 gigabytes.

> **Tip**
>
> *An Oracle **Long** data type has a number of restrictions on its use. Only one **Long** is permitted per table. A column of type **Long** can't be used as part of an index. A stored function can't return a **Long**. The **Where**, **Group By**, **Order By**, **Unique**, or **Connect By** clauses can't reference a **Long** column. A **Long** column can't be included as part of a **Select Distinct** operation.*

Literals An Access **Long** literal consists of a series of numbers, such as 123 or 12345. Note that commas (",") are not permitted in an Access **Long** literal.

See Also **Alter Table** (statement), **Clob** (data type), **Create Table** (statement), **Integer** (data type), **Text** (data type), **Varchar** (data type)

Long Raw

Syntax Long Raw

Usage The **Long Raw** data type is an Oracle extension that represents a variable-length string of binary information. This type is very useful when data is moved from one system to another and shouldn't be converted. Except for its maximum length of 2 gigabytes, a **Long Raw** is identical to a **Raw**, though a **Long Raw** column can't be included in an index.

See Also **Alter Table** (statement), **Blob** (data type), **Create Table** (statement), **Raw** (data type)

Long Varchar

Syntax   **Long Varchar** [(*length*)] [**For Bit Data**]

Usage   The **Long Varchar** data type is a DB2 extension that represents a variable-length string of characters. Except for its length, it is identical to a **Character Varying** or **Varchar** value.

The **For Bit Data** clause is an IBM extension that indicates that the value of the column should be treated as binary data. No code translations are performed when data is exchanged with other systems and binary comparisons are used instead of the system's normal collating sequence.

Literals   All **Long Varchar** literals are identical to **Varchar** literals.

Argument ▪ *length*—the number of characters in the character string, up to a maximum of 32,700. If omitted, this value will default to 1.

Implementation Notes   IBM DB2   **Long Varchar** fields that are greater than 254 characters are not permitted as part of a **Select Distinct** statement, a **Group By** clause, an **Order By** clause, a column function with the **Distinct** operator, or a subselect using any operator other than **Union All**.

See Also   **Alter Table** (statement), **Character** (data type), **Create Table** (statement), **Text** (data type), **Varchar** (data type)

Long Vargraphic

Syntax **Long Vargraphic** [(*length*)]

Usage The **Long Vargraphic** data type is a DB2 extension that represents a variable-length string of characters, where each character occupies two bytes. Except for its length, it is identical to a **Vargraphic** value.

Literals All **Long Vargraphic** literals are identical to **Vargraphic** literals.

Argument ▪ *length*—the number of characters in the character string, up to a maximum of 16,350. If omitted, this value will default to 1.

Implementation Notes IBM DB2

Long Varchar fields that are greater than 254 characters are not permitted as part of a **Select Distinct** statement, a **Group By** clause, an **Order By** clause, a column function with the **Distinct** operator, or a subselect using any operator other than **Union All**.

Note that the database must have MBCS enabled in order to use this data type.

See Also **Alter Table** (statement), **Create Table** (statement), **Graphic** (data type), **Text** (data type), **Vargraphic** (data type)

Longbinary

Syntax **Longbinary**

Usage The **Longbinary** data type in MS Access provides an unstructured, variable-length data type for storing binary data. The maximum size of a **Longbinary** field is about 1.2 gigabytes.

> ### Tip
>
> *While the Access database engine supports the **Longbinary** data type, there is no support for it in the Access programming environment. **Binary** data types must be maintained by other programming languages, such as Visual Basic or Visual C++.*

See Also **Alter Table** (statement), **Binary** (data type), **Create Table** (statement), **Longbinary** (data type), **Varbinary** (data type)

Memo

Syntax **Memo** [(*length*)]

Usage The **Memo** data type represents a variable-length string of characters in Microsoft Access.

Literals A **Memo** literal is constructed by enclosing the desired string of characters in single quotes ('). Two single quotes ('') together are used to indicate an empty string. When two single quotes appear inside a **Memo** literal, they will be treated as a single quote.

Argument ▪ *length*—the number of characters in the character string, up to a maximum of 65,535. If omitted, this value will default to 1.

Implementation Notes   MS Access

The **Memo** data type is essentially the same as the **Varchar** data type. If you use Data Access Objects (found in Visual Basic and Visual C++) to access the database, **Memo** values can exceed the 65,535 limit and range in size up to 2 gigabytes.

See Also   **Alter Table** (statement), **Character Varying** (data type), **Create Table** (statement), **Long Character** (data type), **Text** (data type)

Money

DATA TYPE

Informix • MS SQL Server • Sybase

Syntax   **Money** [(*precision* [, *scale*])]

Usage   The **Money** data type represents a fixed-point decimal number (Informix) or a scaled integer (MS SQL Server and Sybase SQL Server) that is designed for use with monetary calculations. While Informix permits you to specify values for *precision* and *scale*, MS SQL Server and Sybase do not.

Arguments ▪ *precision*—the total number of digits in the number (before and after the decimal point). A maximum of 32 digits is permitted. If omitted, this value will default to 16. This argument applies to Informix only.

▪ *scale*—the number of digits after the decimal point. If omitted, this value will default to 2. This argument applies to Informix only.

Literals   The format of a **Money** literal is:

$ [+ | –] digits [. | . digits]

where *digits* is one or more numbers ("0", "1", . . . "9").

Thus, one million can be expressed as 1000000 or +1000000. The number one-hundredth (1/100) can be expressed as 0.01.

Note that commas (",") are not permitted in a **Money** literal.

| Implementation Notes | MS SQL Server | Microsoft SQL Server uses a scaled integer to store the value with four digits to the right of the decimal point. Legal values for this data type range from -922,337,685,477.5808 to +922,337,685,477.5808. |
| | Sybase | Sybase SQL Server uses a scaled integer to store the value with four digits to the right of the decimal point. Legal values for this data type range from -922,337,685,477.5808 to +922,337,685,477.5808. |

See Also **Alter Table** (statement), **Create Table** (statement), **Currency** (data type), **Decimal** (data type)

Mlslabel

DATA TYPE

Oracle

Syntax **Mlslabel**

Usage The **Mlslabel** data type is an Oracle data type representing the binary form of an operating system label. This data type is included for backward compatibility with Trusted Oracle.

See Also **Alter Table** (statement), **Create Table** (statement)

Nchar

DATA TYPE

Informix • Oracle

Syntax **Nchar** [(*length*)]

Usage The **Nchar** data type represents a fixed-length string of characters in a particular national language. These character strings often occupy more than one character per byte of information.

Literals An **Nchar** literal is constructed by enclosing the desired string of characters in single quotes ('). Two single quotes ('') together are used to indicate an empty string. When two single quotes appear inside a **Nchar** literal, they will be treated as a single quote.

An extended format **Nchar** literal is composed of multiple **Nchar** literals separated by zero or more spaces and a single newline marker. This provides an easy method to create a very large character string.

Argument ▪ *length*—the number of bytes or characters in the character string. (See Implementation Notes for more information.) If omitted, this value will default to 1. (See Table 1-8.)

Database	maximum length
ANSI	implementer defined
IBM DB2	see **Graphic** (data type)
Informix	32,767 bytes
MS Access	see **Text** (data type)
Oracle8	2,000 bytes

*Table 1-8: Maximum length of an **Nchar** value.*

Implementation Notes	Informix	The N in **Nchar** refers to Native Language Support (NLS) that is enabled by using the DBNLS environment variable.
	Oracle	If the character set used with the national language uses fixed-length characters, then *length* refers to the number of characters in the string. If the national language uses variable-length characters, then *length* contains size of the field in bytes.

See Also **Alter Table** (statement), **Character** (data type), **Create Table** (statement), **Nclob** (data type), **Nvarchar** (data type)

Nclob

DATA TYPE

Oracle

Syntax **Nclob**

Usage The **Nclob** data type represents a National Character Large Object that is stored in the database. An **Nclob** can contain up to 4 gigabytes of data.

See Also **Alter Table** (statement), **Clob** (data type), **Create Table** (statement), **Nchar** (data type), **Nvarchar** (data type)

Number

Syntax **Number** [(*precision* [, *scale*])]

Usage The **Number** data type in Oracle represents a packed decimal number that contains the specified number of digits.

Arguments ▪ *precision*—the total number of digits in the number (before and after the decimal point).
▪ *scale*—the number of digits after the decimal point.

Literals The format of a **Number** literal is:

[+ | −] digits [. | . digits]

where *digits* is one or more numbers ("0", "1", . . . "9").
Thus, one million can be expressed as 1000000 or +1000000. The number one-hundredth (1/100) can be expressed as 0.01.
Note that commas (",") are not permitted in a **Number** literal.

See Also **Alter Table** (statement), **Create Table** (statement), **Double Precision** (data type), **Float** (data type), **Money** (data type), **Numeric** (data type)

Numeric

Syntax **Numeric** [(*precision* [, *scale*])]

Usage The **Numeric** data type represents a packed decimal number that contains the specified number of digits. A **Numeric** number contains an exact representation of the number, so no arithmetic errors can occur during calculations.

Argument ▪ *precision*—the total number of digits in the number, before and after the decimal point (see Table 1-9).

Database	maximum precision
ANSI	implementer defined
IBM DB2	see **Decimal** (data type)
Informix	32 digits
MS Access	see **Money** (data type)
MS SQL Server	28 digits
Oracle8	see **Number** (data type)
Sybase SQL Server	38 digits

*Table 1-9: Maximum precision for a **Numeric** value.*

▪ *scale*—the number of digits after the decimal point (see Table 1-10).

Database	default scale
ANSI	implementer defined
IBM DB2	see **Decimal** (data type)
Informix	0
MS Access	see **Money** (data type)
MS SQL Server	0
Oracle8	see **Number** (data type)
Sybase SQL Server	0

*Table 1-10: Default scale for a **Numeric** value.*

Literals   The format of a **Numeric** literal is:

```
[ + | – ] digits [ . | . digits]
```

where *digits* is one or more numbers ("0", "1", . . . "9").

Thus, one million can be expressed as 1000000 or +1000000. The number one-hundredth (1/100) can be expressed as 0.01.

Note that commas (",") are not permitted in a **Numeric** literal.

Implementation Notes   MS SQL Server   Microsoft SQL Server uses a 28-digit number for compatibility; however, you can specify any value from 1 to 38 as the default precision by using the /p option on the SQLSERVR.EXE command line.

See Also   **Alter Table** (statement), **Create Table** (statement), **Double Precision** (data type), **Float** (data type), **Money** (data type), **Number** (data type)

Nvarchar

Syntax **Nvarchar** [(*length*)]

Usage The **Nvarchar** data type represents a variable-length string of characters in a particular national language. These character strings often occupy more than one character per byte of information.

Literals An **Nvarchar** literal is constructed by enclosing the desired string of characters in single quotes ('). Two single quotes ('') together are used to indicate an empty string. When two single quotes appear inside an **Nvarchar** literal, they will be treated as a single quote.

An extended format **Nvarchar** literal is composed of multiple **Nvarchar** literals separated by zero or more spaces and a single newline marker. This provides an easy method to create a very large character string.

Argument ▪ *length*—the number of bytes or characters in the character string. (See Implementation Notes for more information.) If omitted, this value will default to 1. (See Table 1-11.)

Database	maximum length
ANSI	implementer defined
IBM DB2	see **Graphic** (data type)
Informix	32,767 bytes
MS Access	see **Text** (data type)
Oracle8	255 bytes

*Table 1-11: Maximum length of an **Nvarchar** value.*

Implementation Notes	Informix	The N in **Nchar** refers to Native Language Support (NLS), which is enabled by using the DBNLS environment variable.
		Nvarchar fields are limited to a *length* of 254, if used as part of an index.
	Oracle	If the character set used with the national language uses fixed-length characters, then *length* refers to the number of characters in the string. If the national language uses variable-length characters, then *length* contains size of the field in bytes.

See Also **Alter Table** (statement), **Character** (data type), **Create Table** (statement), **Varchar** (data type)

Raw

DATA TYPE

IBM

Syntax **Raw** (`length`)

Usage The **Raw** data type is an Oracle extension that represents a variable-length string of binary information. A **Raw** column is limited to 255 characters in length and is similar to **Varchar** in most aspects. This type is very useful when data is moved from one system to another and shouldn't be converted.

Argument ▪ *length*—the number of bytes in the character string. This value must be specified.

See Also **Alter Table** (statement), **Blob** (data type), **Create Table** (statement), **Long Raw** (data type)

Real

ANSI • IBM • Informix • MS Access • MS SQL Server • Oracle • Sybase

Syntax   **Real**

Usage   The **Real** data type represents a floating point number that consists of a leading digit followed by a fractional part that is raised to a power. Unlike an **Integer** value, a **Real** value is inexact. While the exact size of a **Real** varies from implementation to implementation, the precision of a **Real** will never be more than that of a **Double Precision**. (See Table 1-12.)

Tip

*It is important to note that **Real** numbers are not appropriate in many situations, especially where money values can be computed. While it is possible to represent money as a floating point value, performing calculations on these values can result in small errors. While these errors might not be important to most people, try explaining to your accountant how 2.00 plus 2.00 resulted in 3.99 instead of 4.00.*

Database	size
ANSI	implementer defined
IBM DB2	32 bits
Informix	32 bits
MS Access	see **Single** (data type)
MS SQL Server	32 bits
Oracle8	see **Numeric** (data type)
Sybase SQL Server	32 bits

*Table 1-12: Size and range of values for a **Real** value.*

Literals   The format of a **Real** literal is:

[+ | –] digits [. | . digits] [E [+ | –] digits]

where *digits* is one or more numbers ("0", "1", . . . "9").

Thus one million can be expressed as 1000000, +1000000, 1E7, or 1.0E7. The number one-hundredth (1/100) can be expressed as 0.01 or 1E-2.

Note that commas (",") are not permitted in a **Real** literal.

See Also   **Alter Table** (statement), **Create Table** (statement), **Double Precision** (data type), **Float** (data type)

Serial

Syntax   **Serial** [(*start*)]

Usage   The **Serial** data type is an Informix data type whose value is a system-maintained sequence number. You can also assign a value to this column or let the database assign a value automatically each time a new row is inserted into a table. If not specified, the **Serial** column will be assigned a value that is equal to the largest value in that column plus one. A **Unique Index** should be applied to this column to prevent duplicate values. Only one column can be defined to have a data type of **Serial.**

Argument   ▪ *start*—the first value to be used. If omitted, this value will default to 1.

See Also   **Alter Table** (statement), **Counter** (data type), **Create Table** (statement)

Short

Syntax   **Short**

Usage   The **Short** data type represents a whole number that doesn't contain any fractional part. This value can be either a binary number or a decimal number, but in either case the value stored will always be exact. This is not true for values of type **Single**.

Literals   A **Short** literal consists of a series of numbers, such as 123 or 12345. Note that commas (",") are not permitted in a **Short** literal.

See Also   **Alter Table** (statement), **Byte** (data type), **Create Table** (statement), **Decimal** (data type), **Integer** (data type), **Long** (data type), **Number** (data type), **Numeric** (data type), **Smallint** (data type), **Tinyint** (data type)

Shortdatetime

Syntax   Shortdatetime

Usage   The **Shortdatetime** data type represents year, month, day, hour, minute, and second values. A **Shortdatetime** value can range from 1 January 1900 to 6 June 2079. Time values are accurate to the minute. This data type is similar to the **Datetime** data type, but because it keeps less information, less storage is required.

Literals   Sybase SQL Server accepts most common date and time formats enclosed in single quotes ('). If a two-digit year is specified, then for values between 0 and 50, the twenty-first century is assumed (20xx) and for values between 51 and 99, the nineteenth century is assumed (19xx).

Implementation Notes   Sybase   A **Shortdatetime** value that consists of two 16-bit integers containing the number of days from 1 January 1900 and the number of minutes past midnight.

See Also   **Alter Table** (statement), **Create Table** (statement), **Date** (data type), **Datetime** (data type), **Smalldatetime** (data type), **Time** (data type), **Timestamp** (data type)

Single

Syntax   Single

Usage   The **Single** data type in Access represents a floating point number that consists of a leading digit followed by a fractional part that is raised to a power.

> ### Tip
>
> *It is important to note that **Single** numbers are not appropriate in many situations, especially where money values can be computed. While it is possible to represent money as a floating point value, performing calculations on these values can result in small errors. While these errors might not be important to most people, try explaining to your accountant how 2.00 plus 2.00 resulted in 3.99 instead of 4.00.*

Literals   The format of a **Single** literal is:

[+ | –] digits [. | . digits] [E [+ | –] digits]

where *digits* is one or more numbers ("0", "1", . . . "9").

Thus, one million can be expressed as 1000000, +1000000, 1E7, or 1.0E7. The number one-hundredth (1/100) can be expressed as 0.01 or 1E-2.

Note that commas (",") are not permitted in a **Single** literal.

See Also   **Alter Table** (statement), **Character Varying** (data type), **Create Table** (statement), **Long Character** (data type), **Text** (data type)

Smalldatetime

DATA TYPE

MS SQL Server

Syntax   Smalldatetime

Usage   The **Smalldatetime** data type represents year, month, day, hour, minute, and second values. A **Smalldatetime** value can range from 1 January 1900 to 6 June 2079. Time values are accurate to the minute. This data type is similar to the **Datetime** data type, but because it keeps less information, less storage is required.

Literals   MS SQL Server accepts most common date and time formats enclosed in single quotes ('). If a two-digit year is specified, then for values between 0 and 50, the twenty-first century is assumed (20xx) and for values between 51 and 99, the nineteenth century is assumed (19xx).

Implementation Notes   MS SQL Server   A **Smalldatetime** value that consists of two 16-bit integers containing the number of days from 1 January 1900 and the number of minutes past midnight.

See Also   **Alter Table** (statement), **Create Table** (statement), **Date** (data type), **Datetime** (data type), **Shortdatetime** (data type), **Time** (data type), **Timestamp** (data type)

Smallint

ANSI • IBM • Informix • MS SQL Server • Oracle • Sybase

Syntax   `Smallint`

Usage   The **Smallint** data type represents a whole number which doesn't contain any fractional part. This value can be either a binary number or a decimal number, but in either case the value stored will always be exact. This is not true for values of type **Float**.

     While the exact size of a **Smallint** varies from implementation to implementation, the precision of **Smallint** will never be more than that of an **Integer**, though **Smallint** will generally have lower precision. (See Table 1-13.)

Database	size	values
ANSI	implementer defined	—
IBM DB2	16 bits	-32768 to +32767
Informix	16 bits	-32768 to +32767
MS Access	see **Integer** (data type), **Long** (data type)	—
MS SQL Server	16 bits	-32768 to +32767
Oracle8	16 bits	-32768 to +32767
Sybase SQL Server	16 bits	-32768 to +32767

*Table 1-13: Size and range of values for an **Integer** value.*

Literals   A **Smallint** literal consists of a series of numbers, such as 123 or 12345. Note that commas (",") are not permitted in a **Smallint** literal.

Implementation Notes   Oracle   The exact size of a **Smallint** depends on the host system running the database. Typically, a **Smallint** is a 16-bit value that has a range of -32768 to +32767.

See Also   **Alter Table** (statement), **Create Table** (statement), **Double** (data type), **Integer** (data type), **Long** (data type)

Smallmoney

Syntax   **Smallmoney**

Usage   The **Smallmoney** data type represents a scaled integer similar to **Money** that is designed for use with monetary calculations. Legal values for this data type range from -214,748.3648 to +214,748.3647.

Literals   The format of a **Smallmoney** literal is:

$ [+ | –] digits [. | . digits]

where *digits* is one or more numbers ("0", "1", . . . "9").

     Thus, one million can be expressed as 1000000 or +1000000. The number one-hundredth (1/100) can be expressed as 0.01.

     Note that commas (",") are not permitted in a **Smallmoney** literal.

See Also   **Alter Table** (statement), **Create Table** (statement), **Currency** (data type), **Decimal** (data type), **Money** (data type)

Text

Syntax   **Text** [(*length*)]

Usage   The **Text** data type represents a variable-length string of characters.

Literals   A **Text** literal is constructed by enclosing the desired string of characters in single quotes ('). Two single quotes ('') together are used to indicate an empty string. When two single quotes appear inside a **Text** literal, they will be treated as a single quote.

Argument   ▪ *length*—the number of characters in the character string. If omitted, this value will default to 1.

Implementation Notes	MS Access	The **Text** data type is essentially the same as the **Varchar** data type and has a limit of 255 characters.
	MS SQL Server	The **Text** data type is essentially the same as the **Clob** data type and is limited to approximately 2 gigabytes.
	Sybase	The **Text** data type is essentially the same as the **Clob** data type and is limited to approximately 2 gigabytes.

See Also   **Alter Table** (statement), **Character** (data type), **Clob** (data type), **Create Table** (statement), **Varchar** (data type)

Time

DATA TYPE

ANSI • IBM

Syntax   Time

Usage   The **Time** data type represents hour, minute, and second values. IBM implemented **Time** as a three byte packed decimal number, where the first byte contains the hour, the next byte contains the minute, and the last byte contains the second.

Literals   The ISO standard for time is "hh:mm:ss." The IBM US standard for time is "hh:mm AM" or "hh:mm PM."

See Also   **Alter Table** (statement), **Create Table** (statement), **Date** (data type), **Datetime** (data type), **Shortdatetime** (data type), **Timestamp** (data type)

Timestamp

DATA TYPE

ANSI • IBM • MS SQL Server • Sybase

Syntax `Timestamp`

Usage   The **Timestamp** data type in IBM DB2 represents a date and time value stored in
packed decimal form. Of the ten bytes of storage allocated, the first four bytes contain
the date (year, month, and day), the next three digits contain the time (hour, minute,
second), and the last three digits contain the current microsecond.

The **Timestamp** data type in MS SQL Server and Sybase SQL Server does not
contain an actual date or time value, but rather it contains a monotonically increasing
counter that represents a unique value in the database. This value is stored as a
Binary(8) or a **Varbinary**(8) value if the column is declared **Not Null**. A table can only
have one column with this data type and it will automatically be updated whenever a
record is inserted or updated in the table.

See Also **Alter Table** (statement), **Create Table** (statement), **Date** (data types), **Date** (data type),
Shortdatetime (data type), **Time** (data type)

Tinyint

DATA TYPE

MS SQL Server • Sybase

Syntax `Tinyint`

Usage   The **Tinyint** data type in Microsoft SQL Server represents a whole number that doesn't
contain any fractional part. This value can be either a binary number or a decimal
number, but in either case, the value stored will always be exact. This is not true for
values of type **Float**.

A **Tinyint** can only store values from 0 to 255. If you need to keep a larger number,
see **Integer** (data type) or **Smallint** (data type).

Literals A **Tinyint** literal consists of a series of numbers, such as 12 or 123. Note that commas
(",") are not permitted in a **Tinyint** literal.

See Also **Alter Table** (statement), **Character Varying** (data type), **Create Table** (statement), **Long
Character** (data type), **Text** (data type)

Varbit

Syntax **Varbit** [(*length*)]

Bit Varying [(*length*)]

Usage The **Varbit** data type represents a variable-length array of boolean values, each of which can contain either a 0 or 1 value. Any value other than 0 is treated as a 1.

Argument ▪ *length*—the number of bits in the bit array. If omitted, this value will default to 1 (see Table 1-14).

Database	maximum length
ANSI	implementer defined
IBM DB2	not supported
Informix	not supported
MS Access	not supported
MS SQL Server	not supported
Oracle8	not supported
Sybase SQL Server	not supported

*Table 1-14: Maximum length of a **Varbit** value.*

Literals An ANSI **Bit** literal is constructed by enclosing the desired string of binary digits (0 or 1) inside a pair of single quotes ('') and preceded by a b. Hexadecimal values can be substituted for the binary digits if the string is preceded by an x. Thus, the binary string b'1010' and the hex string x'A' mean the same thing.

See Also **Alter Table** (statement), **Bit** (data type), **Create Table** (statement)

Varbinary

MS Access • MS SQL Server • Sybase

Syntax **Varbinary** [(*length*)]

Binary Varying [(*length*)]

Usage The **Varbinary** data type in MS Access, MS SQL Server, and Sybase SQL Server is used to provide an unstructured, variable-length data type for storing binary data. This data type is similar to the ANSI **Bit Varying** data type.

> **Tip**
>
> *While the Access database engine supports the **Varbinary** data type, there is no support for it in the Access programming environment. **Varbinary** data types must be maintained by other programming languages, such as Visual Basic or Visual C++.*

Argument ▪ *length*—the number of characters in the binary string. If omitted, this value will default to 1. The maximum size of *length* is 255.

See Also **Alter Table** (statement), **Binary** (data type), **Bit** (data type), **Create Table** (statement)

Varchar

ANSI • IBM • Informix • MS SQL Server • Oracle • Sybase

Syntax **Varchar** [(*length* [, *reserved*])] [**For Bit Data**]

Character Varying [(*length* [, *reserved*])] [**For Bit Data**]

Char Varying [(*length* [, *reserved*])] [**For Bit Data**]

Usage The **Varchar** data type represents a variable-length string of characters. Unlike the **Character** data type, no padding will occur during an assignment. However, truncation or an error will occur if the length of the source value is larger than the maximum length of the destination value.

The **For Bit Data** clause is an IBM extension that indicates that the value of the column should be treated as binary data. No code translations are performed when data is exchanged with other systems and binary comparisons are used instead of the system's normal collating sequence.

Literals A **Varchar** literal is constructed by enclosing the desired string of characters in single quotes ('). Two single quotes ('') together are used to indicate a string whose length is zero. When two single quotes appear inside a **Varchar** literal, they will be treated as a single quote.

An extended format **Varchar** literal is composed of multiple **Varchar** literals separated by zero or more spaces and a single newline marker. This provides an easy method to create a very large character string.

Arguments ▪ *length*—the number of characters in the character string. If omitted, this value will default to 1 (see Table 1-15).

Database	maximum length
ANSI	implementer defined
IBM DB2	4,000
Informix	255
MS Access	see **Text** (data type)
MS SQL Server	255
Oracle8	4,000
Sybase SQL Server	255

*Table 1-15: Maximum length of a **Varchar** value.*

▪ *reserved*—the minimum amount of space that will be reserved for the character string. If omitted, this value will default to 0. This value is only supported by Informix databases.

Implementation Notes

IBM DB2 **Varchar** fields that are greater than 254 characters are not permitted as part of a **Select Distinct** statement, a **Group By** clause, an **Order By** clause, a column function with the **Distinct** operator, or a subselect using any operator other than **Union All**.

Informix **Varchar** fields are limited to a *length* of 254, if used as part of an index.

MS Access Because the **Varying** data types are not implemented, you should use the **Text** data type.

Oracle8 Oracle provides a different name for the **Varchar** data type in Oracle8, called **Varchar2**. While there is no difference between the **Varchar** and **Varchar2** at this time, Oracle recommends using **Varchar2**, because the programmers might change how **Varchar** values are compared in a future release.

See Also **Alter Table** (statement), **Character** (data type), **Create Table** (statement)

Vargraphic

Syntax   **Vargraphic** [(*length*)]

Usage   The **Vargraphic** data type is a DB2 extension that represents a variable-length string of characters, in which each character occupies two bytes.

Literals   A **Vargraphic** literal is constructed by enclosing the desired string of characters in single quotes ('). Two single quotes ('') together are used to indicate a string whose length is zero. When two single quotes appear inside a **Vargraphic** literal, they will be treated as a single quote.

An extended format **Vargraphic** literal is composed of multiple **Vargraphic** literals separated by zero or more spaces and a single newline marker. This provides an easy method of creating a very large character string.

Argument   ▪ *length*—the number of characters in the character string, up to a maximum of 2,000. If omitted, this value will default to 1.

Implementation Notes   IBM DB2   **Vargraphic** fields that are greater than 254 characters are not permitted as part of a **Select Distinct** statement, a **Group By** clause, an **Order By** clause, a column function with the **Distinct** operator, or a subselect using any operator other than **Union All**.

Note that the database must have MBCS enabled in order to use this data type.

See Also   **Alter Table** (statement), **Dbclob** (data type), **Create Table** (statement), **Graphic** (data type)

Operators, Functions & Variables

II

+

ANSI • IBM • Informix • MS Access • MS SQL Server • Oracle • Sybase

Syntax   *expr + expr*

Usage   The + operator returns the sum of two expressions.

Argument   ▪ *expr*—an arbitrary expression that can be a column name, a parameter from a stored procedure, a variable, a numeric literal, a function that returns a numeric value, an expression enclosed by parentheses, or a table expression that returns a single numeric expression.

See Also   – (operator), * (operator), / (operator)

–

ANSI • IBM • Informix • MS Access • MS SQL Server • Oracle • Sybase

Syntax   *expr – expr*

– expr

Usage   The – operator returns the difference of two expressions or the negated value of an expression.

Argument   ▪ *expr*—an arbitrary expression that can be a column name, a parameter from a stored procedure, a variable, a numeric literal, a function that returns a numeric value, an expression enclosed by parentheses, or a table expression that returns a single numeric expression.

See Also   + (operator), * (operator), / (operator)

*

ANSI • IBM • Informix • MS Access • MS SQL Server • Oracle • Sybase

Syntax   *expr * expr*

Usage   The * operator returns the product of two expressions.

Argument   ▪ *expr*—an arbitrary expression that can be a column name, a parameter from a stored procedure, a variable, a numeric literal, a function that returns a numeric value, an expression enclosed by parentheses, or a table expression that returns a single numeric expression.

See Also   + (operator), – (operator), / (operator)

/

ANSI • IBM • Informix • MS Access • MS SQL Server • Oracle • Sybase

Syntax   *expr / expr*

Usage   The / operator returns the dividend of two expressions as another expression.

Argument   ▪ *expr*—an arbitrary expression that can be a column name, a parameter from a stored procedure, a variable, a numeric literal, a function that returns a numeric value, an expression enclosed by parentheses, or a table expression that returns a single numeric expression.

See Also   + (operator), – (operator), * (operator)

=

ANSI • IBM • Informix • MS Access • MS SQL Server • Oracle • Sybase

Syntax   `expr1 = expr2`

Usage   The = operator returns **True** if *expr1* is equal to *expr2*; otherwise it returns **False**.

Arguments   ▪ *expr1*—an arbitrary expression that can be a column name, a parameter from a stored procedure, a variable, a numeric literal, a function that returns a numeric value, an expression enclosed by parentheses, or a table expression.

     ▪ *expr2*—an arbitrary expression that can be a column name, a parameter from a stored procedure, a variable, a numeric literal, a function that returns a numeric value, an expression enclosed by parentheses, or a table expression.

See Also   < (operator), <= (operator), > (operator), >= (operator), <> (operator)

<

ANSI • IBM • Informix • MS Access • MS SQL Server • Oracle • Sybase

Syntax   `expr1 < expr2`

Usage   The < operator returns **True** if *expr1* is less than *expr2*; otherwise it returns **False**.

Arguments   ▪ *expr1*—an arbitrary expression that can be a column name, a parameter from a stored procedure, a variable, a numeric literal, a function that returns a numeric value, an expression enclosed by parentheses, or a table expression.

     ▪ *expr2*—an arbitrary expression that can be a column name, a parameter from a stored procedure, a variable, a numeric literal, a function that returns a numeric value, an expression enclosed by parentheses, or a table expression.

See Also   = (operator), <= (operator), > (operator), >= (operator), <> (operator)

<=

ANSI • IBM • Informix • MS Access • MS SQL Server • Oracle • Sybase

Syntax   *expr1* <= *expr2*

Usage   The <= operator returns **True** if *expr1* is less than or equal to *expr2*; otherwise it returns **False**.

Arguments   ▪ *expr1*—an arbitrary expression that can be a column name, a parameter from a stored procedure, a variable, a numeric literal, a function that returns a numeric value, an expression enclosed by parentheses, or a table expression.

▪ *expr2*—an arbitrary expression that can be a column name, a parameter from a stored procedure, a variable, a numeric literal, a function that returns a numeric value, an expression enclosed by parentheses, or a table expression.

See Also   = (operator), < (operator), > (operator), >= (operator), <> (operator)

>

ANSI • IBM • Informix • MS Access • MS SQL Server • Oracle • Sybase

Syntax   *expr1* > *expr2*

Usage   The > operator returns **True** if *expr1* is greater than *expr2*; otherwise it returns **False**.

Arguments   ▪ *expr1*—an arbitrary expression that can be a column name, a parameter from a stored procedure, a variable, a numeric literal, a function that returns a numeric value, an expression enclosed by parentheses, or a table expression.

▪ *expr2*—an arbitrary expression that can be a column name, a parameter from a stored procedure, a variable, a numeric literal, a function that returns a numeric value, an expression enclosed by parentheses, or a table expression.

See Also   = (operator), < (operator), <= (operator), >= (operator), <> (operator)

>=

ANSI • IBM • Informix • MS Access • MS SQL Server • Oracle • Sybase

Syntax   `expr1 >= expr2`

Usage   The < operator returns **True** if *expr1* is greater than or equal to *expr2*; otherwise it returns **False**.

Arguments   ■ *expr1*—an arbitrary expression that can be a column name, a parameter from a stored procedure, a variable, a numeric literal, a function that returns a numeric value, an expression enclosed by parentheses, or a table expression.

■ *expr2*—an arbitrary expression that can be a column name, a parameter from a stored procedure, a variable, a numeric literal, a function that returns a numeric value, an expression enclosed by parentheses, or a table expression.

See Also   = (operator), < (operator), <= (operator), > (operator), <> (operator)

<>

ANSI • IBM • Informix • MS Access • MS SQL Server • Oracle • Sybase

Syntax   `expr1 <> expr2`

`expr1 != expr2`

`expr1 ^= expr2`

Usage   The <> operator returns **True** if *expr1* is not equal to *expr2*; otherwise it returns **False**.

Arguments   ■ *expr1*—an arbitrary expression that can be a column name, a parameter from a stored procedure, a variable, a numeric literal, a function that returns a numeric value, an expression enclosed by parentheses, or a table expression.

■ *expr2*—an arbitrary expression that can be a column name, a parameter from a stored procedure, a variable, a numeric literal, a function that returns a numeric value, an expression enclosed by parentheses, or a table expression.

See Also   = (operator), < (operator), <= (operator), > (operator), >= (operator)

( )

ANSI • IBM • Informix • MS Access • MS SQL Server • Oracle • Sybase

Syntax   (*expr*)

Usage   The () operator returns the value of *expr*, which will be evaluated before any operators outside the parentheses.

Argument ▪ *expr*—an arbitrary expression that can be a column name, a parameter from a stored procedure, a variable, a numeric literal, a function that returns a numeric value, an expression enclosed by parentheses, or a table expression that returns a single numeric expression.

See Also   + (operator), – (operator), * (operator), / (operator)

%found

Oracle

Syntax   *cursor*%**found**

          cursor%**notfound**

Usage   **%found** returns **True** if the latest **Delete**, **Insert**, **Select**, or **Update** successfully completed. **False** is returned if the previous operation failed. **Null** will be returned if the cursor has been opened but no rows have been fetched. **%notfound** will return **True** where **%found** returned **False** and **False** when **%found** returned **True**.

Argument ▪ *cursor*—a valid cursor created with the **Declare Cursor** statement.

See Also   **Declare Cursor** (statement), **Delete** (statement), **Insert** (statement), **Select** (statement), **Update** (statement)

%isopen

Syntax   *cursor***%isopen**

Usage   **%isopen** returns **True** if *cursor* has been opened and **False** if it has not.

Argument   ▪ *cursor*—a valid cursor created with the **Declare Cursor** statement.

See Also   **Close** (statement), **Declare Cursor** (statement), **Open** (statement)

%rowcount

Syntax   *cursor***%rowcount**

Usage   **%rowcount** returns zero if no rows were affected by the latest **Delete**, **Insert**, **Select**, or **Update** statement. It will return one if only one row was affected and two if more than one row was affected.

Argument   ▪ *cursor*—a valid cursor created with the **Declare Cursor** statement.

See Also   **Declare Cursor** (statement), **Delete** (statement), **Insert** (statement), **Select** (statement), **Update** (statement)

%rowtype

Syntax   { *cursor* | [*user.*]*table*}**%rowtype**

Usage   **%rowtype** returns a record structure based on a declared *cursor*, or an existing table or view. This value can be used inside a **Declare** section to create local storage for the entire record.

Arguments   ■ *cursor*—a valid cursor created with the **Declare Cursor** statement.

        ■ *user*—the name of a user that is used to qualify the name of a table or view in the database. If this value is omitted, then the current userid will be assumed.

        ■ *table*—the name of a table in the database.

See Also   **Declare Cursor** (statement)

%type

Syntax   { *variable* | [*user.*]*table.column*}**%rowtype**

Usage   **%type** returns the type of a particular column or variable.

Arguments   ■ *varible*—the name of a previously declared variable.

        ■ *user*—the name of a user that is used to qualify the name of a table or view in the database. If this value is omitted, then the current userid will be assumed.

        ■ *table*—the name of a table in the database.

        ■ *columnr*—a valid column from *table*.

See Also   **Declare** (statement)

||

Syntax   *expr* || *expr*

Usage   The || operator returns the concatenation of two character strings or two bit strings.

Argument ▪ *expr*—an arbitrary expression that can be a column name, a parameter from a stored procedure, a variable, a numeric literal, or a function that returns a character or bit string.

See Also **Bit_length** (function), **Character_length** (function)

Abs

Syntax   **Abs** (*expr*)

         Absval (*expr*)

Usage   **Abs** returns the absolute value of *expr*.

Argument ▪ *expr*—a numeric expression.

See Also **Double Precision** (data type), **Integer** (data type), **Smallint** (data type)

Acos

IBM • Informix • MS SQL Server • Oracle • Sybase

Syntax **Acos** (*expr*)

Usage **Acos** returns a **Double** that contains the arccosine of an angle expressed in radians. If *expr* is **Null**, then **Null** will be returned.

Argument ▪ *expr*—a numeric expression that can be a column name, a parameter from a stored procedure, a variable, or a function that returns a numeric value.

See Also **Double Precision** (data type)

And

ANSI • IBM • Informix • MS Access • MS SQL Server • Oracle • Sybase

Syntax *expr* **And** *expr*

Usage The **And** operator returns the **True** if both *expr* are **True**, otherwise **False** will be returned.

Argument ▪ *expr*—an arbitrary expression that can be a column name, a parameter from a stored procedure, a variable, a numeric literal, a function that returns a numeric value, an expression enclosed by parentheses, or a table expression that returns a **True** or **False** expression.

See Also **Between** (operator), **Exists** (operator), **In** (operator), **Like** (operator), **Not** (operator), **Null** (operator), **Or** (operator)

Ascii

IBM • Informix • MS SQL Server • Oracle • Sybase

Syntax **Ascii** (*string*)

Usage **Ascii** returns an **Integer** value that contains the ASCII code of the left-hand character of *string*.

Argument ▪ *string*—an arbitrary string expression that can be a column name, a parameter from a stored procedure, a variable, or a function that returns a character string.

See Also **Integer** (data type)

Asin

IBM • Informix • MS SQL Server • Oracle • Sybase

Syntax **Asin** (*expr*)

Usage **Asin** returns a **Double** that contains the arcsine of an angle expressed in radians. If *expr* is **Null**, then **Null** will be returned.

Argument ▪ *expr*—a numeric expression that can be a column name, a parameter from a stored procedure, a variable, or a function that returns a numeric value.

See Also **Double Precision** (data type)

Atan

IBM • Informix • MS SQL Server • Oracle • Sybase

Syntax **Atan (*expr*)**

Usage **Atan** returns a **Double** that contains the arctangent of an angle expressed in radians. If *expr* is **Null**, then **Null** will be returned.

Argument ▪ *expr*—a numeric expression that can be a column name, a parameter from a stored procedure, a variable, or a function that returns a numeric value.

See Also **Double Precision** (data type)

Atan2

IBM • Informix • MS SQL Server • Oracle • Sybase

Syntax **Atan2 (*xcoord, ycoord*)**

Usage **Atan2** returns a **Double** that contains the arctangent of an angle specified by x and y coordinates.

Arguments ▪ *xcoord*—a numeric expression that can be a column name, a parameter from a stored procedure, a variable, or a function that returns a numeric value that represents the x coordinate of an angle.

▪ *ycoord*—a numeric expression that can be a column name, a parameter from a stored procedure, a variable, or a function that returns a numeric value that represents the y coordinate of an angle.

See Also **Double Precision** (data type)

Avg

ANSI • IBM • Informix • MS SQL Server • Oracle • Sybase

Syntax **Avg** (*colexpr*)

Usage **Avg** returns the average of *colexpr* when computed across the entire set of retrieved rows. The function is legal only as part of a **Select** statement's list of columns.

Argument ■ *colexpr*—a numeric expression that can be a column name, a parameter from a stored procedure, a variable, or a function that returns a numeric value.

Example

```
Select DeptNo, Lname, Salary from Employees;

DEPTNO LNAME                SALARY
------ ---------------- ------------
    0. James              125000.00
    0. Ashley             100000.00
   10. Heyer              100000.00
   10. Bucky               90000.00
   20. Williams            35000.00
   20. Applegate           25000.00
   30. Freeze              90000.00
   30. Fleming             80000.00
   30. Blumgart            70000.00
   40. Osborne             20000.00
   40. Smith               15000.00
   50. Kelly               30000.00
   50. Tigger              27000.00
   50. Dudley              25000.00
   50. Jean                23000.00
   50. Brigham             21000.00
   60. Wyler               65000.00
   60. Dau                 60000.00

   18 record(s) selected.

Select Avg(Salary) from Employees;

1
-------------------------------
   55611.111111111111111111111

   1 record(s) selected.
```

```
Select DeptNo, Avg(Salary) from Employees Group By DeptNo;

DEPTNO 2
------ --------------------------------
    0.    112500.0000000000000000000000
   10.     95000.0000000000000000000000
   20.     30000.0000000000000000000000
   30.     80000.0000000000000000000000
   40.     17500.0000000000000000000000
   50.     25200.0000000000000000000000
   60.     62500.0000000000000000000000

 7 record(s) selected.
```

In the first **Select** statement, you see the Salary and DeptNo for each employee in the Employee table. In the second statement, you see the average salary for all employees. In the third table, you see the average salary for all the employees in a specific department.

See Also **Double Precision** (data type), **Select** (statement)

Between

OPERATOR

ANSI • IBM • Informix • MS Access • MS SQL Server • Oracle • Sybase

Syntax *expr1* **Between** *expr* and *expr*

expr1 **Not Between** *expr2* and *expr2*

Usage The **Between** operator returns **True** if the value of *expr1* is greater than or equal to *expr2* and less than or equal to *expr3*. The **Not** keyword is used to reverse the result (i.e., **False** if the value of *expr1* is greater than or equal to *expr2* and less than or equal to *expr3*).

Arguments
- *expr1*—an arbitrary expression that can be a column name, a parameter from a stored procedure, a variable, a numeric literal, a function that returns a numeric value, an expression enclosed by parentheses, or a table expression that returns a single numeric expression.

- *expr2*—an arbitrary expression that can be a column name, a parameter from a stored procedure, a variable, a numeric literal, a function that returns a numeric value, an expression enclosed by parentheses, or a table expression that returns a single numeric expression.

- *expr3*—an arbitrary expression that can be a column name, a parameter from a stored procedure, a variable, a numeric literal, a function that returns a numeric value, an expression enclosed by parentheses, or a table expression that returns a single numeric expression.

Example Select DeptNo, Lname from Employees;

```
DEPTNO LNAME
------ ----------------
    0. James
    0. Ashley
   10. Heyer
   10. Bucky
   20. Williams
   20. Applegate
   30. Freeze
   30. Fleming
   30. Blumgart
   40. Osborne
   40. Smith
   50. Kelly
   50. Tigger
   50. Dudley
   50. Jean
   50. Brigham
   60. Wyler
   60. Dau

  18 record(s) selected.
```

```
Select DeptNo, Lname from Employees Where DeptNo between 00 and 20;

DEPTNO LNAME
------ ----------------
    0. James
    0. Ashley
   10. Heyer
   10. Bucky
   20. Williams
   20. Applegate

   6 record(s) selected.
```

In the first **Select** statement, you see the Lname and DeptNo for each employee in the Employee table. In the second statement, you see the same information for the employees in all departments from 00 to 20 inclusive.

See Also **And** (operator), **Exists** (operator), **In** (operator), **Like** (operator), **Not** (operator), **Null** (operator), **Or** (operator)

Bit_Length

Syntax `Bit_length ( ` *string* ` )`

Usage **Bit_length** returns the length of *string* in bits.

Argument ▪ *string*—an arbitrary string expression.

See Also **Bit** (data type), **Character** (data type)

Blob

Syntax `Blob ( ` *string* ` [, ` *length* ` ] )`

Usage **Blob** returns a **Blob** that contains the value from *string*.

Arguments ▪ *string*—a string expression that can be a column name, a parameter from a stored procedure, a variable, or a function that returns a string value.
▪ *length*—the length of the **Blob** to be created. If not specified, *length* will default to the length of *string*.

See Also **Blob** (data type)

Case

Syntax
```
Case [ selector ]
        When expr Then value
    [ When expr Then value ]
        .
        .
        .
        Else value
    End
```

Usage   **Case** operator returns a single value that corresponds to the first expression that is **True** when *selector* is not specified or matches the value of *selector* when *selector* is specified. If no **When** clauses are **True** or match the value of *selector*, the *value* associated with the **Else** clause will be returned.

Arguments   ▪ *selector*—an arbitrary expression that can be a column name, a parameter from a stored procedure, a variable, a numeric literal, a function that returns a numeric value, an expression enclosed by parentheses, or a table expression that returns a single numeric expression.

   ▪ *expr*—if *selector* is not specified, *expr* is any expression that results in a **True** or **False** value. If *selector* is specified, *expr* can be any single value that is the same type as *selector*.

   value—the value that will be returned as the value of the **Case** operator.

Example
```
Select CustNo, Address,
    Case Locate('Maryland', Address)
        when 0 then 'Out of state'
        else 'Local'
    end
from Customers;
```

```
CUSTNO ADDRESS                           3
------ ------------------------------ ------------
 2001. Davis, South Dakota           Out of state
 2002. Beltsville, Maryland          Local
 2003. Parkville, Maryland           Local
 2004. Baltimore, Maryland           Local
 2005. Parkton, Maryland             Local
 2006. College Park, Maryland        Local
 2007. Laurel, Maryland              Local
 2008. Tulsa, Oklahoma               Out of state
 2009. Duluth, Minnesota             Out of state
 2010. Scaggsville, Maryland         Local
 2011. Dallas, Texas                 Out of state
 2012. Bowie, Maryland               Local
 2013. Richmond, Virginia            Out of state
 2014. Marion, South Dakota          Out of state
 2015. El Segundo, California        Out of state
 2016. Clarksville, Maryland         Local

  16 record(s) selected.
```

In this example, the **Case** operator is used to determine if the word 'Maryland' is found in Address. If it's found, a value of 'Local' is returned, otherwise a value of 'Out of state' is returned.

See Also   **Nullif** (function)

Cast

OPERATOR

ANSI

Syntax   **Cast** (*expr* **As** { *datatype* | *domain* })

Usage   **Cast** operator is used to convert an expression to the specified data type or domain.

> ### Tip
>
> *Use caution when using the **Cast** statement. While many data types can be converted from one type to another, some combinations do not make sense. Improper use can result in overflows, underflows, and other unexpected results.*

Arguments   ▪ *expr*—an arbitrary expression that can be a column name, a parameter from a stored procedure, a variable, a numeric literal, a function that returns a numeric value, an expression enclosed by parentheses, or a table expression that returns a single numeric expression.

   ▪ *datatype*—any datatype available with the database system.

   domain—any domain that was created by the **Create Domain** statement.

See Also   **Create Domain** (statement)

Ceiling

FUNCTION

IBM • Informix • MS SQL Server • Oracle • Sybase

Syntax   **Ceil[ing]** (*expr*)

Usage   **Ceiling** returns the smallest integer that is greater than or equal to the value of *expr*. A **Smallint** expression will return a **Smallint** value. An **Integer** expression will return an **Integer** value. A **Double** value is returned if a **Double**, **Decimal,** or **Real** expression is supplied. If a **Decimal** value with more than 15 digits is supplied, a loss of precision can occur in the conversion to a **Double**.

Argument   ▪ *expr*—a numeric expression that can be a column name, a parameter from a stored procedure, a variable, or a function that returns a numeric value.

Example   `values ceiling(4.5),floor(4.5)`

```
1
-----------------------
   +5.00000000000000E+000
   +4.00000000000000E+000
```

The **Values** statement is used to show that the **Ceiling** of 4.5 is 5.0 and the **Floor** of 4.5 is 4.0.

See Also   **Floor** (function), **Double Precision** (data type)

Char

FUNCTION

IBM • MS SQL Server • Sybase

Syntax   **Char** (*dateexpr* [, { ISO | USA | EUR | JIS | Local }])

Char (*string* [, *length*])

Char (*number* [, *decimalchar*])

Usage   **Char** is used to convert a value into a fixed-length character string. Three different types of values are supported: *dateexpr*, *string*, and *number*. Note that MS SQL Server and Sybase SQL Server support only the *number* parameter.

Arguments ▪ *dateexpr*—an expression that can be a column name, a parameter from a stored procedure, a variable, or a function that returns a **Date**, **Time,** or **Timestamp** value. The return value for a **Date** value will be 10 characters long. The return value for a **Time** value will be 8 characters long. The return value for a **Timestamp** value will be 26 characters long. **ISO**, **USA**, **EUR**, **JIS**, and **Local** specify the date/time format and should not be included with **Timestamp** values.

▪ *string*—a string of characters from a **Char**, **Varchar**, **Long Varchar**, or **Clob**. **Char** will return a fixed-length string whose length is *length*, or the length of *string* if *length* is not specified. If the length of *string* is greater than 254 characters, the result will be truncated and a warning will be generated.

▪ *length*—specifies the length of the returned character string. If omitted, the length of the returned string will be the same as *string*, up to a maximum length of 254.

■ *number*—any number. If a **Smallint** is specified, the length of the return value will be 6. An **Integer** will have a return length of 11. **Real** and **Double** will return a character string of length 26. **Decimal** will return a character string that is two places larger than the precision of the number.

■ *decimalchar*—a character that will be displayed as the decimal point. It can't be a number, a plus sign ("+"), a minus sign ("-"), or a space. Applies only when *number* is a **Decimal**.

See Also   **Character** (data type), **Date** (data type), **Decimal** (data type), **Double Precision** (data type), **Integer** (data type), **Real** (data type), **Smallint** (data type), **Time** (data type), **Timestamp** (data type)

Chr

FUNCTION

IBM • Oracle

Syntax   **Chr** (*charcode*)

Usage   **Chr** returns a **Char**(1) value that contains the character corresponding to *charcode*.

Argument   ■ *charcode*—a numeric expression that contains the ASCII value of a character.

Example
```
values chr(65)

1
-
A

  1 record(s) selected.
```

The **Values** statement is used to show that the ASCII character with a numeric value of 65 is 'A.'

See Also   **Character** (data type)

Character_length

FUNCTION

ANSI

Syntax   **Character_length** (*string*)

Char_length (*string*)

Usage   **Character_length** returns the length of *string* in characters.

Argument   ▪ *string*—an arbitrary string expression.

See Also   **Character** (data type)

Clob

FUNCTION

IBM

Syntax   **Clob** (*string* [, *length*])

Usage   **Clob** returns a **Clob** that contains the value from *string*.

Arguments   ▪ *string*—a string expression that can be a column name, a parameter from a stored procedure, a variable, or a function that returns a string value.

▪ *length*—the length of the **Clob** to be created. If not specified, *length* will default to the length of *string*.

See Also   **Clob** (data type)

Coalesce

FUNCTION

IBM • MS SQL Server • Sybase

Syntax   **Coalesce** (*value* [, *value*] . . .)

Usage   **Coalesce** returns the first non-**Null** value from the list of values. If all of the values in the list are **Null**, then **Null** will be returned.

> **Tip**
>
> *This is the same function as **Value**.*

Argument   ▪ *value*—an arbitrary expression that can be a column name, a parameter from a stored procedure, a variable, a numeric literal, a function that returns a value, an expression enclosed by parentheses, or a table.

See Also   **Case** (operator), **Value** (function)

Collchar

VARIABLE

Informix

Syntax   **Collchar**

Usage   **Collchar** returns a value which, when not defined, means the user can create tables containing both **Char** and **Nchar** columns. When **Collchar** is set to 1, then the user can only create **Nchar** columns. **DBNLS** must be set for 1 or 2 for this value to have any effect.

See Also   **Set** (statement)

Concat

IBM

Syntax **Concat** (*string, string*)

Usage **Concat** returns a string value that results from appending the second *string* to the end of the first *string*.

> **Tip**
>
> *This function returns the same value as the concatenation operator ("||"). Because the concatenation operator is included in all SQL database systems, you might want to use that operator rather than the **Concat** function.*

Argument ▪ *string*—an arbitrary expression that can be a column name, a parameter from a stored procedure, a variable, a numeric literal, or a function that returns a string value.

See Also | | (operator)

@@Connections

VARIABLE

MS SQL Server

Syntax **@@Connections**

Usage **@@Connections** contains the number of logins or attempted logins since the database server was started.

See Also **@@Max_connections** (statement)

Convert

Syntax **Convert** (*string* **Using** *conversion*)

Usage **Convert** returns a string of characters where each character has been transformed according to the rules specified in *conversion*.

> **Tip**
>
> The **Translate** *function offers a more general-purpose solution to translating character strings.*

Arguments ▪ *string*—an arbitrary string expression.

▪ *conversion*—the name of the conversion.

See Also **Translate** (function)

Cos

Syntax **Cos** (*expr*)

Usage **Cos** returns a **Double** that contains the cosine of an angle expressed in radians. If *expr* is **Null**, then **Null** will be returned.

Argument ▪ *expr*—a numeric expression that can be a column name, a parameter from a stored procedure, a variable, or a function that returns a numeric value.

See Also **Double Precision** (data type)

Cosh

Syntax **Cosh** (*expr*)

Usage **Cos** returns a **Double** that contains the hyperbolic cosine of an angle expressed in radians. If *expr* is **Null**, then **Null** will be returned.

Argument ▪ *expr*—a numeric expression that can be a column name, a parameter from a stored procedure, a variable, or a function that returns a numeric value.

See Also **Double Precision** (data type)

Cot

Syntax **Cot** (*expr*)

Usage **Cot** returns a **Double** that contains the cotangent of an angle expressed in radians. If *expr* is **Null**, then **Null** will be returned.

Argument ▪ *expr*—a numeric expression that can be a column name, a parameter from a stored procedure, a variable, or a function that returns a numeric value.

See Also **Double Precision** (data type)

Count

ANSI • IBM • Informix • MS SQL Server • Oracle • Sybase

Syntax **Count** (*colexpr* | *)

Usage **Count** returns the number of rows retrieved where *colexpr* is not **Null**. If an asterisk (*) is specified, the total number of rows retrieved will be returned without consideration for **Null** values.

Argument ▪ *colexpr*—a numeric expression that can be a column name, a parameter from a stored procedure, a variable, or a function that returns a value.

Example Select DeptNo, Lname, Fname from Employees;

```
DEPTNO LNAME             FNAME
------ ----------------- ------------
    0. James             Christopher
    0. Ashley            Samantha
   10. Heyer             Jill
   10. Bucky             Raymond
   20. Williams          Wanda
   20. Applegate         Susan
   30. Freeze            Wayne
   30. Fleming           Shaun
   30. Blumgart          Ian
   40. Osborne           Chris
   40. Smith             Walter
   50. Kelly             Robert
   50. Tigger            Elwyn
   50. Dudley            Richard
   50. Jean              Bonnie
   50. Brigham           Linda
   60. Wyler             Robert
   60. Dau               Veronica

18 record(s) selected.
```

```
Select Count(*) from Employees;

1
-----------
        18

 1 record(s) selected.


Select DeptNo, Count(*) from Employees Group By DeptNo;

DEPTNO 2
------ -----------
    0.         2
   10.         2
   20.         2
   30.         3
   40.         2
   50.         5
   60.         2

 7 record(s) selected.
```

In the first **Select** statement, you see the names of each employee in the Employee table. In the second statement, you see the total number of employees. In the third statement, you see the total number of employees in each department.

See Also   **Double Precision** (data type), **Select** (statement)

@@Cpu_busy

VARIABLE

MS SQL Server

Syntax   **@@Cpu_busy**

Usage   @@Cpu_busy contains the number of ticks (3.33 milliseconds = 1 tick) of CPU time that was used by the database server since it was last started.

See Also   **@@Idle** (variable), **@@Io_busy** (variable), **@@Timeticks** (variable)

Current Date
VARIABLE

IBM

Syntax `Current Date`

Usage **Current Date** returns a **Date** value that contains the current date from the system's time-of-day clock.

See Also **Current Time** (variable), **Current Timestamp** (variable), **Date** (data type), **Time** (data type), **Timestamp** (data type) , **Values** (statement)

Current_date
VARIABLE

ANSI

Syntax `Current_date`

Usage **Current_date** returns a **Date** value that contains the current date from the system's time-of-day clock.

See Also **Current_Time** (variable), **Current_Timestamp** (variable), **Date** (data type), **Time** (data type), **Timestamp** (data type)

Current Degree
VARIABLE

IBM

Syntax `Current Degree`

Usage **Current Degree** returns a **Char**(5) value that contains the degree of intra-partition parallelism for the execution of a dynamic SQL statement. When it returns a value of 'ANY,' then the database manager will determine the degree of intra-partition parallelism. Otherwise this value will contain the character equivalent to the degree of parallelism, which can range in value from 1 to 32767.

See Also **Set** (statement) , **Values** (statement)

Current Explain Mode

VARIABLE

IBM

Syntax **Current Explain Mode**

Usage **Current Explain Mode** returns a **Char**(8) value that, when 'YES,' means that the explain facility is enabled and explain information will be saved while a dynamic statement is compiled. 'EXPLAIN' is the same as 'YES,' but the statement won't be executed. A returned value of 'NO' means that the explain facility is disabled. The default value is 'NO.'

See Also **Set** (statement) , **Values** (statement)

Current Explain Snapshot

VARIABLE

IBM

Syntax **Current Explain Snapshot**

Usage **Current Explain Snapshot** returns a **Char**(8) value that, when 'YES,' means that the explain facility is enabled and explain snapshot information will be saved while a dynamic statement is compiled. 'EXPLAIN' is the same as 'YES,' but the statement won't be executed. A returned value of 'NO' means that the explain facility is disabled. The default value is 'NO.' This variable is only used by the **Delete**, **Insert**, **Select**, **Select Into**, **Set**, **Update**, **Values,** and **Values Into** statements.

See Also **Delete** (statement), **Insert** (statement), **Select** (statement), **Select Into** (statement), **Set** (statement), **Update** (statement), **Values** (statement), **Values Into** (statement)

Current Function Path

VARIABLE

IBM

Syntax   `Current Function Path`

Usage   **Current Function Path** returns a **Varchar**(254) value that contains a list of schema-names that will be searched to resolve function names and data types. Each schema-name must be enclosed in double quotes. The default value for this variable is ('"SYSIBM","SYSFUN",x') where x contains the value of the **User** variable enclosed in double quotes.

See Also   **Set** (statement), **Values** (statement)

Current Node

VARIABLE

IBM

Syntax   `Current Node`

Usage   **Current Node** returns an **Integer** value that contains the coordinator node number. A value of zero means that the database instance does not support partitioning.

See Also   **Values** (statement)

Current Query Optimization

Syntax   `Current Query Optimization`

Usage   **Current Query Optimization** returns an **Integer** value, as specified in Table 2-1 below.

Current Query Optimization	Description
0	Minimal optimization is performed. Good value for typical dynamic queries.
1	Optimization equivalent to DB2 version 1 is performed.
2	Optimization higher than DB2 version 1 and lower than DB2 version 3 is performed.
3	A moderate amount of optimization is performed.
5	A significant amount of optimization is performed. Uses heuristic rules to limit the amount of time spent selecting an access plan for complex dynamic queries.
7	Similar to 5, but without the heuristic rules.
9	A maximal amount of optimization is performed. Good for long-running queries and very complex queries.

Table 2-1: **Current Query Optimization** *values.*

See Also   **Set** (statement), **Values** (statement)

Current Server

Syntax   `Current Server`

Usage   **Current Server** returns a **Varchar**(18) value that contains the name of the active database server.

See Also   **Values** (statement)

Current Time

VARIABLE

IBM

Syntax `Current Time`

Usage **Current Time** returns a **Time** value that contains the current time from the system's time-of-day clock.

See Also **Current Date** (variable), **Current Timestamp** (variable), **Date** (data type), **Time** (data type), **Timestamp** (data type) , **Values** (statement)

Current_time

VARIABLE

ANSI

Syntax `Current_Time`

Usage **Current_time** returns a **Time** value that contains the current time from the system's time-of-day clock.

See Also **Current_date** (variable), **Current_timestamp** (variable), **Date** (data type), **Time** (data type), **Timestamp** (data type) , **Values** (statement)

Current Timestamp

VARIABLE

IBM

Syntax `Current Timestamp`

Usage **Current Timestamp** returns a **Timestamp** value that contains the current date and time from the system's time-of-day clock.

See Also **Current Date** (variable), **Current Time** (variable), **Date** (data type), **Time** (data type), **Timestamp** (data type)

Current_timestamp

VARIABLE

ANSI • MS SQL Server • Sybase

Syntax   `Current_timestamp`

Usage   **Current_timestamp** returns a **Timestamp** value that contains the current date and time from the system's time-of-day clock.

See Also   **Current_date** (variable), **Current_time** (variable), **Date** (data type), **Time** (data type), **Timestamp** (data type)

Current Timezone

VARIABLE

IBM

Syntax   `Current Timezone`

Usage   **Current Timezone** returns a **Decimal**(6,0) value that contains a value that can be subtracted from any **Time** or **Timestamp** value to determine the equivalent UTC (or GMT) time value.

See Also   **Current Date** (variable), **Current Time** (variable), **Date** (data type), **Time** (data type), **Timestamp** (data type) , **Values** (statement)

Current_user

VARIABLE

ANSI • MS SQL Server • Sybase

Syntax   `Current_user`

Usage   **Current_user** returns a character string that contains the current user authentication id.

See Also   **User** (variable)

@@Cursor_rows

Syntax **@@Cursor_rows**

Usage @@**Cursor_rows** contains the number of rows in the most recently opened cursor. If this value is negative, the cursor is being populated asynchronously and the absolute value of this value is the current number of rows in the keyset; otherwise, this value contains the number of rows in the fully populated keyset. If this value is zero, then no cursors have been opened or the last cursor has been closed.

See Also **Select** (statement)

Date

Syntax **Date** (*expr*)

Usage **Date** returns a **Date, Time,** or **Timestamp** value that is computed from *expr*.

Argument ▪ *expr*—a numeric expression that can be a column name, a parameter from a stored procedure, a variable, or a function that returns a numeric value. If *expr* contains a **Date** or **Timestamp** value, then only the date information will be returned. If *expr* is a numeric value, then the return value will be the number of days minus one past 1 January 0001. If *expr* contains a 7 character string, the **Date** function expects the format to be yyyyddd, where yyyy is a four-digit year and ddd is a three-digit day of year. Otherwise, the **Date** function will attempt to convert the string into a **Date** value.

Example
```
values date('8-13-1994')

1
----------
08/13/1994

  1 record(s) selected.
```

The **Values** statement is used to show how the character string '8-13-1994' can be converted to a **Date** value.

See Also   **Date** (data type), **Time** (data type), **Timestamp** (data type)

@@Datefirst

VARIABLE

MS SQL Server

Syntax   **@@Datefirst**

Usage   **@@Datefirst** contains a value from 1 through 7 that indicates the first day of a week (Monday through Sunday).

See Also   **DBTS** (variable)

Day

FUNCTION

IBM

Syntax   **Day** (*expr*)

Usage   **Day** returns a number that contains the day of month from a **Date** or **Timestamp** value or the day part of a **Date** or **Timestamp** duration.

Argument   ▪ *expr*—a **Date**, a **Timestamp**, or a **Date** or a **Timestamp** duration value.

Example
```
values day('8-13-1994')

1
----------
        13
```
The **Values** statement is used to show that the day part of the date '8-13-1994' is 13.

See Also   **Date** (data type), **Timestamp** (data type)

Dayname

Syntax **Dayname (*expr*)**

Usage **Dayname** returns a **Varchar**(100) value that contains the name of the weekday (i.e, "Sunday," "Monday," etc.) based on the **Date** value computed from *expr*.

Argument ▪ *expr*—a **Date** or **Timestamp** value that can be a column name, a parameter from a stored procedure, a variable, or a function that returns a numeric value. It can also be a character string that contains a date in the proper format.

Example
```
values dayname(date('4-16-1993'))

1
-----------------------------
Friday
```
The **Values** statement is used to show that '4-16-1993' is Friday.

See Also **Date** (data type), **Timestamp** (data type)

Dayofweek

Syntax **Dayofweek (*expr*)**

Usage **Dayofweek** returns an **Integer** value that contains the relative number of the weekday (i.e, Sunday = 1, Monday = 2, etc.) based on the **Date** value computed from *expr*.

Argument ▪ *expr*—a **Date** or **Timestamp** value that can be a column name, a parameter from a stored procedure, a variable, or a function that returns a numeric value. It can also be a character string that contains a date in the proper format.

See Also **Date** (data type), **Dayofyear** (function), **Timestamp** (data type)

Dayofyear

Syntax **Dayofyear** (*expr*)

Usage **Dayofyear** returns an **Integer** value that contains the day of the year (i.e., 1 January = 1, 1 February = 32, 31 December = 365 or 366 depending on leap year).

Argument ▪ *expr*—a **Date** or **Timestamp** value that can be a column name, a parameter from a stored procedure, a variable, or a function that returns a numeric value. It can also be a character string that contains a date in the proper format.

Example
```
values dayofweek(date('4-16-1993'))
```

```
1
----------
         6
```

The **Values** statement is used to show that '4-16-1993' is Friday, the sixth day of the week.

See Also **Date** (data type), **Dayofweek** (function), **Timestamp** (data type)

Days

Syntax **Days** (*expr*)

Usage **Days** returns an **Integer** value that contains the number of days plus one from 1 January 0001. This value can be used as input to the **Date** function.

Argument ▪ *expr*—a **Date** or **Timestamp** value that can be a column name, a parameter from a stored procedure, a variable, or a function that returns a numeric value. It can also be a character string that contains a date in the proper format.

See Also **Date** (data type), **Date** (function), **Timestamp** (data type)

Dbansiwarn

Syntax   **Dbansiwarn**

Usage   **Dbansiwarn** contains either 'Y' or 'N'. A value of 'Y' means that a warning message will be generated any time an Informix extension to the ANSI SQL standard is used. While the default value for this variable is 'N', it can set to 'Y' by using the -ANSI flag when running the utility program.

See Also   **Set** (statement)

Dbapicode

Syntax   **Dbapicode**

Usage   **Dbapicode** contains a reference to the language and code page used for terminal access to the database. The data stored in the database is stored using the standard code page available in the **Lang** variable.

See Also   **Dblang** (variable), **Lang** (variable), **Set** (statement)

Dbblobbuf

Syntax   **Dbblobbuf**

Usage   **Dbblobbuf** contains the size of an internal memory buffer in kilobytes to hold a **Blob**. **Blobs** smaller than this size are stored in the buffer, while those greater than this size are stored as a temporary disk file. **Dbblobbuf** defaults to a value of 10 (10 kilobytes of storage).

See Also   **Set** (statement)

Dbclob

Syntax **Dbclob** (*graphic* [, *length*])

Usage **Dbclob** returns a **Dbclob** that contains the value from the double-byte string *graphic*.

Arguments ▪ *graphic*—a graphic string expression that can be a column name, a parameter from a stored procedure, a variable, or a function that returns a string value.

▪ *length*—the length of the **Dbclob** to be created. If not specified, *length* will default to the length of *graphic*.

See Also **Dbclob** (data type), **Graphic** (data type), **Vargraphic** (data type)

Dbdate

Syntax **Dbdate**

Usage **Dbdate** contains information about how date values are displayed. The format for this value is:

dateparm separatorparm
dateparm
MDY2
MDY4
DMY2
DMY4
Y2MD
Y2DM
Y4MD
Y4DM
separatorparm
/
.
,
0

If not specified, **Dbdate** will default to MDY4/.

See Also **Dbtime** (variable), **Set** (statement)

Dbdelimiter

VARIABLE

Informix

Syntax   **Dbdelimiter**

Usage   **Dbdelimiter** contains a single character that will be used as a field delimiter with the Dbexport utility and with the **Load** and **Unload** statements. This character can be any character except for 0 to 9, a to f, A to F, newline, Ctrl-J, or \. By default, **Dbdelimiter** is set to |.

See Also   **Load** (statement), **Set** (statement), **Unload** (statement)

Dbedit

VARIABLE

Informix

Syntax   **Dbedit**

Usage   **Dbedit** contains the name of the editor to be used with SQL statements and command files in DB-Access. For Windows NT, this will be the Notepad editor.

> **Tip**
>
> *While any editor can be used, Informix expects that the files will be saved as a normal ASCII text file. So be sure to save your changes properly if you use a word processor as your editor.*

See Also   **Set** (statement)

Dblang

VARIABLE

Informix

Syntax   **Dblang**

Usage   **Dblang** contains the path name that stores the compiled message files used by your application. This path can be relative to **Informixdir** or the full path name. The default value is %**Informixdir**%\msg.

See Also   **Lang** (variable), **Set** (statement)

Dbmoney

Syntax   **Dbmoney**

Usage   **Dbmoney** contains information about how monetary values are displayed. The format for this value is:

[*front*] { . | , } [*back*]

    If not specified, **Dbmoney** will default to a dollar sign followed by a period ("$."). If **Dbnls** is set, then the value of **Lc_monetary** will override the value of this variable.

See Also   **Dbtime** (variable), **Set** (statement)

Dbnls

Syntax   **Dbnls**

Usage   **Dbnls** contains a value that determines how an NLS database will operate. A value of 1 means that the NLS value for the application must match the NLS value for the database or an error will occur. A value of 2 means that the NLS values of the client and server can differ and the server will operate under the NLS value assigned at its creation.

See Also   **Set** (statement)

Dbpath

Syntax   **Dbpath**

Usage   **Dbpath** contains a list of one or more database servers up to a maximum of 16. This information is used to resolve the location of the server on the **Connect, Database, Start Database,** and **Drop Database** statements when the location of the database is not specified or when the database can't be located on the default server.

   Each database server name is preceded by a double backslash (\ \). Multiple servers are separated by semicolons, as follows:

servername [; *servername*] . . .

Each server name must be less than 128 characters; the total length of **Dbpath** depends on the platform on which you are running.

See Also   **Set** (statement)

Dbspacetemp

Syntax   **Dbspacetemp**

Usage   **Dbspacetemp** contains a list of one or more dbspaces where temporary tables can be built. Semicolons (;) are used to separate dbspace names as follows:

dbspace [; *dbspace*] . . .

This information is used by the **Select Into Temp** statement and **Create Temp Table** when the **Into** clause is not used to determine a location for the temporary table.

See Also   **Create Temp Table** (statement), **Select Into Temp** (statement), **Set** (statement)

Dbtime

Syntax   **Dbtime**

Usage   **Dbtime** contains information about how date and time values are displayed. The formatting characters used to display the date and time are listed in Table 2-2.

Formatting Characters	Description
%b	Abbreviated month name.
%B	Full month name.
%d	Day of month number (01 to 31).
%Fn	Value of the fraction where n specifies the number of digits after the decimal point.
%H	Twenty-four hour clock (00-23).
%I	Twelve hour clock (01-12).
%M	Minutes number (00-59).
%m	Month number (01-12).
%p	A.M. or P.M.
%S	Seconds number (00-59).
%y	Four-digit year.
%Y	Four-digit year. User must enter four digits.
%%	Display a percent sign (%).

Table 2-2: **Dbtime** *formatting characters.*

Other characters can be included in the format string and will be displayed without change. Thus, the format string %m/%d/%y will display the date 14 September 1991 as 09/14/91.

See Also   **Dbdate** (variable), **Set** (statement)

@@Dbts

VARIABLE

MS SQL Server

Syntax **@@Dbts**

Usage **@@Dbts** contains the current value for the **Timestamp** data type.

See Also **Timestamp** (data type)

Dbupspace

VARIABLE

Informix

Syntax **Dbupspace**

Usage **Dbupspace** contains the amount of space in kilobytes that the **Update Statistics** statement can use when analyzing a table. If you try to set this variable to less than 1,024 kilobytes, it will automatically be set to 1,024 without generating an error or warning message.

See Also **Set** (statement), **Update Statistics** (statement)

Decimal

FUNCTION

IBM

Syntax **Dec[imal]** (*number* [, *precision* [, *scale*]])

Dec[imal] (*string* [, *precision* [, *scale* [, *decimalchar*]]])

Usage **Decimal** is used to convert a character string or number into a **Decimal** value.

Arguments ▪ *number*—an arbitrary expression that can be a column name, a parameter from a stored procedure, a variable, a numeric literal, a function that returns a numeric value, an expression enclosed by parentheses, or a table expression that returns a single numeric expression.

- *precision*—the number of digits in the result.
- *scale*—the scale of the result.
- *string*—a string of characters from a **Char**, or **Varchar.**
- *decimalchar*—a character that is used in *string* as the decimal point. It can't be a number, a plus sign ("+"), a minus sign ("-") or a space (" ").

See Also   **Character** (data type), **Decimal** (data type)

Degrees

FUNCTION

IBM • MS SQL Server • Sybase

Syntax   **Degrees (*expr*)**

Usage   **Degrees** converts radians into degrees.

Argument   ▪ *expr*—a number that contains a measurement in radians.

See Also   **Cos** (function), **Radians** (function), **Sin** (function)

Delimident

VARIABLE

Informix

Syntax   **Delimident**

Usage   **Delimident** specifies that strings delimited by double quotes (") are delimited identifiers. This means that reserved words, such as **Table** or **Update,** can be used as identifiers. Also, delimited identifiers can contain spaces and other non-alphanumeric characters.

See Also   **Set** (statement)

Difference

FUNCTION

IBM • MS SQL Server

Syntax **Difference** (*string, string*)

Usage **Difference** compares two character strings and returns an **Integer** value from 0 to 4 that describes how close the two strings sound. A value of 4 means that the two strings sound very similar. The **Soundex** function is used to determine how the strings sound.

Argument ▪ *string*—a **Char** or **Varchar** string that contains one or more words to be compared.

Example
```
select lname, fname from employees where difference(lname,'Smythe') > 3

LNAME             FNAME
----------------  -------------
Smith             Walter

 1 record(s) selected.
```

The **Difference** function is used to find a person in the Employee table whose name sounds like 'Smythe.'

See Also **Soundex** (function)

Digits

FUNCTION

IBM

Syntax **Digits** (*expr*)

Usage **Digits** converts a numeric expression into a fixed-length (**Char**) string.

Argument ▪ *expr*—an arbitrary expression that can be a column name, a parameter from a stored procedure, a variable, a numeric literal, a function that returns a numeric value, an expression enclosed by parentheses, or a table expression that returns a single numeric expression.

See Also **Decimal** (function)

Double

Syntax   **Double[_precision]** (*number*)

Double[_precision] (*string*)

Usage   **Double** is used to convert a character string or number into a **Double** value.

> **Tip**
>
> *This function is the same as the **Float** function.*

Arguments   ▪ *number*—an arbitrary expression that can be a column name, a parameter from a stored procedure, a variable, a numeric literal, a function that returns a numeric value, an expression enclosed by parentheses, or a table expression that returns a single numeric expression.

▪ *string*—a string of characters from a **Char**, or **Varchar.**

See Also   **Character** (data type), **Double Precision** (data type)

@@Error

Syntax   **@@Error**

Usage   **@@Error** contains the error code for the most recently executed statement. A value of 0 means that no error occurred.

See Also   **@@Total_errors** (variable)

Event_mon_state

FUNCTION

IBM

Syntax **Event_mon_state** (*monitorname*)

Usage **Event_mon_state** returns an **Integer** value of 0 when the event monitor is inactive and a value of 1 when the event monitor is active.

Argument ▪ *monitorname*—the name of an event monitor. This value must exist in the table Syscat.Eventmonitors in the Evmonname column.

See Also **Character** (data type), **Double Precision** (data type)

Exists

OPERATOR

ANSI • IBM • Informix • MS Access • MS SQL Server • Oracle • Sybase

Syntax **Exists** (*selectstatement*)

Usage The **Exists** operator returns **True** if *selectstatement* returns at least one row. If no rows are returned, **False** will be returned.

Argument ▪ *selectstatement*—a valid **Select** statement.

Example

```
select Lname, Fname from employees e
    where exists
        (select * from departments where
            e.empno = manager)
```

LNAME	FNAME
James	Christopher
Heyer	Jill
Williams	Wanda
Freeze	Wayne
Osborne	Chris
Kelly	Robert
Wyler	Robert

```
 7 record(s) selected.
```

The **Exists** operator is used to find all employees who are listed as managers in the department table.

See Also   **And** (operator), **Between** (operator), **In** (operator), **Like** (operator), **Not** (operator), **Null** (operator), **Or** (operator), **Select** (statement)

Exp

FUNCTION

IBM • Informix • MS SQL Server • Oracle • Sybase

Syntax   **Exp** (*expr*)

Usage   **Exp** returns a **Double** value that contains the exponential value of *expr*.

Argument ▪ *expr*—an arbitrary expression that can be a column name, a parameter from a stored procedure, a variable, a numeric literal, a function that returns a numeric value, an expression enclosed by parentheses, or a table expression that returns a single numeric expression.

See Also   **Ln** (function)

Extract

FUNCTION

ANSI

Syntax   Extract (field From expr)

Usage   **Extract** returns a numeric value from a **Datetime** or **Interval**.

Arguments ▪ *field*—one of the following items: Year, Month, Day, Hour, Minute, Second, Timezone_hour, Timezone_minute.

▪ *expr*—a Datetime or Interval expression.

See Also   **Datetime** (data type), **Interval** (data type)

Fet_buf_size

VARIABLE

Informix

Syntax   **Fet_buf_size**

Usage   **Fet_buf_size** contains the size of the fetch buffer for all data types except for **Blobs**.

See Also   **Set** (statement)

@@Fetch_status

VARIABLE

MS SQL Server

Syntax   **@@Fetch_status**

Usage   **@@Fetch_status** contains the current status of the **Fetch** command. A value of 0 means it was successful, a value of -1 means that the **Fetch** failed or the row was beyond the results set, and a value of -2 means that the row was missing.

See Also   **Fetch** (statement)

Float

FUNCTION

IBM

Syntax   **Float** (*number*)

        Float (*string*)

Usage   **Float** is used to convert a character string or number into a **Double** value.

> **Tip**
>
> *This function is the same as the **Double** function.*

Arguments ▪ *number*—an arbitrary expression that can be a column name, a parameter from a stored procedure, a variable, a numeric literal, a function that returns a numeric value, an expression enclosed by parentheses, or a table expression that returns a single numeric expression.

▪ *string*—a string of characters from a **Char**, or **Varchar**.

See Also **Character** (data type), **Double Precision** (data type)

Floor

FUNCTION

IBM • Informix • MS SQL Server • Oracle • Sybase

Syntax **Floor** (*expr*)

Usage **Floor** returns the smallest integer that is less than or equal to the value of *expr*. A **Smallint** expression returns a **Smallint** value. An **Integer** expression returns an **Integer** value. A **Double** value is returned if a **Double, Decimal,** or **Real** expression is supplied. If a **Decimal** value with more than 15 digits is supplied, a loss of precision can occur in the conversion to a **Double**.

Argument ▪ *expr*—a numeric expression that can be a column name, a parameter from a stored procedure, a variable, or a function that returns a numeric value.

Example

```
values ceiling(4.5),floor(4.5)

1
------------------------
  +5.00000000000000E+000
  +4.00000000000000E+000
```

The **Values** statement is used to show that the **Ceiling** of 4.5 is 5.0 and the **Floor** of 4.5 is 4.0.

See Also **Ceiling** (function)

Generate_unique

Syntax **Generate_unique ( )**

Usage **Generate_unique** returns a **Char**(13) **For Bit Data** value that contains a unique value. This function is preferred to using the **Timestamp** data type, because a unique value will be generated on each row of a multiple-row insert.

> **Tip**
>
> *The return value is based in part on the server's clock. If the server's clock is moved backwards, then it is possible for duplicate values to be generated.*

See Also **Timestamp** (data type)

Graphic

Syntax **Graphic (*graphic* [, *length*])**

Usage **Graphic** returns a **Graphic** that contains the value from *graphic*.

Arguments ▪ *graphic*—a graphic string expression that can be a column name, a parameter from a stored procedure, a variable, or a function that returns a string value.

▪ *length*—the length of the **Graphic** to be created. This value must be less than or equal to 127.

See Also **Graphic** (data type)

Hex

Syntax **Hex** (*expr*)

Usage **Hex** returns a character string that contains the hexadecimal equivalent of *expr* as defined by the server. If *expr* is a number, this value reflects how the number is stored internally on the server. If *expr* is a character string, each pair of bytes in the return value represents a single character in *expr*. If *expr* is a **Graphic**, then each character in *expr* will occupy four characters in the result.

> ### Tip
>
> *The values returned by this function reflect how the server stores the information. You should use caution when the server is EBCDIC and the client is ASCII, or vice versa, because the return value will not be consistent with the native character set of the client. Also, numeric values will be stored as the server stores them in memory. This could mean that the bytes are arranged from the high-order byte to the low-order byte, which is what you expect, or from the low-order byte to the high-order byte, which is typical of Intel-based computers.*

Argument ▪ *expr*—a numeric or character string expression that can be a column name, a parameter from a stored procedure, a variable, or a function that returns a numeric or character string value.

See Also **Graphic** (data type)

Hextoraw

Syntax **Hextoraw** (*string*)

Usage **Hextoraw** returns the binary value of *string* which contains a string of hexadecimal characters.

Argument ▪ *string*—a character string expression that can be a column name, a parameter from a stored procedure, a variable, or a function that returns character string value containing a hexadecimal number.

See Also **Character** (data type)

Hour

Syntax   **Hour** (*expr*)

Usage   **Hour** returns an **Integer** value that contains the hour of day expressed as a number. It can also represent the difference between two **Time** or **Timestamp** values in the range of -99 to +99.

Argument   ▪ *expr*—a **Time** or **Timestamp** value that can be a column name, a parameter from a stored procedure, a variable, or a function that returns a numeric value. It can also be a character string that contains a time in the proper format.

See Also   **Time** (data type), **Timestamp** (data type)

@@Identity

Syntax   `@@Identity`

Usage   **@@Identity** contains the most recent value that would be assigned into an **Identity** column during an **Insert** or **Select Into** statement.

See Also   **Identity** (data type), **Insert** (statement), **Select Into** (statement)

@@Idle

Syntax   `@@Idle`

Usage   **@@Idle** contains the number of ticks (3.33 milliseconds = 1 tick) that the server was not performing useful work since it was last started.

See Also   **@@Cpu_busy** (variable), **@@Io_busy** (variable), **@@Timeticks** (variable)

In

ANSI • IBM • Informix • MS Access • MS SQL Server • Oracle • Sybase

Syntax   { *expr1* | (*expr2* [, *expr2*] . . .) } [**Not**] **IN** { (*selectstatement*)
| (*expr3* [, *expr3*] . . .) }

Usage   The **In** operator returns **True** if *expr1* is found in the result set of *selectstatement* or in the list of *expr3* values. If a list of values are specified for *expr2*, then each value in the list must correspond to a column of *selectstatement*. The **Not** keyword is used to reverse the result of this operator.

Arguments   ▪ *expr1*—an arbitrary expression that can be a column name, a parameter from a stored procedure, a variable, a numeric literal, a function that returns a numeric value, an expression enclosed by parentheses, or a table expression that returns a single numeric expression.

▪ *expr2*—an arbitrary expression that can be a column name, a parameter from a stored procedure, a variable, a numeric literal, a function that returns a numeric value, an expression enclosed by parentheses, or a table expression that returns a single numeric expression.

▪ *expr3*—an arbitrary expression that can be a column name, a parameter from a stored procedure, a variable, a numeric literal, a function that returns a numeric value, an expression enclosed by parentheses, or a table expression that returns a single numeric expression.

▪ *selectstatement*—a valid select statement.

Example   Select ItemName from Items where ItemNo in (3002, 3005, 3007, 3008)

```
ITEMNAME
------------------------------------------
The Tower Computer of Babel
The Itsy Bitsy Teenie Weenie Palmtop
The Modemraker
The Backup to the Future Tape Drive

 4 record(s) selected.
```

This **Select** statement uses the **In** operator to select ItemNames from the Items table where the ItemNo is specified in the list of numbers.

See Also   **And** (operator), **Between** (operator), **Exists** (operator), **Like** (operator), **Not** (operator), **Null** (operator), **Or** (operator)

Informixconretry

Syntax   `Informixconretry`

Usage   **Informixconretry** contains the number of times after the initial connection attempt that the client can attempt to connect to the server.

See Also   **Connect** (statement), **Informixcontime** (variable), **Set** (statement)

Informixcontime

Syntax   `Informixcontime`

Usage   **Informixcontime** contains the minimum number of seconds that must pass before a connection error is returned. After the initial connection attempt, the remaining attempts will be spread over the **Informixcontime** interval. For instance, if **Informixconretry** is set to 2 and **Informixcontime** is set to 30, the connection will be retried at 15 seconds and 30 seconds.

See Also   **Connect** (statement), **Informixconretry** (variable), **Set** (statement)

Informixdir

Syntax   `Informixdir`

Usage   **Informixdir** contains the full path to the directory that contains the Informix product files. This variable is useful when you have multiple copies of the server installed on a single machine.

See Also   **Set** (statement)

Informixserver

VARIABLE

Informix

Syntax   `Informixserver`

Usage   **Informixserver** contains the name of the preferred database server. This value must be set even if your application always specifies the name of the server when connecting to the server.

See Also   **Dbpath** (variable), **Set** (statement)

Informixstacksize

VARIABLE

Informix

Syntax   `Informixstacksize`

Usage   **Informixstacksize** contains the stack size in kilobytes for a client session.

See Also   **Set** (statement)

Informixserver

VARIABLE

Informix

Syntax   `Informixserver`

Usage   **Informixserver** contains the name of the preferred database server. This value must be set even if your application always specifies the name of the server when connecting to the server.

See Also   **Dbpath** (variable), **Set** (statement)

Insert

Syntax **Insert** (`string, start, delchars, insertstring`)

Usage **Insert** returns a **Varchar**(4000) if *string* is a **Varchar** or **Char**. If *string* is a **Blob** or **Clob**, then the return value will be a **Blob** or **Clob,** respectively. The **Insert** function will delete the specified number of characters beginning at *start* and then insert *insertstring* at the same location. The characters that follow *start* will remain in the string and follow the characters in *insertstring*.

Arguments ▪ *string*—a string value which can be a column name, a parameter from a stored procedure, a variable, or a function that returns a string value.

▪ *start*—a numeric value that is the starting position inside *string* where the characters will be deleted and inserted.

▪ *delchars*—the number of characters to be deleted.

▪ *insertstring*—a string of characters that are to be inserted at *start*.

Example ```
values insert ('I hate SQL!', 3, 4, 'really love')

1

I really love SQL!
```

The **Values** statement demonstrates how to use the **Insert** function to replace the word starting at the third character and extending for four characters and replace it with the phrase 'really love.'

**See Also**  **Blob** (data type), **Character** (data type), **Clob** (data type), **Varchar** (data type)
```

Integer

FUNCTION

IBM

Syntax **Integer** ({ *number* | *string* })

Usage **Integer** is used to convert a character string or number into an **Integer** value.

Arguments ■ *number*—an arbitrary expression that can be a column name, a parameter from a stored procedure, a variable, a numeric literal, a function that returns a numeric value, an expression enclosed by parentheses, or a table expression that returns a single numeric expression.

■ *string*—a string of characters from a **Char**, or **Varchar.**

See Also **Character** (data type), **Integer** (data type), **Smallint** (function)

@@Io_busy

VARIABLE

MS SQL Server

Syntax **@@Io_busy**

Usage **@@Io_busy** contains the number of ticks (3.33 milliseconds = 1 tick) that the server was performing I/O activities since it was last started.

See Also **@@Cpu_busy** (variable), **@@Idle** (variable), **@@Timeticks** (variable)

Julian_day

Syntax   `Julian_day ( expr )`

Usage   **Julian_day** returns the number of days between 1 January 4712 BC (the start of the Julian calendar) and the date specified by *expr*.

Argument   ▪ *expr*—a **Date** or a **Timestamp** value or a character string that contains a valid date.

See Also   **Date** (data type), **Timestamp** (data type)

Lang

Syntax   **Lang**

Usage   **Lang** contains a reference to the language, country, and code page that will be used for access to the database. The format for this value is:

language [*_country*][*.codepage*]

Arguments   ▪ *language*—name of the language (ex: English, French, etc.).

▪ *country*—name of the country where the language is spoken (ex: Swiss French).

▪ *codepage*—modifies the settings in *language* and *country*.

The exact values for *language*, *country*, and *codepage* depend on your operating system and can vary from system to system.

Setting this variable will also update the contents of **Lc_collate**, **Lc_ctype**, **Lc_monetary**, **Lc_numeric** and **Lc_time** to correspond to the particular value of **Lang**. These values can be modified after **Lang** is set to further customize how information is presented to the user. If **Lang** is not specified, then it will default to English.

See Also   **Dblang** (variable), **Lc_collate** (variable), **Lc_ctype** (variable), **Lc_monetary** (variable), **Lc_numeric** (variable), **Lc_time** (variable), **Set** (statement)

@@Langid

VARIABLE

MS SQL Server

Syntax   `@@Langid`

Usage   **@@Langid** contains the currently used language ID.

See Also   **@@Language** (variable)

@@Language

VARIABLE

MS SQL Server

Syntax   `@@Language`

Usage   **@@Language** contains the name of the currently used language.

See Also   **@@Langid** (variable)

Lc_collate

VARIABLE

Informix

Syntax   `Lc_collate`

Usage   **Lc_collate** contains a reference to the language, country, and code page that will be used to sort data in **Nchar** and **Nvarchar** columns in the database. The format for this value is:

`language [ _country ][ .codepage ]`

Arguments   ▪ *language*—name of the language (ex: English, French, etc.).

▪ *country*—name of the country where the language is spoken (ex: Swiss French).

▪ *codepage*—modifies the settings in *language* and *country*.

The exact values for *language, country,* and *codepage* depend on your operating system and can vary from system to system.

See Also   **Dblang** (variable), **Lang** (variable), **Lc_ctype** (variable), **Lc_monetary** (variable), **Lc_numeric** (variable), **Lc_time** (variable), **Nchar** (data type), **Nvarchar** (data type), **Set** (statement)

Lc_ctype

Syntax   `Lc_ctype`

Usage   **Lc_ctype** contains a reference to the language, country, and code page that will be used to specify character attributes such as spaces, punctuation, uppercase letters, etc. in **Nchar** and **Nvarchar** columns in the database. The format for this value is:

     language [*_country*][*.codepage*]

Arguments   ▪ *language*—name of the language (ex: English, French, etc.).

     ▪ *country*—name of the country where the language is spoken (ex: Swiss French).

     ▪ *codepage*—modifies the settings in *language* and *country*.

     The exact values for *language*, *country*, and *codepage* depend on your operating system and can vary from system to system.

See Also   **Dblang** (variable), **Lang** (variable), **Lc_collate** (variable), **Lc_monetary** (variable), **Lc_numeric** (variable), **Lc_time** (variable), **Nchar** (data type), **Nvarchar** (data type), **Set** (statement)

Lc_monetary

Syntax   `Lc_monetary`

Usage   **Lc_monetary** contains a reference to the language, country, and code page that will be used to display monetary values. The format for this value is:

     language [*_country*][*.codepage*]

Arguments   ▪ *language*—name of the language (ex: English, French, etc.).

     ▪ *country*—name of the country where the language is spoken (ex: Swiss French).

     ▪ *codepage*—modifies the settings in *language* and *country*.

     The exact values for *language*, *country*, and *codepage* depend on your operating system and can vary from system to system.

See Also   **Dblang** (variable), **Lang** (variable), **Lc_ctype** (variable), **Lc_collate** (variable), **Lc_numeric** (variable), **Lc_time** (variable), **Nchar** (data type), **Nvarchar** (data type), **Set** (statement)

Lc_numeric

VARIABLE

Informix

Syntax `Lc_numeric`

Usage **Lc_numeric** contains a reference to the language, country, and code page that will be used to display numeric values. This value will modify the decimal separator and digits separator. The format for this value is:

`language [ _country ][ .codepage ]`

Arguments ▪ *language*—name of the language (ex: English, French, etc.).

▪ *country*—name of the country where the language is spoken (ex: Swiss French).

▪ *codepage*—modifies the settings in *language* and *country*.

The exact values for *language, country,* and *codepage* depend on your operating system and can vary from system to system.

See Also **Dblang** (variable), **Lang** (variable), **Lc_ctype** (variable), **Lc_collate** (variable), **Lc_monetary** (variable), **Lc_time** (variable), **Nchar** (data type), **Nvarchar** (data type), **Set** (statement)

Lc_time

VARIABLE

Informix

Syntax `Lc_time`

Usage **Lc_time** contains a reference to the language, country, and code page that will be used to display time and date values. The format for this value is:

`language [ _country ][ .codepage ]`

Arguments ▪ *language*—name of the language (ex: English, French, etc.).

▪ *country*—name of the country where the language is spoken (ex: Swiss French).

▪ *codepage*—modifies the settings in *language* and *country*.

The exact values for *language, country,* and *codepage* depend on your operating system and can vary from system to system.

See Also **Dblang** (variable), **Lang** (variable), **Lc_ctype** (variable), **Lc_collate** (variable), **Lc_monetary** (variable), **Lc_numeric** (variable), **Nchar** (data type), **Nvarchar** (data type), **Set** (statement)

Lcase

Syntax **Lcase** (*string*)

Usage **Lcase** converts all of the uppercase characters contained in *string* to lowercase. Characters that have diacritical marks will not be converted to lowercase.

Argument ▪ *string*—a **Char, Varchar, Long Varchar,** or **Clob** value.

Example   Select Lcase(Name) from Customers

```
1
-------------------------------------------
bucky's country roundup
jill's just plane crazy
maries's onsite mainframes
waldo's antique computers and stuff
barbara's ondisplays
terry's catnip farm
sargent scott's seafood and steakhouse
becky's kids place
tracy's treehouse
peter's puppet boutique
joan's technology shop
barbie's house of laptops
rosie's garden shop
goose's kitty katt kitchen
jennifer's collectable wheels
randy's universal import-export

   16 record(s) selected.
```

This examples selects all of the Names and converts them to lowercase from the Customer table.

See Also **Character** (data type), **Clob** (data type), **Long Varchar** (data type), **Ucase** (function), **Varchar** (data type)

Left

Syntax   **Left** (*string*, *chars*)

Usage   **Left** returns the left-hand *chars* characters from *string*. The return value is a
Varchar(4000) if *string* is a **Varchar** or **Char**. If *string* is a **Blob** or **Clob**, then the return
value will be a **Blob** or **Clob**, respectively.

Arguments   ▪ *string*—a string value that can be a column name, a parameter from a stored procedure,
a variable, or a function that returns a string value.

   ▪ *chars*—the number of characters to be returned.

Example
```
Select Left(ItemName,25) from Items

1
------------------------
The Big Comfy Laptop
The Tower Computer of Bab
The Desktop Daemon
The Big Bad Unix Workstat
The Itsy Bitsy Teenie Wee
The Monster Mainframe
The Modemraker
The Backup to the Future
The Smokey and the Disk D

  9 record(s) selected.
```

This examples selects only the first 25 characters for each ItemName in the Items table.

See Also   **Blob** (data type), **Character** (data type), **Clob** (data type), **Right** (function), **Varchar**
(data type)

Length

Syntax **Length (*expr*)**

Usage **Length** returns the number of bytes of storage that is occupied by *expr*, except for **Graphic** and **Dbclob,** which return the number of double-byte characters.

Argument ▪ *expr*—a numeric or character string expression that can be a column name, a parameter from a stored procedure, a variable, or a function that returns a numeric or character string value.

See Also **Dbclob** (data type), **Graphic** (data type), **Vargraphic** (data type)

Like

Syntax *expr* [**Not**] **Like** *pattern* [**Escape** *escape*]

Usage The **Like** operator returns **True** if the specified string expression (*expr*) matches the specified *pattern* string. The **Not** operator is used to reverse the result of this operator.

Arguments ▪ *expr*—an arbitrary expression that can be a column name, a parameter from a stored procedure, a variable, a numeric literal, a function that returns a numeric value, an expression enclosed by parentheses, or a table expression that returns a string expression.

▪ *pattern*—a string expression that contains a pattern where the underline character ("_") will match any single character, the percent sign ("%") matches a string of zero or more characters and any other character matches only itself.

▪ *escape*—a string expression containing a single character that when used in front of the underline or percent sign characters means that the underline character or percent sign character should be used as a single character rather than a pattern matching expression.

Example Select Name, Address from Customers Where Address Like '%Maryland%'

NAME	ADDRESS
Jill's Just Plane Crazy	Beltsville, Maryland
Marie's Onsite Mainframes	Parkville, Maryland
Waldo's Antique Computers and Stuff	Baltimore, Maryland
Barbara's OnDisplays	Parkton, Maryland
Terry's Catnip Farm	College Park, Maryland

```
Sargent Scott's Seafood and Steakhouse   Laurel, Maryland
Peter's Puppet Boutique                   Scaggsville, Maryland
Barbie's House of Laptops                Bowie, Maryland
Randy's Universal Import-Export          Clarksville, Maryland

 9 record(s) selected.
```

This examples selects records from Customers that have Maryland somewhere in the Address column.

See Also **And** (operator), **Between** (operator), **Exists** (operator), **In** (operator), **Not** (operator), **Null** (operator), **Or** (operator)

Locate

FUNCTION

IBM

Syntax **Locate** (*search*, *string*, [*start*])

Usage **Locate** returns the position of the *search* string within *string* optionally starting at the *start* character. If the *search* string isn't found, then 0 will be returned.

Arguments ▪ *search*—a string of characters to be searched for.

▪ *string*—a string value that can be a column name, a parameter from a stored procedure, a variable, or a function that returns a string value.

▪ *start*—a numeric value that is the starting position inside *string* for the search.

Example
```
select Name, Address from Customers where Locate('Maryland', Address) = 0

NAME                                     ADDRESS
------------------------------------     --------------------------------
Bucky's Country Roundup                  Davis, South Dakota
Becky's Kids Place                       Tulsa, Oklahoma
Tracy's Treehouse                        Duluth, Minnesota
Joan's Technology Shop                   Dallas, Texas
Rosie's Garden Shop                      Richmond, Virginia
Goose's Kitty Katt Kitchen               Marion, South Dakota
Jennifer's Collectible Wheels            El Segundo, California

 7 record(s) selected.
```

This examples selects records from Customers that do not have Maryland anywhere in the Address column.

See Also **Blob** (data type), **Character** (data type), **Clob** (data type), **Posstr** (function), **Varchar** (data type)

Log

FUNCTION

IBM • Informix • MS Access • MS SQL Server • Oracle • Sybase

Syntax **Log** (*number*)

Ln (*number*)

Usage **Log** returns a **Double** that contains the natural logarithm of *number*.

Argument ▪ *number*—an arbitrary expression that can be a column name, a parameter from a stored procedure, a variable, a numeric literal, a function that returns a numeric value, an expression enclosed by parentheses, or a table expression that returns a single numeric expression.

See Also **Double Precision** (data type), **Exp** (function)

Log10

FUNCTION

IBM • MS SQL Server • Sybase

Syntax **Log10** (*number*)

Usage **Log** returns a **Double** that contains the base 10 logarithm of *number*.

Argument ▪ *number*—an arbitrary expression that can be a column name, a parameter from a stored procedure, a variable, a numeric literal, a function that returns a numeric value, an expression enclosed by parentheses, or a table expression that returns a single numeric expression.

See Also **Double Precision** (data type), **Exp** (function)

Long_varchar

FUNCTION

IBM

Syntax **Long_varchar (*string*)**

Usage **Long_varchar** returns a **Long_varchar** value that contains the value from *string*.

Argument ▪ *string*—a string expression that can be a column name, a parameter from a stored procedure, a variable, or a function that returns a string value.

See Also **Long Varchar** (data type)

Long_vargraphic

FUNCTION

IBM

Syntax **Long_vargraphic (*graphic*)**

Usage **Long_vargraphic** returns a **Long Vargraphic** that contains the value from *graphic*.

Argument ▪ *graphic*—a graphic string expression that can be a column name, a parameter from a stored procedure, a variable, or a function that returns a string value.

See Also **Long Vargraphic** (data type)

Lower

FUNCTION

ANSI • MS SQL Server • Oracle • Sybase

Syntax **Lower (*string*)**

Usage **Lower** returns a string where all uppercase characters have been translated to lowercase.

Argument ▪ *string*—a character string.

See Also **Upper** (function)

Ltrim

IBM • MS SQL Server • Oracle • Sybase

Syntax   **Ltrim** (*string*)

Usage   **Ltrim** deletes the leading spaces from *string* and returns the result. If *string* is a **Char** or **Varchar**, then a **Varchar** (4000) will be returned. A **Clob** will be returned if *string* is a **Clob** or a **Long Varchar**.

Argument   ▪ *string*—a string expression that can be a column name, a parameter from a stored procedure, a variable, or a function that returns a string value.

Example
```
values ltrim('   No more leading spaces')

1
-----------------------------------------
No more leading spaces
```
The leading spaces are deleted from the string by using the **Ltrim** function.

See Also   **Rtrim** (function), **Trim** (function)

Max

ANSI • IBM • Informix • MS SQL Server • Oracle • Sybase

Syntax   **Max** (*colexpr*)

Usage   **Max** returns the largest value found in *colexpr* when computed across the entire set of retrieved rows. The function is legal only as part of a **Select** statement's list of columns.

Argument   ▪ *colexpr*—a numeric expression that can be a column name, a parameter from a stored procedure, a variable, or a function that returns a value.

Example   `select max(salary) from employees`

       1

          125000.00

       1 record(s) selected.

The **Select** statement returns the largest value for Salary in the Employees table.

See Also   **Double Precision** (data type), **Select** (statement)

@@Max_connections

VARIABLE

MS SQL Server

Syntax   **@@Max_connections**

Usage   **@@Max_connections** contains the maximum number of concurrent connections that can be made to the database server.

See Also   **@@Connections** (variable)

@@Max_precision

VARIABLE

MS SQL Server

Syntax   **@@Max_precision**

Usage   **@@Max_precision** contains the maximum precision of a **Decimal** or **Numeric** value. This value defaults to 28 digits, however it can be as large as 38 digits, which can be specified with the /p parameter when the database server is started.

See Also   **Decimal** (data type), **Numeric** (data type)

Microsecond

FUNCTION

IBM

Syntax   **Microsecond** (*expr*)

Usage   **Microsecond** returns an **Integer** value that contains the number of microseconds from *expr*. It can also represent the difference between two **Time** or **Timestamp** values in the range of -999,999 to +999,999.

Argument   ▪ *expr*—a **Time** or **Timestamp** value that can be a column name, a parameter from a stored procedure, a variable, or a function that returns a numeric value. It can also be a character string that contains a time in the proper format.

See Also   **Time** (data type), **Timestamp** (data type)

@@Microsoftversion

VARIABLE

MS SQL Server

Syntax   **@@Microsoftversion**

Usage   **@@Microsoftversion** contains the internal version number of the database server.

See Also   **@@Version** (variable)

Midnight_seconds

FUNCTION

IBM

Syntax   **Midnight_seconds** (*expr*)

Usage   **Midnight_seconds** returns the number of seconds past midnight and the time specified by *expr*.

> **Tip**
>
> *Note that ('00:00:00') and ('24:00:00') are considered to be the start and end of a day.*

Argument   ▪ *expr*—a **Time** or a **Timestamp** value or a character string that contains a valid time.

See Also   **Time** (data type), **Timestamp** (data type)

Min

FUNCTION

ANSI • IBM • Informix • MS SQL Server • Oracle • Sybase

Syntax   **Min** (*colexpr*)

Usage   **Min** returns the smallest value of *colexpr* when computed across the entire set of retrieved rows. The function is legal only as part of a **Select** statement's list of columns.

Argument   ▪ *colexpr*—a numeric expression that can be a column name, a parameter from a stored procedure, a variable, or a function that returns a value.

Example
```
select min(salary) from employees

1
------------
    15000.00

 1 record(s) selected.
```

The **Select** statement returns the smallest value for Salary in the Employees table.

See Also   **Double Precision** (data type), **Select** (statement)

Minute

Syntax   **Minute (*expr*)**

Usage   **Minute** returns an **Integer** value that contains the number of minutes from *expr*. It can also represent the difference between two **Time** or **Timestamp** values in the range of –99 to +99.

Argument   ▪ *expr*—a **Time** or a **Timestamp** value or a character string that contains a valid time.

See Also   **Time** (data type), **Timestamp** (data type)

Mod

Syntax   **Mod (*expr, expr*)**

Usage   **Mod** returns an **Integer** value (or **Smallint** value if both expressions are **Smallints**) that is the remainder after the first expression divided by the second.

Argument   ▪ *expr*—an **Integer** or **Smallint** expression that can be a column name, a parameter from a stored procedure, a variable, a numeric literal, a function, an expression enclosed by parentheses, or a table expression that returns a single numeric expression.

See Also   **Time** (data type), **Timestamp** (data type)

Month

FUNCTION

IBM

Syntax **Month** (*expr*)

Usage **Month** returns an **Integer** value that contains the number of minutes from *expr*. It can also represent the difference between two **Date** or **Timestamp** values in the range of -99 to +99.

Argument ▪ *expr*—a **Date** or a **Timestamp** value or a character string that contains a valid date.

Example
```
values month(date('8-13-1994'))

1
----------
        8
```

The **Month** function returns the number of the specified month.

See Also **Date** (data type), **Timestamp** (data type)

Monthname

FUNCTION

IBM

Syntax **Monthname** (*expr*)

Usage **Monthname** returns a **Varchar** (100) value that contains the name of the month from *expr*.

Argument ▪ *expr*—a **Date** or a **Timestamp** value or a character string that contains a valid date.

Example
```
values monthname(date('8-13-1994'))

1
----------------------------------------
August
```

The **Monthname** function returns the name of the specified month.

See Also **Date** (data type), **Timestamp** (data type)

@@Nestlevel

VARIABLE

MS SQL Server

Syntax **@@Nestlevel**

Usage @@**Nestlevel** contains the current nesting level of execution for stored procedures. The first procedure has a nesting level of 0; a stored procedure called from this procedure would have a nesting level of 1. The maximum nesting level is 16.

See Also @@**Cursor_rows** (variable)

Nodefdac

VARIABLE

Informix

Syntax **Nodefdac**

Usage **Nodefdac** contains either 'Yes' or 'No.' 'Yes' means that default table privileges (**Delete, Insert, Select,** and **Update**) are not granted to **Public** in a database that is not ANSI compliant. It also prevents the **Execute** privilege from being granted to **Public** on a stored procedure. 'No' means that default table privileges and the **Execute** privilege to a stored procedure are granted to **Public**.

See Also **Set** (statement)

Nodenumber

FUNCTION

IBM

Syntax **Nodenumber** (*columnname*)

Usage **Nodenumber** returns an **Integer** value that contains the partition number of the row.

Argument ▪ *columnname*—the name of a column. Because the information applies to the entire row, it doesn't matter which column is used.

See Also **Partition** (function)

Not

OPERATOR

ANSI • IBM • Informix • MS Access • MS SQL Server • Oracle • Sybase

Syntax   **Not** *expr*

Usage   The **Not** operator returns **True** if *expr* is **False** and **False** if *expr* is **True**.

Argument   ▪ *expr*—an arbitrary expression that can be a column name, a parameter from a stored procedure, a variable, a numeric literal, a function that returns a numeric value, an expression enclosed by parentheses, or a table expression.

See Also   **And** (operator), **Between** (operator), **Exists** (operator), **In** (operator), **Like** (operator), **Null** (operator), **Or** (operator)

Null

OPERATOR

ANSI • IBM • Informix • MS Access • MS SQL Server • Oracle • Sybase

Syntax   *expr* **Is** [**Not**] **Null**

Usage   The **Null** operator returns **True** if *expr* contains a **Null** value and **False** if *expr* does not contain a **Null** value. The **Not** keyword reverses the inverse value (i.e., **False** if *expr* contains a **Null** value and **True** if *expr* does not contain a **Null** value).

Argument   ▪ *expr*—an arbitrary expression that can be a column name, a parameter from a stored procedure, a variable, a numeric literal, a function that returns a numeric value, an expression enclosed by parentheses, or a table expression.

See Also   **And** (operator), **Between** (operator), **Exists** (operator), **In** (operator), **Like** (operator), **Not** (operator), **Or** (operator)

Nullif

Syntax   **Nullif** (*expr, expr*)

Usage   **Nullif** returns **Null** if both expressions are equal. Otherwise, it returns the value of the first *expr*.

> **Tip**
>
> *This function is the same as the following line of code:*
>
> **Case When** expr1 = expr2 **Then Null Else** expr1 **end**

Argument   ■ *expr*—an arbitrary expression that can be a column name, a parameter from a stored procedure, a variable, a literal, a function's return value, an expression enclosed by parentheses, or a table expression that returns a single value.

Example
```
values nullif(1,1),nullif(1,2)

1
-----------
          -
          1

2 record(s) selected.
```

The first call to **NullIf** returns **Null** since both values are identical. The second call to **NullIf** returns 1 since the values are not the same and first value is 1.

See Also   **Case** (operator)

Octet_length

FUNCTION

ANSI

Syntax **Octet_length (*string*)**

Usage **Octet_length** returns the length of *string* in octets. This is the equivalent of the **Bit_length** function, but the result is divided by 8.

Argument ▪ *string*—an arbitrary character or bit string expression.

See Also **Bit_length** (function)

Onconfig

VARIABLE

Informix

Syntax **Onconfig**

Usage **Onconfig** contains the file name in the %**Informixdir**%\etc directory that contains the server's initialization parameters. By default this file is called onconfig.std.

See Also **Set** (statement)

Or

OPERATOR

ANSI • IBM • Informix • MS Access • MS SQL Server • Oracle • Sybase

Syntax *expr* **Or** *expr*

Usage The **Or** operator returns the **False** if both *expr* are **False**, otherwise **True** will be returned.

Argument ▪ *expr*—an arbitrary expression that can be a column name, a parameter from a stored procedure, a variable, a numeric literal, a function that returns a numeric value, an expression enclosed by parentheses, or a table expression that returns a **True** or **False** expression.

See Also **And** (operator), **Between** (operator), **Exists** (operator), **In** (operator), **Like** (operator), **Not** (operator), **Null** (operator)

@@Pack_received

MS SQL Server

Syntax   **@@Pack_received**

Usage   **@@Pack_received** contains the number of packets received by the database server since it was last started.

See Also   **@@Pack_sent** (variable), **@@Packet_errors** (variable)

@@Pack_sent

MS SQL Server

Syntax   **@@Pack_sent**

Usage   **@@Pack_sent** contains the number of packets sent by the database server since it was last started.

See Also   **@@Pack_received** (variable), **@@Packet_errors** (variable)

@@Packet_errors

MS SQL Server

Syntax   **@@Packet_errors**

Usage   **@@Packet_errors** contains the number of packets received by the database server since it was last started.

See Also   **@@Pack_received** (variable), **@@Pack_sent** (variable)

Partition

FUNCTION

IBM

Syntax   **Partition (*columnname*)**

Usage   **Partition** returns an **Integer** value from 0 to 4,095 that contains the partitioning map index for the row.

Argument   ▪ *columnname*—the name of a column. Because the information applies to the entire row, it doesn't matter which column is used.

See Also   **Nodenumber** (function)

Path

VARIABLE

Informix

Syntax   **Path**

Usage   **Path** contains the directories that will be searched for executable programs. This value is taken directly from the operating system's path information.

See Also   **Set** (statement)

Pi

FUNCTION

MS SQL Server • Sybase

Syntax   **Pi()**

Usage   Pi returns the value 3.141592653589793.

See Also   **Cos** (function), **Sin** (function), **Tan** (function)

Position

Syntax   **Position** (*string1* **In** *string2*)

Usage   **Position** returns the location of *string1* in *string2*. If the length of *string2* is zero, then a value of one will be returned. If *string1* is not found in *string2*, then a value of zero will be returned.

Arguments   ▪ *string1*—an arbitrary string expression.

▪ *string2*—the string to be searched for *string1*.

See Also   **Character** (data type)

Posstr

Syntax   **Posstr** (*string, search*)

Usage   **Posstr** returns the position of the *search* string within *string*, optionally starting at the *start* character. If the *search* string isn't found, then 0 will be returned. The search string can contain special characters from the **Like** clause.

Arguments   ▪ *search*—a string of characters to be searched for.

▪ *string*—a string value that can be a column name, a parameter from a stored procedure, a variable, or a function that returns a string value.

See Also   **Blob** (data type), **Character** (data type), **Locate** (function), **Varchar** (data type)

Power

IBM • Informix • MS SQL Server • Oracle • Sybase

Syntax **Power** (*expr1, expr2*)

Usage **Power** returns a **Double** value (or **Integer** if *expr1* and *expr2* are both **Integer** or **Smallint**) that contains the value of *expr1* raised to the *expr2* power.

Arguments ▪ *expr1*—a numeric expression that can be a column name, a parameter from a stored procedure, a variable, a numeric literal, a function, an expression enclosed by parentheses, or a table expression that returns a single numeric expression.

▪ *expr2*—a numeric expression that can be a column name, a parameter from a stored procedure, a variable, a numeric literal, a function, an expression enclosed by parentheses, or a table expression that returns a single numeric expression.

See Also **Exp** (function), **Log** (function)

@@Procid

MS SQL Server

Syntax **@@Procid**

Usage **@@Procid** contains the name of the currently executing stored procedure.

See Also **@@Remserver** (variable), **@@Spid** (variable)

Quarter

Syntax   **Quarter** (*expr*)

Usage   **Quarter** returns an **Integer** value that contains the quarter of the year from *expr*.

Argument   ▪ *expr*—a **Date** or a **Timestamp** value or a character string that contains a valid date.

See Also   **Date** (data type), **Timestamp** (data type)

Radians

Syntax   **Radians** (*expr*)

Usage   **Radians** converts degrees into radians and returns the value as a **Double**.

Argument   ▪ *expr*—a number that contains a measurement in degrees.

See Also   **Cos** (function), **Degrees** (function), **Double Precision** (data type), **Sin** (function)

Raise_error

Syntax   **Raise_error** (*state, diagnostic*)

Usage   **Raise_error** forces a stored procedure to set the SQL State to *state* and returns a *diagnostic* character with a text description of the SQL state. Executing this will immediately terminate the stored procedure.

Arguments   ▪ *state*—a **Char** (5) or **Varchar** (5) or greater that contains the SQL State. All characters must be in the range of '0' to '9' and 'A' to 'Z.' No lowercase characters are permitted. The first two characters can not be '00,' '01,' or '02,' because these are not valid error codes. If the first two characters begin with '0' to '6' or 'A' to 'H,' then the last three characters must begin with 'I' to 'Z.'

  ▪ *diagnostic*—a character string that contains the text message associated with the SQL State.

See Also **Signal Sqlstate** (statement)

Rand

FUNCTION

IBM • Informix • MS SQL Server • Sybase

Syntax **Rand** ([*expr*])

Usage **Rand** returns a **Double** that contains a random number.

> **Tip**
>
> *To use this routine to generate a repeatable sequence of random numbers, call **Rand** the first time with a specific value for* expr. *Then for all subsequent calls, call **Rand** without specifying a value for* expr. *To repeat the sequence, simply call **Rand** with the same seed value.*

Argument ▪ *expr*—an **Integer** or **Smallint** that provides a seed for the random number. When the same value of *expr* is specified, the same random number will be returned.

See Also **Double Precision** (data type)

Real

FUNCTION

IBM

Syntax **Real** (*number*)

Usage **Real** is used to convert a number into a **Real** value.

Argument ▪ *number*—an arbitrary expression that can be a column name, a parameter from a stored procedure, a variable, a numeric literal, a function that returns a numeric value, an expression enclosed by parentheses, or a table expression that returns a single numeric expression.

See Also **Real** (data type)

@@Remserver

VARIABLE

MS SQL Server

Syntax **@@Remserver**

Usage **@@Remserver** contains the server's names contained in the login record.

See Also **@@Procid** (variable), **@@Servername** (variable), **@@Spid** (variable)

Repeat

FUNCTION

IBM

Syntax **Repeat** (*string*, *number*)

Usage **Repeat** returns a value that consists of *string* repeated *number* of times. If *string* is a **Char** or **Varchar**, a **Varchar** will be returned. When a **Clob** or **Long Varchar** is passed as *string*, a **Clob** will be returned. If a **Blob** is passed to the function, a **Blob** will be returned.

Arguments ▪ *string*—a **Char**, **Varchar**, **Blob**, or **Clob** expression.

▪ *number*—an **Integer** or **Smallint** that specifies how many times to repeat *string*.

See Also **Character** (data type), **Double Precision** (data type)

Replace

FUNCTION

IBM

Syntax **Replace** (*string1*, *string2*, *string3*)

Usage **Replace** returns a **Varchar**(4000) if *string* is a **Varchar** or **Char**. If *string* is a **Blob** or **Clob**, then the return value will be a **Blob** or **Clob**, respectively. This function will scan *string1* and replace all occurrences of *string2* with *string3*.

Arguments ▪ *string1*—a string value that can be a column name, a parameter from a stored procedure, a variable, or a function that returns a string value.

▪ *string2*—a string value that can be a column name, a parameter from a stored procedure, a variable, or a function that returns a string value.

▪ *string3*—a string value that can be a column name, a parameter from a stored procedure, a variable, or a function that returns a string value.

Example
```
values replace('1234567890', '456', 'abcdef')

1
------------
123abcdef7890

  1 record(s) selected.
```

The **Replace** function is used to substitute 'abcdef' for '456' in the string '1234567890'.

See Also **Blob** (data type), **Character** (data type), **Clob** (data type), **Varchar** (data type)

Right

FUNCTION

IBM

Syntax **Right** (*string*, *chars*)

Usage **Right** returns the right most *chars* characters from *string*. The return value is a
Varchar(4000) if *string* is a **Varchar** or **Char**. If *string* is a **Blob** or **Clob**, then the return
value will be a **Blob** or **Clob**, respectively.

Arguments ▪ *string*—a string value that can be a column name, a parameter from a stored procedure,
a variable, or a function that returns a string value.

▪ *chars*—the number of characters to be returned.

See Also **Blob** (data type), **Character** (data type), **Clob** (data type), **Left** (function), **Varchar** (data
type)

Round

IBM • Informix • MS SQL Server • Oracle • Sybase

Syntax **Round** (*expr, decimalplaces*)

Usage **Round** rounds the value of *expr* to the number of decimal places specified in *decimalplaces*. If *expr* is an **Integer** or **Smallint,** then an **Integer** will be returned. If *expr* is anything else, a **Double** will be returned.

Arguments ▪ *expr*—a numeric value that can be a column name, a parameter from a stored procedure, a variable, or a function that returns a numeric value.

▪ *decimalplaces*—the number of decimal places to be returned.

See Also **Decimal** (data type), **Double Precision** (data type), **Integer** (data type), **Real** (data type), **Smallint** (data type), **Truncate** (function)

@@Rowcount

MS SQL Server

Syntax **@@Rowcount**

Usage **@@Rowcount** contains the number of rows affected by the last statement.

See Also **@@Cursor_rows** (variable)

Rtrim

IBM • Informix • MS SQL Server • Oracle • Sybase

Syntax **Rtrim** (*string*)

Usage **Rtrim** deletes the trailing spaces from *string* and returns the result. If *string* is a **Char** or **Varchar**, then a **Varchar** (4000) will be returned. A **Clob** will be returned if *string* is a **Clob** or a **Long Varchar**.

Argument ▪ *string*—a string expression that can be a column name, a parameter from a stored procedure, a variable, or a function that returns a string value.

Example

```
values rtrim('No more trailing spaces    ')

1
-------------------------------------------
No more trailing spaces
```

The trailing spaces are deleted from the string by using the **Rtrim** function.

See Also **Ltrim** (function), **Trim** (function)

Second

FUNCTION

IBM

Syntax **Second (*expr*)**

Usage **Second** returns an **Integer** value that contains the number of seconds from *expr*. It can also represent the difference between two **Time** or **Timestamp** values in the range of –99 to +99.

Argument ▪ *expr*—a **Time** or a **Timestamp** value or a character string that contains a valid time.

See Also **Time** (data type), **Timestamp** (data type)

@@Servername

VARIABLE

MS SQL Server

Syntax **@@Servername**

Usage **@@Servername** contains the name of the database server.

See Also **@@Remserver** (variable), **@@Spid** (variable)

Session_user

VARIABLE

ANSI • MS SQL Server • Sybase

Syntax **Session_user**

Usage **Session_user** returns a character string that contains the current SQL session authentication id.

See Also **Current_user** (variable), **System_user** (variable), **User** (variable)

Sign

FUNCTION

IBM

Syntax **Sign** (*number*)

Usage **Sign** returns -1 if *number* is less than zero, 0 if *number* is equal to zero, or +1 if *number* is greater than zero. A **Smallint** will be returned if *number* is a **Smallint**. An **Integer** will be returned if *number* is an **Integer**. Any other numeric data type will return a **Double**.

Argument ▪ *number*—an arbitrary expression that can be a column name, a parameter from a stored procedure, a variable, a numeric literal, a function that returns a numeric value, an expression enclosed by parentheses, or a table expression that returns a single numeric expression.

See Also **Double Precision** (data type), **Integer** (data type), **Smallint** (data type)

Sin

FUNCTION

IBM • Informix • MS SQL Server • Oracle • Sybase

Syntax **Sin** (*expr*)

Usage **Sin** returns a **Double** that contains the sine of an angle expressed in radians. If *expr* is **Null**, then **Null** will be returned.

Argument ▪ *expr*—a numeric expression that can be a column name, a parameter from a stored procedure, a variable, or a function that returns a numeric value.

See Also **Double Precision** (data type)

Sinh

FUNCTION

Oracle

Syntax **Sinh (*expr*)**

Usage **Sin** returns a **Double** that contains the hyperbolic sine of an angle expressed in radians. If *expr* is **Null**, then **Null** will be returned.

Argument ▪ *expr*—a numeric expression that can be a column name, a parameter from a stored procedure, a variable, or a function that returns a numeric value.

See Also **Double Precision** (data type)

Smallint

FUNCTION

IBM

Syntax **Smallint ({ *number* | *string* })**

Usage **Smallint** is used to convert a character string or number into a **Smallint** value.

Arguments ▪ *number*—an arbitrary expression that can be a column name, a parameter from a stored procedure, a variable, a numeric literal, a function that returns a numeric value, an expression enclosed by parentheses, or a table expression that returns a single numeric expression.

▪ *string*—a string of characters from a **Char**, or **Varchar.**

See Also **Character** (data type), **Integer** (function), **Smallint** (data type)

Soundex

Syntax **Soundex** (*string*)

Usage **Soundex** returns a **Char**(4) string that contains a four-character code that represents the sound of the words in *string*.

> **Tip**
>
> *Use this routine to find matches where you know how a word sounds, but not how it is spelled, like searching for a particular name.*

Argument ▪ *string*—a **Char** or **Varchar** string that contains one or more works to be compared.

Example   select fname, soundex(fname) from employees

```
FNAME           2
------------    ----
Christopher     C623
Samantha        S553
Jill            J400
Raymond         R553
Wanda           W530
Susan           S250
Wayne           W500
Shaun           S500
Ian             I500
Chris           C620
Walter          W436
Robert          R163
Elwyn           E450
Richard         R263
Bonnie          B500
Linda           L530
Robert          R163
Veronica        V652
```

   18 record(s) selected.

The Fname and the **Soundex** value for Fname are listed for each row in the Employees table.

See Also   **Difference** (function)

Space

FUNCTION

IBM • MS SQL Server • Sybase

Syntax **Space** (*count*)

Usage **Space** returns a **Varchar**(4000) that contains the specified number of spaces.

Argument ▪ *count*—an **Integer** or **Smallint** value that contains the number of spaces to be returned.

See Also **Varchar** (data type)

@@Spid

VARIABLE

MS SQL Server

Syntax **@@Spid**

Usage **@@Spid** contains the process id of the database server process.

See Also **@@Servername** (variable)

Sqrt

FUNCTION

IBM • Informix • MS SQL Server • Oracle • Sybase

Syntax **Sqrt** (*number*)

Usage **Sqrt** returns a **Double** that contains the square root of *number*.

Argument ▪ *number*—an arbitrary expression that can be a column name, a parameter from a stored procedure, a variable, a numeric literal, a function that returns a numeric value, an expression enclosed by parentheses, or a table expression that returns a single numeric expression.

See Also **Double Precision** (data type)

Substr

FUNCTION

IBM • Informix • Oracle

Syntax **Substr** (*string*, *start* [, *length*])

Usage **Substr** returns a string of *length* characters from *string* beginning with *start*. If *length* is omitted, all the characters beginning with *start* until the end of the string will be returned.

Arguments ▪ *string*—an arbitrary string expression.
▪ *start*—a numeric value that indicates the starting position of the substring.
▪ *length*—a numeric value that contains the number of characters to be extracted.

See Also **Character** (data type)

Substring

FUNCTION

ANSI • MS SQL Server • Sybase

Syntax **Substring** (*string* **From** *start* [**For** *length*])

Usage **Substring** returns a string of *length* characters from *string* beginning with *start*. If *length* is omitted, the characters beginning with *start* until the end of the string will be returned.

Arguments ▪ *string*—an arbitrary string expression.
▪ *start*—a numeric value that indicates the starting position of the substring.
▪ *length*—a numeric value that contains the number of characters to be extracted.

See Also **Character** (data type)

Sum

ANSI • IBM • Informix • MS SQL Server • Oracle • Sybase

Syntax **Sum** (*colexpr*)

Usage **Sum** returns the total of all of the values of *colexpr* when computed across the entire set of retrieved rows. The function is legal only as part of a **Select** statement's list of columns.

Argument ▪ *colexpr*—a numeric expression that can be a column name, a parameter from a stored procedure, a variable, or a function that returns a numeric value.

Example

```
Select DeptNo, Lname, Salary from Employees;

DEPTNO LNAME              SALARY
------ ------------------ ------------
    0. James              125000.00
    0. Ashley             100000.00
   10. Heyer              100000.00
   10. Bucky               90000.00
   20. Williams            35000.00
   20. Applegate           25000.00
   30. Freeze              90000.00
   30. Fleming             80000.00
   30. Blumgart            70000.00
   40. Osborne             20000.00
   40. Smith               15000.00
   50. Kelly               30000.00
   50. Tigger              27000.00
   50. Dudley              25000.00
   50. Jean                23000.00
   50. Brigham             21000.00
   60. Wyler               65000.00
   60. Dau                 60000.00

18 record(s) selected.


Select Sum(Salary) from Employees;

1
----------------------------------
                       1001000.00

1 record(s) selected.
```

```
Select DeptNo, Avg(Salary) from Employees Group By DeptNo;

DEPTNO 2
------ -------------------------------
    0.                        225000.00
   10.                        190000.00
   20.                         60000.00
   30.                        240000.00
   40.                         35000.00
   50.                        126000.00
   60.                        125000.00

 7 record(s) selected.
```

In the first **Select** statement, you see the Salary and DeptNo for each employee in the Employee table. In the second statement, you see the sum of the salaries for all employees. In the third table, you see the sum of the salaries for all the employees in a specific department.

See Also   **Double Precision** (data type), **Select** (statement)

System_user   VARIABLE

ANSI • MS SQL Server • Sybase

Syntax   **System_user**

Usage   **System_user** returns a character string that contains the operating system userid for the SQL server.

See Also   **Current_user** (variable), **Session_user** (variable), **User** (variable)

Table_name   FUNCTION

ANSI

Syntax   **Table_name** (*objectname* [, *objectschema*])

Usage   **Table_name** returns a **Varchar**(18) that contains the unqualified name of an object by resolving the alias chains.

Arguments • *objectname*—a character string that contains the unqualified object name to be resolved. This argument must be a **Char** or **Varchar** that contains between 1 and 18 characters.

• *objectschema*—a character string that contains the schema name that is used to qualify *objectname*. If not specified, the default schema will be used. This argument must be a **Char** or **Varchar** that contains between 1 and 8 characters.

See Also   **Table_schema** (function)

Table_schema

FUNCTION

ANSI

Syntax   **Table_schema** (*objectname* [, *objectschema*])

Usage   **Table_schema** returns a **Varchar**(8) that contains the unqualified name of an object's schema by resolving the alias chains.

Arguments • *objectname*—a character string that contains the unqualified object name to be resolved. This argument must be a **Char** or **Varchar** that contains between 1 and 18 characters.

• *objectschema*—a character string that contains the schema name that is used to qualify *objectname*. If not specified, the default schema will be used. This argument must be a **Char** or **Varchar** that contains between 1 and 8 characters.

See Also   **Table_name** (function)

Tan

FUNCTION

IBM • Informix • MS SQL Server • Oracle • Sybase

Syntax   **Tan** (*expr*)

Usage   **Tan** returns a **Double** that contains the tangent of an angle expressed in radians. If *expr* is **Null**, then **Null** will be returned.

Argument • *expr*—a numeric expression that can be a column name, a parameter from a stored procedure, a variable, or a function that returns a numeric value.

See Also   **Double Precision** (data type)

Tanh

FUNCTION

Oracle

Syntax | **Tanh** (*expr*)

Usage | **Tan** returns a **Double** that contains the hyperbolic tangent of an angle expressed in radians. If *expr* is **Null**, then **Null** will be returned.

Argument | ▪ *expr*—a numeric expression that can be a column name, a parameter from a stored procedure, a variable, or a function that returns a numeric value.

See Also | **Double Precision** (data type)

@@Textsize

VARIABLE

MS SQL Server

Syntax | **@@Textsize**

Usage | **@@Textsize** contains the maximum amount of data that will be retrieved from a **Text** or **Image** column. The default value for this field is 4,096 bytes. To change this value, use the **Set** statement.

See Also | **Image** (data type), **Set** (statement), **Text** (data type)

Time

FUNCTION

IBM

Syntax | **Time** (*expr*)

Usage | **Time** returns a **Time** value that is computed from *expr*.

Argument | ▪ *expr*—a numeric expression that can be a column name, a parameter from a stored procedure, a variable, or a function that returns a numeric value. If *expr* contains a **Time** or **Timestamp** value, only the time information will be returned. Otherwise, the **Time** function will attempt to convert the string into a **Time** value.

See Also | **Date** (function), **Time** (data type), **Timestamp** (data type)

Timestamp

Syntax   **Timestamp** (*timestamp*)

Timestamp (*date, time*)

Usage   **Timestamp** returns a **Timestamp** value that is computed from a character string that has the complete timestamp value or from two character strings that contain date and time information.

Arguments   ▪ *timestamp*—a **Char**(14) or **Varchar**(14) that contains date and time values in the following format: yyyymmddhhnnss, where yyyy is the year, mm is the month, dd is the day of month, hh is the hour of the day, nn is the minute of the hour, and ss is the second of the minute.

▪ *date*—a **Char** or **Varchar** that contains a valid date.

▪ *timestamp*—a **Char** or **Varchar** that contains a valid time.

See Also   **Date** (function), **Time** (function), **Timestamp** (data type)

Timestamp_iso

Syntax   **Timestamp_iso** ({ *timestamp* | *date* | *time* })

Usage   **Timestamp_iso** returns a **Timestamp** value that is computed from a character string that has date and time information. If only date information is supplied, a time value of midnight is assumed. If only time information is supplied, then **Current_date** is assumed for the date information.

Arguments   ▪ *timestamp*—a **Timestamp** value or a **Char** or **Varchar** string that contains valid date and time values.

▪ *date*—a **Date** value or a **Char** or **Varchar** string that contains a valid date value.

▪ *time*—a **Time** value or a **Char** or **Varchar** string that contains a valid time value.

See Also   **Current_date** (variable), **Date** (function), **Time** (function), **Timestamp** (data type)

Timestampdiff

Syntax   **Timestampdiff** (*range, difference*)

Usage   **Timestampdiff** returns an **Integer** value that returns the difference between two **Timestamp** values in the specified range. The calculations assume that there are 365 days in a year, 30 days in a month, 24 hours in a day, 60 minutes in an hour, and 60 seconds in a minute. For example, assuming there is a one-month difference between **Timestamp** values, the difference in days will always be 30 days.

Arguments   ▪ *range*—an **Integer** or **Smallint** value that contains the desired interval. (See Table 2-3.)

range value	Description
1	Fractions of a second.
2	Seconds.
4	Minutes.
8	Hours.
16	Days.
32	Weeks.
64	Months.
128	Quarters.
256	Years.

Table 2-3: Range formatting characters.

▪ *difference*—a **Char**(22) value that contains the difference between two **Timestamp** values.

See Also   **Date** (function), **Time** (function), **Timestamp** (function)

@@Timeticks

Syntax   **@@Timeticks**

Usage   **@@Timeticks** contains the size of a tick in microseconds. This is generally 1/32 of a second, or 31,250 microseconds.

See Also   **@@Cpu_busy** (variable), **@@Idle** (variable), **@@Io_busy** (variable)

To_binary_integer

Syntax **To_binary_integer** (*expr*)

Usage **To_binary_integer** returns an **Integer** value that contains the integer equivalent *expr*.

Argument ▪ *expr*—a **Character**, **Varchar2** or a **Number** value to be converted into a binary integer.

See Also **Character** (data type), **Integer** (data type), **Number** (data type), **Varchar2** (data type)

To_char

Syntax **To_char** (*expr* , *format*)

Usage **To_char** returns the character equivalent of a date or number.

Arguments ▪ *expr*—a **Date** or a **Number** value to be converted into a string.
▪ *format*—a string containing instructions on how to format *expr*. (See Tables 2-4 and 2-5.)

format value	Description
A.D.	Uppercase A.D. or B.C.
a.d.	Lowercase a.d. or b.c.
AD	Uppercase AD or BC.
ad	Lowercase ad or bc.
A.M.	Uppercase A.M. or P.M.
a.m.	Lowercase a.m. or p.m.
AM	Uppercase AM or PM.
am	Lowercase am or pm.
B.C.	Uppercase A.D. or B.C.
b.c.	Lowercase a.d. or b.c.
BC	Uppercase AD or BC.
bc	Lowercase ad or bc.
CC	Two-digit century.
D	Number of the day of the week.
DAY	Name of day (all uppercase).

➡

format value	Description
Day	Name of day (first character uppercase, the rest lowercase).
day	Name of day (all lowercase).
DD	Number of the day of the month.
DDD	Number of the day of the year.
DY	Three character abbreviation of the day (all uppercase).
Dy	Three character abbreviation of the day (first character uppercase, the rest lowercase).
Dy	Three character abbreviation of the day (all lowercase).
HH	Hour of the day (1-12).
HH12	Hour of the day (1-12).
HH24	Hour of the day (1-24).
I	Last digit of an ISO year.
IW	Two-digit week of an ISO year
IY	Last two digits of an ISO year.
IYY	Last three digits of an ISO year.
IYYY	Four digit ISO standard year.
J	Julian days since December 31, 4713 B.C.
MI	Minute of the hour.
MM	Number of the month (0-12).
MOM	Three character abbreviation of the month (all uppercase).
Mom	Three character abbreviation of the month (first character uppercase, the rest lowercase).
mom	Three character abbreviation of the month (all lowercase).
MONTH	Name of month (all uppercase).
Month	Name of month (first character uppercase, the rest lowercase).
month	Name of month (all lowercase).
P.M.	Uppercase A.M. or P.M.
p.m.	Lowercase a.m. or p.m.
PM	Uppercase AM or PM.
pm	Lowercase am or pm.
Q	Number of the quarter.
RM	Roman numeral for the month.
RR	Last two digits of the year, possibly a different century.
SCC	Signed two-digit century (centuries before 0 AD are negative).

format value	Description
SS	Second of the minute.
SSSSS	Seconds since midnight.
SYYYY	Signed four-digit year (years before 0 AD are negative).
W	Number of the week of the month.
WW	Number of the week of the year.
Y	Last digit of the year.
YEAR	Four-digit year spelled out as words (all uppercase).
Year	Four-digit year spelled out as words (first character uppercase, the rest lowercase).
year	Four-digit year spelled out as words (all lowercase).
YY	Last two digits of the year.
YYY	Last three digits of the year.
YYYY	Four-digit year.

Table 2-4: Date formats.

format value	Description
,	Place holder for a comma if needed.
$	Display a dollar sign in front of the number.
0	Place holder for a digit. Leading zeros will be displayed as zero.
9	Place holder for a digit. Leading zeros will be displayed as spaces.
B	Place holder for a digit. Leading zeros will be displayed as spaces.
C	Display the ISO currency symbol in this position.
D	Display a decimal point.
EEEE	Display an exponent.
L	Display the local currency symbol.
MI	Display a minus sign or blank.
PR	Display negative numbers in parentheses.
RN	Display the number as a roman numeral.
S	Display a minus sign or blank.
V	Add a zero to the display for every 9 that follows the V.

Table 2-5: Number formats.

See Also   **Character** (data type), **Number** (data type)

To_date

Syntax **To_date** (*expr* , *format*)

Usage **To_date** returns a **Date** value containing the data value specified by *expr*.

Arguments
- *expr*—a string value to be converted into a **Date**.
- *format* - a string containing instructions on how the date was formatted. (See Table 2-6.)

format value	Description
A.D.	Uppercase A.D. or B.C.
a.d.	Lowercase a.d. or b.c.
AD	Uppercase AD or BC.
ad	Lowercase ad or bc.
A.M.	Uppercase A.M. or P.M.
a.m.	Lowercase a.m. or p.m.
AM	Uppercase AM or PM.
am	Lowercase am or pm.
B.C.	Uppercase A.D. or B.C.
b.c.	Lowercase a.d. or b.c.
BC	Uppercase AD or BC.
bc	Lowercase ad or bc.
CC	Two digit century.
D	Number of the day of the week.
DAY	Name of day (all uppercase).
Day	Name of day (first character uppercase, the rest lowercase).
day	Name of day (all lowercase).
DD	Number of the day of the month.
DDD	Number of the day of the year.
DY	Two-character abbreviation of the day (all uppercase).
Dy	Two-character abbreviation of the day (first character uppercase, the rest lowercase).
dy	Two-character abbreviation of the day (all lowercase).
HH	Hour of the day (1-12).
HH12	Hour of the day (1-12).
HH24	Hour of the day (1-24).

format value	Description
I	Last digit of an ISO year.
IW	Two-digit week of an ISO year
IY	Last two digits of an ISO year.
IYY	Last three digits of an ISO year.
IYYY	Four-digit ISO standard year.
J	Julian days since December 31, 4713 B.C.
MI	Minute of the hour.
MM	Number of the month (0-12).
MOM	Three-character abbreviation of the month (all uppercase).
Mom	Three-character abbreviation of the month (first character uppercase, the rest lowercase).
mom	Three-character abbreviation of the month (all lowercase).
MONTH	Name of month (all uppercase).
Month	Name of month (first character uppercase, the rest lowercase).
month	Name of month (all lowercase).
P.M.	Uppercase A.M. or P.M.
p.m.	Lowercase a.m. or p.m.
PM	Uppercase AM or PM.
pm	Lowercase am or pm.
Q	Number of the quarter.
RM	Roman numeral for the month.
RR	Last two digits of the year, possibly a different century.
SCC	Signed two-digit century (centuries before 0 AD are negative).
SS	Second of the minute.
SSSSS	Seconds since midnight.
SYYYY	Signed four-digit year (years before 0 AD are negative).
W	Number of the week of the month.
WW	Number of the week of the year.
Y	Last digit of the year.
YEAR	Four-digit year spelled out as words (all uppercase).
Year	Four-digit year spelled out as words (first character uppercase, the rest lowercase).
year	Four-digit year spelled out as words (all lowercase).
YY	Last two digits of the year.
YYY	Last three digits of the year.
YYYY	Four-digit year.

Table 2-6: Date formats.

See Also   **Character** (data type), **Date** (data type)

To_multi_byte

Syntax **To_multi_byte** (*expr*)

Usage **To_multi_byte** returns a string containing the multi-byte equivalent of the single byte *expr*.

Argument ▪ *expr*—a single byte **Character** or a **Varchar2** value to be converted into a multi-byte string.

See Also **Character** (data type), **Varchar2** (data type)

To_number

Syntax **To_number** (*expr*)

Usage **To_number** returns a **Number** containing the numeric equivalent of the string value *expr*.

Argument ▪ *expr*—a **Character** or a **Varchar2** value to be converted into a **Number**.

See Also **Character** (data type), **Number** (data type), **Varchar2** (data type)

To_single_byte

Syntax **To_single_byte** (*expr*)

Usage **To_single_byte** returns a string containing the single byte equivalent of the multi-byte *expr*.

Argument ▪ *expr*—a multi-byte **Character** or a **Varchar2** value to be converted into a single byte string.

See Also **Character** (data type), **Varchar2** (data type)

Translate

Syntax   **Translate** (*string* **Using** *translation*)

Usage   **Translate** is used to translate one string into another.

Arguments   ▪ *string*—an arbitrary string expression.

▪ *translate*—either a predefined translation or a translation defined by the **Create Translation** statement.

See Also   **Create Translation** (statement), **Character** (data type)

Translate

Syntax   **Translate** (*string* [, *tostring*, *fromstring* [, *pad*]])

Usage   **Translate** is used to translate characters in a character string. Both *tostring* and *fromstring* are required if *string* is either **Graphic** or **Vargraphic**. *String* is searched one character at a time for characters in *fromstring*. If a match is found, then the corresponding character in *tostring* will be substituted. If *tostring* and *fromstring* are not specified, the characters in *string* are changed to uppercase.

Arguments   ▪ *string*—an arbitrary string expression, which can be **Char**, **Varchar**, **Graphic**, or **Vargraphic**.

▪ *tostring*—a string that contains a set of replacement characters for the characters in *fromstring*.

fromstring—a string that contains a set of characters that will be searched for in *string*.

See Also   **Character** (data type), **Graphic** (data type), **Varchar** (data type), **Vargraphic** (data type)

Trim

FUNCTION

ANSI

Syntax   **Trim ([Leading | Trailing | Both] [** *char* **] [From]** *string* **)**

Usage   **Trim** returns a string where leading, trailing, or both leading and trailing *char* characters are deleted. If the **Leading, Trailing,** or **Both** keywords are omitted, **Both** will be assumed.

> ### Tip
>
> Use the **Trim** function to remove trailing spaces from a **Char Varying** string before storing it in the database to save space.

Arguments ▪ *char*—a single character that will be removed from the front or the back of the string. If omitted, it will default to a space.

▪ *string*—an arbitrary string expression.

See Also   **Character** (data type), **Ltrim** (function)

@@Total_errors

VARIABLE

MS SQL Server

Syntax   **@@Total_errors**

Usage   **@@Total_errors** contains the number of errors encountered by the database server since it was started.

See Also   **@@Error** (variable)

@@Total_read

Syntax `@@Total_read`

Usage **@@Total_read** contains the number of physical disk reads (not cache reads) by the database server since it was started.

See Also **@@Io_busy** (variable)

@@Total_write

Syntax `@@Total_write`

Usage **@@Total_write** contains the number of physical disk writes by the database server since it was started.

See Also **@@Io_busy** (variable)

@@Trancount

Syntax `@@Trancount`

Usage **@@Trancount** contains the number of current active transactions for the current user.

See Also **@@Total_errors** (variable)

Truncate

FUNCTION

IBM

Syntax   **Truncate** (`expr, decimalplaces`)

Usage   **Truncate** truncates the value of *expr* to the number of decimal places specified in *decimalplaces*. If *expr* is an **Integer** or **Smallint**, then an **Integer** will be returned. If *expr* is anything else, a **Double** will be returned.

Arguments   ▪ *expr*—a numeric value that can be a column name, a parameter from a stored procedure, a variable, or a function that returns a numeric value.

     ▪ *decimalplaces*—the number of decimal places to be returned.

See Also   **Decimal** (data type), **Double Precision** (data type), **Integer** (data type), **Real** (data type), **Round** (function), **Smallint** (data type)

Ucase

FUNCTION

IBM

Syntax   **Ucase** (`string`)

Usage   **Ucase** converts all of the lowercase characters contained in *string* to uppercase. Because characters that have diacritical marks will be converted to uppercase only if they exist, it is possible that **Ucase** (**Lcase** (*string*)) will not be the same as *string*.

Argument   ▪ *string*—a **Char**, **Varchar**, **Long Varchar,** or **Clob** value.

See Also   **Character** (data type), **Clob** (data type), **Long Varchar** (data type), **Lcase** (function), **Varchar** (data type)

Upper

FUNCTION

ANSI • Informix • MS SQL Server • Oracle • Sybase

Syntax **Upper** (*string*)

Usage **Upper** returns a string in which all lowercase characters have been translated to uppercase.

Argument ▪ *string*—a character string.

See Also **Lower** (function)

User

VARIABLE

IBM • MS SQL Server • Sybase

Syntax **User**

Usage **User** returns a **Char** value that contains the name of the active user.

See Also **Values** (statement)

Value

FUNCTION

IBM

Syntax **Value** (*value* [, *value*] . . .)

Usage **Value** returns the first non-**Null** value from the list of values. If all of the values in the list are **Null**, then **Null** will be returned.

Tip

*This is the same function as **Coalesce**.*

Argument ▪ *value*—an arbitrary expression which can be a column name, a parameter from a stored procedure, a variable, numeric literal, a function that returns a value, an expression enclosed by parentheses, or a table.

See Also **Case** (operator), **Coalesce** (function)

Varchar

Syntax **Varcbar** (*dateexpr*)

Varchar (*string* [, *length*])

Usage **Varchar** is used to convert a value into a fixed-length character string.

Arguments ▪ *dateexpr*—an expression that can be a column name, a parameter from a stored procedure, a variable, or a function that returns a **Date**, **Time**, or **Timestamp** value.

▪ *string*—a string of characters from a **Char**, **Varchar**, **Long Varchar**, or **Clob**. **Char** will return a fixed-length string whose length is *length* or the length of *string*, if *length* is not specified. If the length of *string* is greater than 254 characters, the result will be truncated and a warning will be generated.

▪ *length*—specifies the length of the returned character string. If omitted, the length of the returned string will be the same as *string* up to a maximum length of 4,000.

See Also **Character** (data type), **Date** (data type), **Time** (data type), **Timestamp** (data type)

Vargraphic

Syntax **Vargraphic** (*graphic*)

Vargraphic (*string* [, *length*])

Usage **Vargraphic** is used to convert a **Graphic**, **Char**, or **Varchar** value into a variable-length graphic string.

Arguments ▪ *graphic*—an expression that can be a column name, a parameter from a stored procedure, a variable, or a function that returns a **Graphic** value.

▪ *string*—a string of characters from a **Char** or **Varchar** string. **Vargraphic** will return a variable-length **Graphic** whose length is *length* or the length of *string*, if *length* is not specified.

▪ *length*—specifies the length of the returned character string. If omitted, the length of the returned string will be the same as *string* up to a maximum length of 2,000.

See Also **Character** (data type), **Graphic** (data type), **Time** (data type), **Timestamp** (data type), **Vargraphic** (data type)

@@Version

VARIABLE

MS SQL Server

Syntax **@@Version**

Usage **@@Version** contains the version number, date, and processor type for the database server.

See Also **@@Microsoftversion** (variable)

Week

FUNCTION

IBM

Syntax **Week** (*expr*)

Usage **Week** returns an **Integer** value that contains the week of the year (1 to 54) from *expr*. Weeks are assumed to begin on a Sunday.

Argument ▪ *expr*—a **Date** or a **Timestamp** value or a character string that contains a valid date.

See Also **Date** (data type), **Timestamp** (data type)

Year

Syntax   **Year** (*expr*)

Usage   **Year** returns an **Integer** value that contains the year from *expr*. It can also represent the difference between two **Date** or **Timestamp** values in the range of -9999 to +9999.

Argument   ▪ *expr*—a **Date** or a **Timestamp** value or a character string that contains a valid date.

See Also   **Date** (data type), **Timestamp** (data type)

Statements

III

Alter Bufferpool

Syntax   Alter Bufferpool *bufferpool*
    {
    [Node *nodenumber*] Size *numberpages* |
    [Not] Extended Storage |
    Add Nodegroup *nodegroup*
    }

Usage   The **Alter Bufferpool** statement modifies a buffer pool definition. The **Node** clause is used to limit the changes to a specific node. The **Extended Storage** allows pages that are migrated from the buffer pool to be cached in extended storage (assuming that extended storage is available). **Not Extended Storage** means that the pages will not be cached. **Add Nodegroup** adds a new nodegroup to the list of nodegroups that use this buffer pool. The nodegroup must already be defined to the database before it is added to the buffer pool.

Authorization   You must have the **SYSCTRL** or **SYSADM** authority to change buffer pool definitions.

Arguments   ▪ *bufferpool*—the name of the buffer pool to be changed. This buffer pool must already exist in the catalog.

    ▪ *nodenumber*—the number of the partition in which the buffer pool will be changed. If this clause is not specified, then all nodes containing the buffer pool will be updated.

    ▪ *numberpages*—the number of pages in the buffer pool.

    ▪ *nodegroup*—specifies the name of a new nodegroup that will be added to the list of nodes using this buffer pool. The node groups IBMCATGROUP and IBMTEMPGROUP can't be specified.

See Also   **Create Bufferpool** (statement)

Alter Cluster

Syntax   Alter Cluster [*user.*]*cluster*
               {
                  Pctused *pctused* |
                  Pctfree *pctfree* |
                  Size *size* [K | M] |
                  Initrans *initrans* |
                  Maxtrans *maxtrans* |
                  Storage (
                     [Initial *initial* [K | M]]
                     [Next *next* [K | M]]
                     [Pctincrease *increase*]
                     [Minextents *minext*]
                     [Maxextents { *maxext* |
                  Unlimited }]
                     [Optimal { *optimal* [K | M] |
                  Null }]
                     [Freelists *freelists*]
                     [Freelist Groups *freelistgroup*
                  ]

                  |

                  Allocate Extent [(
                     {
                     Size *size* [K | M] |
                     Datafile *filename* |
                     Instance *instance*
                     } . . .) |
                  Deallocate Unused [Keep *value* [K | M]]
               } . . .
               [Parallel [Degree *degree*][Instances *instance*]
                  | Noparallel]

Usage   The **Alter Cluster** statement modifies a cluster that contains one or more tables.
         Changes to the **Pctused, Pctfree, Initrans, Maxtrans, Tablespace,** and **Storage** do not
         affect any current cluster blocks, but will apply for all future cluster blocks.

Authorization   You must either own the cluster or have the **Alter Any Cluster** privilege to alter a
                 cluster.

Arguments ■ *user*—the name of the user creating the cluster.

■ *cluster*—the name of the cluster.

■ *pctused*—the amount of space in a data block that must be used before another data block is allocated. There must be at least *pctused* space available in a block before a row can be inserted. If not specified, this value will default to 40 percent.

■ *pctfree*—the amount of space in a data block that is reserved for future updates. Any insert that will result in less than *pctfree* space available will cause a new block to be created. If not specified, this value will default to 10 percent.

■ *size*—this value should be the average amount of space to store all the rows in all the tables for a single cluster key. The physical block size should be evenly divisible by this value. Specifying too large a value might decrease the time to access the data, but can waste space.

■ *initrans*—specifies the initial number of transactions that might update a block. It can range from 1 to 255. If not specified, this value will default to 1.

■ *maxtrans*—specifies the maximum number of transactions that might update a block. It can range from 1 to 255. If not specified, this value will default to 255.

■ *initial*—specifies the amount of storage in bytes for the first extent. **K** or **M** indicates that this value is in kilobytes or megabytes respectively. If not specified, this value will default to two data blocks.

■ *next*—specifies the amount of storage in bytes for the rest of the extents. **K** or **M** indicates that this value is in kilobytes or megabytes respectively. If not specified, this value will default to five data blocks.

■ *increase*—specifies the percentage increase that the next extent should be over the previous extent. If zero is specified, the next extent will be the same size as the previous extent. The default value is 50 percent.

■ *minext*—specifies the minimum number of extents. If not specified this value defaults to 1.

■ *maxext*—specifies the maximum number of extents or **Unlimited**.

■ *optimal*—specifies the optimal size of a rollback segment in bytes. **K** or **M** indicates that this value is in kilobytes or megabytes respectively. **Null** indicates that the database doesn't deallocate any rollback extents.

■ *freelists*—specifies the number of free lists for each free list group.

■ *freelistgroups*—specifies the number of free list groups.

■ *filename*—the name of the cluster file enclosed in single quotes (').

■ *instance*—specifies the number of instances that should be used with the Parallel Query option.

■ *value*—specifies the amount of space to be kept when unused storage is deallocated.

■ *degree*—specifies the number of parallel query servers to use.

See Also   **Create Cluster** (statement)

Alter Database

Syntax

MS SQL Server

```
Alter Database database
   [ On
      {
      Default [= dbsize ]|
      dbdevice [= dbsize ] [,dbdevice [= dbsize ] ] . . .
      }
   [ For Load ]
```

Oracle

```
Alter Database database
   { Mount [ Standby Database ] [ Exclusive | Parallel ] |
   Convert |
   Open [ Resetlogs | Noresetlogs ] |
   Activate Standby Database |
   Archivelog |
   Noarchivelog |
   Recover [ Automatic ]
      [ From location ]
      [ { [ [ [ Standby ] Database ]
         [ Until Cancel |
         Until Time datetime |
         Until Change changenum |
         Using Backup Controlfile ] . . . |
      Tablespace tablespace [, tablespace ] . . . |
      Database fdatabasefile [, databasefile ] . . . |
      Logfile logfile [, logfile ] . . . |
      Continue [ Default ] |
      Cancel } ]
      [ Parallel [ Degree degree ][ Instances instance ]
| Noparallel ]
      Add Logfile Member filename [ Reuse ] [, filename [ Reuse ] ] . . .
   To { Group group | filename | ( ( filename [, filename ] . . . ) }
      [, filename [ Reuse ] ] . . .
         To { Group group | filename | ( filename [, filename ] . . . ) } |
      Drop Logfile {
         { Group group | filename | ( ( filename [, filename ] . . . ) }
         [, { Group group | filename | ( ( filename [, filename ] . . . ) } ] . . . |
      Drop Logfile Member filename [, filename ] . . .
```

```
Clear [ Unarchived ] Logfile
    { Group group | filename | ( ( filename [, filename ] . . . ) }
      [, { Group group | filename | ( ( filename [, filename ] . . . ) } ] . . . [
Unrecoverable Datafile ] |
    Rename File filename [, filename ] . . . To filename [, filename ] . . . |
    Create Standby Controlfile As filename [ Reuse ]
    Backup Controlfile { To filename [ Reuse ] | To Trace [ Resetlogs | Noresetlogs ] } |
    Rename Global_name To database[.domain] |
    Reset Compatibility |
    Set { Dblow = dblow | Dbhigh = dbhigh | Dbmac { On | Off } |
    Enable [ Public ] Thread thread |
    Disable Thread thread |
    Create Datafile filename [, filename ] As filename [ Size size [ K | M ] [ Reuse ] ]
|
    Datafile filename [ filename ] . . . { Online | Offline [ Drop ] | Resize size [ K |
M ] |
    Autoextend { Off | On [ Next next [ K | M ] ] [ Maxsiz { Unlimited | maxsiz [ K | M ]
} } |
    End Backup } }
```

Usage The **Alter Database** statement is used to change the characteristics of a database.

Arguments
- *database*—the name of an existing database.
- *dbdevice*—the logical name of the database device where the database will be stored.
- *dbsize*—specifies the number of megabytes to be allocated on the *dbdevice*.
- *location*—specifies the location of the redo logfile group to be recovered.
- *datetime*—specifies the last date and time that should be recovered.
- *changenum*—specifies the last system change number to be recovered.
- *tablespace*—the name of the tablespace to be used.
- *databasefile*—specifies the name of a database file to be used.
- *logfile*—specifies the name of the redo log file to be used.
- *degree*—specifies the number of parallel query servers to use.
- *instance*—specifies the number of instances that should be used with the Parallel Query option.
- *filename*—the name of a physical disk file. This name must be enclosed in single quotes (' ').
- *group*—identifies the set of log files.
- *domain*—the name of a database domain.
- *dblow*—an operating system string.
- *dbhigh*—an operating system string.

- *thread*—a thread inside the database server.
- *size*—of the *filename* in bytes. If **K** is specified, then *size* is in kilobytes. If **M** is specified, then *size* is in megabytes.
- *next*—specifies the size that the data file will be expanded to when it runs out of space.
- *maxsiz*—specifies the maximum size of the file in bytes. **K** or **M** indicates that this value is in kilobytes or megabytes respectively. If not specified, this value will default to five data blocks.

Implementation Notes	MS SQL Server	This statement is used to create and add storage to an existing database. You can specify the size and location of the database files. Specifying **Default** will build the database on the default *dbdevice*.
		The **For Load** clause prevents anyone but the database owner from accessing the database until after the database has been loaded.
	Oracle	This statement allows you to **Mount** and **Activate** a standby database. You can **Archive** the redo logs or **Recover** from the redo logs. You can also **Add** or **Drop** **Logfiles** or **Logfile Members**. By specifying **Create Standby Controlfile**, you can create a backup for the control file. The **Enable** and **Disable Thread** clauses let you start and stop threads in the database.

See Also   **Alter Database** (statement), **Create Controlfile** (statement), **Drop Database** (statement)

Alter Function

STATEMENT

Oracle

Syntax   Alter Function [*user.*]*function* Compile

Usage   The **Alter Function** statement allows you to recompile a PL/SQL function.

Argument   ▪ *user*—the name of the creator of the function. If omitted, this value will default to the current user's name.
▪ *function*—the name of the function you want to recompile.

See Also   **Create Function** (statement), **Drop Function** (statement)

Alter Index

Syntax **Informix**

```
Alter Index indexname To [ Not ] Cluster
```

Oracle

```
Alter Index indexname
    [ Rebuild [
        { Parallel [ Degree degree ][ Instances instance ] | Noparallel } |
        { Logging | Nologging } |
        { Reverse | Noreverse } |
        [ Pctused pctused ] |
        [ Pctfree pctfree ] |
        [ Initrans initrans ] |
        [ Maxtrans maxtrans ] |
        [ Storage (
            [ Initial initial [ K | M ] ]
            [ Next next [ K | M ]
            [ Pctincrease increase ]
            [ Minextents minext ]
            [ Maxextents { maxext | Unlimited } ]
            [ Optimal { optimal [ K | M ] | Null } ]
            [ Freelists freelists ]
            [ Freelist Groups freelistgroup
          storage ] |
            [ Tablespace tablespace ]
            ] . . . )
        ]
    [ Deallocate Unused [ Keep keep [ K | M ] ] |
    Allocate Extent [ ( {
        Size size [ K | M ] |
        Datafile filename |
        Instance instance } . . . )
    [ { Parallel [ Degree degree ][ Instances instance ] | Noparallel } ] |
    [ Pctused pctused ] |
    [ Pctfree pctfree ] |
    [ Initrans initrans ] |
    [ Maxtrans maxtrans ] |
    [ Storage (
        [ Initial initial [ K | M ] ]
```

```
            [ Next next [ K | M ]
            [ Pctincrease increase ]
            [ Minextents minext ]
            [ Maxextents { maxext | Unlimited } ]
            [ Optimal { optimal [ K | M ] | Null } ]
            [ Freelists freelists ]
            [ Freelist Groups freelistgroup
            ] . . . ) |
      [ { Logging | Logging } ] ] |
      Rename To newindex |
      Modify Partition partition
            [ Pctused pctused ] |
            [ Pctfree pctfree ] |
            [ Initrans initrans ] |
            [ Maxtrans maxtrans ] |
            [ Storage (
                [ Initial initial [ K | M ] ]
                [ Next next [ K | M ]
                [ Pctincrease increase ]
                [ Minextents minext ]
                [ Maxextents { maxext | Unlimited } ]
                [ Optimal { optimal [ K | M ] | Null } ]
                [ Freelists freelists ]
                [ Freelist Groups freelistgroup
            storage ] |
                ] . . . ) |
            { Logging | Nologging } |
            Unusable ] |
      Rename Partition partition To newpartition |
      Drop Partition partition |
          Split Partition partition At ( value [, value ] . . . ) [ Into (
                { Partition [ newpartition ]
                [ Storage (
                [ Initial initial [ K | M ] ]
                [ Next next [ K | M ]
                [ Pctincrease increase ]
                [ Minextents minext ]
                [ Maxextents { maxext | Unlimited } ]
                [ Optimal { optimal [ K | M ] | Null } ]
                [ Freelists freelists ]
                [ Freelist Groups freelistgroup
            storage ] ] . . . ) |
                [ Tablespace tablespace ] |
                [ { Logging | Nologging } ]
                } . . . ) |
```

```
        [ { Parallel [ Degree degree ][ Instances instance ] | Noparallel } ] |
   Rebuild partition
            [ { Parallel [ Degree degree ][ Instances instance ] | Noparallel } ] |
         [ Pctused pctused ] |
         [ Pctfree pctfree ] |
         [ Initrans initrans ] |
         [ Maxtrans maxtrans ] |
         [ Storage (
            [ Initial initial [ K | M ] ]
            [ Next next [ K | M ]
            [ Pctincrease increase ]
            [ Minextents minext ]
            [ Maxextents { maxext | Unlimited } ]
            [ Optimal { optimal [ K | M ] | Null } ]
         [ Freelists freelists ]
         [ Freelist Groups freelistgroup
         ] . . . ) |
         [ { Logging | Logging } ] |
   Unusable
```

Usage   The **Alter Index** statement changes some aspects of an index. In most cases, you will
need to drop the index and recreate it.

Arguments   ▪ *indexname*—the name of the index. This value might include any optional qualifiers.

▪ *degree*—specifies the number of parallel query servers to use.

▪ *instance*—specifies the number of instances that should be used with the Parallel Query
option.

▪ *pctused*—the amount of space in a data block that must be used before another data
block is allocated. There must be at least *pctused* space available in a block before a row
can be inserted. If not specified, this value will default to 40 percent.

▪ *pctfree*—the amount of space in a data block that is reserved for future updates. Any
insert that will result in less than *pctfree* space available will cause a new block to be
created. If not specified, this value will default to 10 percent.

▪ *initrans*—specifies the initial number of transactions that might update a block. It can
range from 1 to 255. If not specified, this value will default to 1.

▪ *maxtrans*—specifies the maximum number of transactions that might update a block. It
can range from 1 to 255. If not specified, this value will default to 255.

▪ *initial*—specifies the amount of storage in bytes for the first extent. **K** or **M** indicates
that this value is in kilobytes or megabytes respectively. If not specified, this value will
default to two data blocks.

▪ *next*—specifies the amount of storage in bytes for the rest of the extents. **K** or **M**
indicates that this value is in kilobytes or megabytes respectively. If not specified, this
value will default to five data blocks.

- *increase*—specifies the percentage increase that the next extent should be over the previous extent. If zero is specified, the next extent will be the same size as the previous extent. The default value is 50 percent.
- *minext*—specifies the minimum number of extents. If not specified this value defaults to 1.
- *maxext*— specifies the maximum number of extents or **Unlimited**.
- *optimal*—specifies the optimal size of a rollback segment in bytes. **K** or **M** indicates that this value is in kilobytes or megabytes respectively. **Null** indicates that the database doesn't deallocate any rollback extents.
- *freelists*—specifies the number of free lists for each free list group.
- *freelistgroups*—specifies the number of free list groups.
- *value*—specifies the amount of space to be kept when unused storage is deallocated.
- *tablespace*—the name of the tablespace where the index will reside.
- *keep*—total space left in the index after deallocating the rest of the space.
- *size*—total size of the extent.
- *filename*—the name of the file that contains the extent in single quotes (').
- *instance*—specifies the database instance.
- *newindex*—the new name for *index*.
- *partition*—the name of the partition.
- *newpartition*—the new name for the partition.

Implementation Notes	Informix	The **Alter Index** statement is limited to changing the index to or from a clustering index. If **To Cluster** is specified, the table is physically sorted in order of the index. Any inserts will also maintain that ordering. You must use the **To Not Cluster** clause before changing another index to become the clustering index.
	Oracle	The **Alter Index** statement allows you to change some of the storage characteristics. You can rebuild an index with the **Rebuild** clause. You can free unneeded storage with the **Deallocate Unused** clause. You can add more space by using the **Allocate Extent** clause. You can rename the index with the **Rename** clause. For partitions, you can modify characteristics with the **Modify Partition** clause, you can rename it with the **Rename Partition**, you can delete a partition with the **Drop Partition** clause, split an existing partition into one or more new partitions with the **Split Partition** clause, or you can rebuild a partition with the **Rebuild** clause.

See Also   **Create Index** (statement), **Drop Index** (statement)

Alter Nodegroup

Syntax
```
Alter Nodegroup nodegroup
    {
    Add { Nodes | Node } ( nodenum [ To nodenum ] [, nodenum [ To nodenum ] . . . )
        [
        Like Node nodenum ] |
        Without Tablespaces
        |
    Drop { Nodes | Node } ( nodenum [ To nodenum ] [, nodenum [ To nodenum ] ] . . . )
    }
```

Usage   The **Alter Nodegroup** statement can add or delete nodes to a node group. Use the **Add** clause to include new nodes in *nodegroup* and the **Drop** clause to delete existing nodes from *nodegroup*. You can also specify a range of node numbers using the **To** keyword.

Authorization   You must have the **SYSCTRL** or **SYSADM** authority to define a node group.

Arguments   ▪ *nodegroup*—the name of the nodegroup. This name can't be qualified.
   ▪ *nodenum*—a specific partition number. Node numbers are defined in the db2nodes.cfg file.

See Also   **Create Nodegroup** (statement), **Drop Nodegroup** (statement)

Alter Procedure

Syntax   `Alter Procedure [user.]procedure Compile`

Usage   The **Alter Procedure** statement allows you to recompile a PL/SQL procedure.

Arguments   ▪ *user*—the name of the creator of the procedure. If omitted, this value will default to the current user's name.
   ▪ *procedure*—the name of the procedure you want to recompile.

See Also   **Create Procedure** (statement), **Drop Procedure** (statement)

Alter Table

Syntax   **IBM**

```
Alter Table tablename (
    {Add [ Column ] column datatype
        [
        Not Null |
        [ With ] Default
            [
            constant |
            variable |
            castfunction ( { constant | variable } ) |
            Null
            ] |
        [ Logged | Not Logged ] [ Compact | Not Compact ] |
        [ Constraint constraint ]
            [
            Primary Key |
            Unique |
            References reftable [ ( refcolumn [, refcolumn ] . . . ) ]
                [
                On Delete No Action |
                On Delete Restrict |
                On Delete Cascade |
                On Delete Set Null
                ]
                [
                On Update No Action |
                On Update Restrict
                ] |
            Check ( checkcondition )
            ]
            ] . . . |
        [ Constraint constraint ] { Unique | Primary Key } ( column [ , column ] . . . ) |
        [ Constraint constraint ] Foreign Key ( column [ , column ] . . . ) References
    reftable [ ( refcolumn [, refcolumn ] . . . ) ]
            [
            On Delete No Action |
            On Delete Restrict |
            On Delete Cascade |
            On Delete Set Null
            ]
            [
```

```
            On Update No Action |
            On Update Restrict
            ] |
      [ Constraint constraint ] Check ( checkcondition ) ]|
  Drop
      {
      Primary Key |
      { Foreign Key | Unique | Check | Constraint } constraint |
      Partitioning Key
      }
  } . . .
  [ Data Capture None | Data Capture Changes ]
```

Informix

```
Alter Table table
    {
    { Add | Modify } column datatype
        [ Default {
            constant |
            variable |
            Null }
        [ Not Null
            [ Constraint constraint [
            Disabled |
            Enabled |
            Filtered [ Without Error | With Error ] ] ]
        [ { Unique |
            Distinct |
            Primary Key |
            References table [ ( column [, column ] . . . ) ] [ On Delete Cascade ] |
            Check ( checkcondition ) } ]
                [ Constraint constraint [
                Disabled |
                Enabled |
                Filtered [ Without Error | With Error ] ] ] ]
        [ Before column ] |
    { Add | Modify } ( { column datatype
    [ Default {
        constant |
        variable |
    Null }
    [ Not Null
    [ Constraint constraint [
            Disabled |
            Enabled |
            Filtered [ Without Error | With Error ] ] ]
```

```
                [ { Unique |
                    Distinct |
                    Primary Key |
                    References table [ ( column [, column ] . . . ) ] [ On Delete Cascade ] |
                    Check ( checkcondition ) } ]
                       [ Constraint constraint [
                       Disabled |
                       Enabled |
                       Filtered [ Without Error | With Error ] ] ] ] |
                [ Before column ]
                [,] } . . . ) |
        Drop column |
        Drop ( column [, column ] . . . ) |
        Add Constraint constraint [
            Disabled |
            Enabled |
            Filtered [ Without Error | With Error ] ] ]
            [ { Unique |
                Distinct |
                Primary Key |
                References table [ ( column [, column ] . . . ) ] [ On Delete Cascade ] |
                Check ( checkcondition ) } ]
                   [ Constraint constraint [
                   Disabled |
                   Enabled |
                   Filtered [ Without Error | With Error ] ] ] ] |
        Add Constraint ( {constraint [
            Disabled |
            Enabled |
            Filtered [ Without Error | With Error ] ] ]
            [ { Unique |
                Distinct |
                Primary Key |
                References table [ ( column [, column ] . . . ) ] [ On Delete Cascade ] |
                Check ( checkcondition ) } ]
                   [ Constraint constraint [
                   Disabled |
                   Enabled |
                   Filtered [ Without Error | With Error ] ] ] ] [,] } . . . ) |
        Drop Constraint constraint |
        Drop Constraint ( constraint [, constraint ] . . . ) |
        Modify Next Size next |
        Lock Mode ( { Page | Row } )
```

MS SQL Server

```
Alter Table table
  [ With Nocheck ](
  Add column datatype
      [ Null | Not Null | Identity [ ( seed, increment ) ] ]
      [ Constraint constraint
          { { Primary Key | Unique } [ Clustered | Nonclustered ] ( column [, column ] . . .
  ) [ On segment ] |
          [ Foreign Key ( column, [, column ] . . . ) ] References table [ ( column [,
  column ] . . . ) ] |
          Default { constant | variable | Null } |
          Check [ Not For Replication ] ( checkcondition ) ] |
  Drop [ Constraint ] constraint [, constraint ] . . .
```

Oracle

```
Alter Table table
  ( Add {
      column datatype
          [ Default constant ]
          [ With Rowid ] [ Scope Is scopetable ]
          Constraint constraint {
              [ Not ] Null |
              { Unique | Primary Key }
              [ Using Index ]
              [ References table ( column ) ] [ On Delete Cascade ]
              [ Check ( checkcondition ) ]
              [ Exceptions Into table ]
              [ Disable ] } |
      Constraint constraint {
          [ Not ] Null |
          { Unique | Primary Key }
          [ Using Index ]
          [ References table ( column ) ] [ On Delete Cascade ]
          [ Check ( checkcondition ) ]
          [ Exceptions Into table ]
          [ Disable ] } |
      Ref ( column ) With Rowid |
      Scope For ( column ) Is table }
  Modify ( column [ datatype ]
      } [,] . . . )
      [ Default constant ]
      [ With Rowid ] [ Scope Is scopetable ]
      Constraint constraint {
```

```
              [ Not ] Null |
              { Unique | Primary Key }
              [ Using Index ]
              [ References table ( column ) ] [ On Delete Cascade ] |
              [ Check ( checkcondition ) ]
              [ Exceptions Into table ]
              [ Disable | Enable ] } |
    Drop ( column [, column ] . . . )
    Allocate Extent [ Size size [ K | M ] | Datafile filename | Instance instance ] |
    Deallocate Unused [ Keep keep [ K | M ] ] |
    Modify ( lob )
        ( Storage storage |
        Pctversion pctversion |
        Cache |
        Nocache Logging |
        Nocache Nologging |
        Allocate Extent [ Size size [ K | M ] | Datafile filename | Instance instance ] |
        Deallocate Unused [ Keep keep [ K | M ] ] |
        Rename To newtable |
    Overflow
        [ Pctfree pctfree |
        Pctused pctused |
        Initrans initrans |
        Maxtrans maxtrans |
        Storage storage |
        Including column ]
        Datafile filename | Instance instance ] |
        Deallocate Unused [ Keep keep [ K | M ] ] |
    Add Overflow
        [ Pctfree pctfree |
        Pctused pctused |
        Initrans initrans |
        Maxtrans maxtrans |
        Storage storage |
        Pcthreshold pcthreshold |
        Including column |
        Tablespace tablespace ] |
    Modify Partition partition
        { Pctfree pctfree |
        Pctused pctused |
        Initrans initrans |
        Maxtrans maxtrans |
        Storage storage ]
        [ Logging | Nologging ] }
```

```
Modify Partition partition
    { Pctfree pctfree |
    Pctused pctused |
    Initrans initrans |
    Maxtrans maxtrans |
    Storage storage ]
    [ Logging | Nologging ] |
    Tablespace tablespace |
    Parallel   [ Degree degree ][ Instances instance ] | Noparallel } |
Add Partition partition
    Values Less Than ( constant [, constant ] . . . )
    { Pctfree pctfree |
    Pctused pctused |
    Initrans initrans |
    Maxtrans maxtrans |
    Storage storage ]
    [ Logging | Nologging ] |
    Tablespace tablespace |
Drop Partition partition |
Truncate Partition partition [ Drop Storage | Reuse Storage ] |
Split Partition partition At ( value [, value ] . . . ) [ Into (
    { Partition [ newpartition ] |
    [ Storage (
        [ Initial initial [ K | M ] ]
        [ Next next [ K | M ]
        [ Pctincrease increase ]
        [ Minextents minext ]
        [ Maxextents { maxext | Unlimited } ]
        [ Optimal { optimal [ K | M ] | Null } ]
        [ Freelists freelists ]
        [ Freelist Groups freelistgroup
    storage ] ] . . . ) |
        [ Tablespace tablespace ] |
        [ { Logging | Nologging } ]
        } . . . ) |
Exchange Partition partition With Table table [ ( Including | Excluding ) ] Indexes ] [
{ With | Without } Validation ] |
Modify Partition Unusable Local Indexes |
Modify Partition Rebuild Unusable Local Indexes }
```

Usage   The **Alter Table** statement is used to change an existing table. Within the table, you can
Add or **Drop** columns, constraints, check conditions, partitioning information, primary
keys, and foreign keys.

When adding a column to the table, it must be assigned a valid data type. Then **Not Null** can be specified to insure that the column always contains data. You can also specify a default value for the column to be used when a new row is inserted into the table and a value is not specified or specified as **Default**. This is done by using the **With Default** clause. The default value can be **Null**, a standard constant, a system variable such as **Current Date** or **User**, or a function that will cast a value from one data type to another.

For large objects (LOB) such as **Blobs**, **Clobs**, **Dbclobs**, or any **Long** data type, you can choose not to log any changes to this column. While you can log changes up to one gigabyte in size, you probably shouldn't log changes any larger than 10 megabytes. **Not Logged** has no impact on normal **Rollback** or **Commit** operations; however, in the event you have to recover the database from a backup copy and try to roll forward with the database log, the information necessary to recover the LOBs will not be available. In this case, the large object will be assigned a value of zero.

You can also free any unused pages in the LOBs by specifying **Compact;** the disadvantage with specifying this option is that there might be a performance hit when you update a LOB with a larger size.

For each column, you can specify a constraint that will define the column as a **Primary Key**, insuring that the column has a **Unique** value in the table or that it acts as a value for a foreign key in another table using **References** clause. This means that the value must exist in the other table before the new row can be inserted or the current row can be updated. Note that no LOBs can be included as part of the foreign key.

When a record is deleted in the referred table, you have the option either to take no action and not process any constraints (**On Delete No Action**), process all constraints and then take no action (**On Delete Restrict**), process all constraints and pass the delete on to any dependent tables (**On Delete Cascade**), or set each foreign key value in the dependent table to **Null** (**On Delete Set Null**). When a record is updated in the referred table, you have the option to either take no action and not process any constraints (**On Update No Action**) or process all constraints and then take no action (**On Update Restrict**).

The **Check** clause is used to verify the value of a column or the contents of a row any time the row is inserted or updated. If the *checkcondition* is included as part of a column definition, then it might only refer to that column. Otherwise, it might refer to any column in the table. You can't use subqueries, column functions, host variables, parameter markers, system variables, or user functions that return variants, use **External Action**, or use **Scratchpad**.

You can also specify **Constraints** that define a **Primary Key** for the table or define a particular column or set of columns to be **Unique**. Also, you can define a **Foreign Key** that means the value in the list of columns must exist in another table.

You can also enable or disable **Data Capture** status by specifying **Changes** or **None**. Remember that **Data Capture Changes** must be specified so that the Capture program can get the information it needs to capture all changes needed for replication.

The **Drop** clause can be used to drop the **Primary Key**, the **Partitioning Key**, and any **Foreign Key**, **Unique**, **Check**, and **Constraint** clauses by specifying *constraint*.

On Informix database, you can also modify the size of the next extent by using the **Modify Next Size** clause. You can also change the locking scheme from **Row** to **Page** or **Page** to **Row**.

Authorization

You must have the **SYSCTRL** or **SYSADM** authority, plus the appropriate authority to use each of the statements included, to create a schema using any *schema* or *authorization* name. Without these capabilities, you can only create a schema where the *schema* and *authorization* match your user id.

Arguments

- *tablename*—the name of the table. It must not already exist in the database. This name might be qualified with either a schema name or a user id followed by a period and the name of the table.
- *column*—refers to the name of a column in the table.
- *datatype*—a valid data type.
- *constant*—a literal.
- *variable*—one of the following system variables: **Current Date**, **Current Time**, **Current Timestamp**, or **User**. Note that the *column* must be of the same data type as the variable.
- *castfunction*—a function that is used to convert a value to the same data type as *column*.
- *constraint*—the name of the constraint. This value must not duplicate the name of any constraint already defined. If not specified, a name will be generated by the system.
- *reftable*—the name of a base table holding the foreign key's columns.
- *refcolumn*—the name of a column in *reftable* that will be used as part of the foreign key.
- *checkcondition*—an expression that verifies the contents of the column any time a row is inserted or updated. If the *checkcondition* is included as part of a column definition, then it might only refer to that column. Otherwise, it might refer to any column in the table. You can't use subqueries, column functions, host variables, parameter markers, system variables, or user functions that return variants, use **External Action**, or use **Scratchpad**.
- *tablespace*—the name of the table space where the table will be placed. If not specified, this value will default to the **IBMDEFAULTGROUP** table space. If **IBMDEFAULTGROUP** table space does not exist, then the database will place it in the user's table space or the **USERSPACE1** table space. If none of these table spaces exist, an error will be returned. Also, unless otherwise specified, this table space will be used to store all long values (**Blob**, **Clob**, **Dbclob,** or any **Long** value) and any indexes.
- *indexspace*—the name of the table space where any indexes will be placed. It must be a **Regular** Database Managed Space (DMS) table space and part of the same nodegroup as the table space that contains the base table. If not specified, the indexes will be placed in the same table space as the base table.

- *longspace*—the name of the table space where long values (**Blob, Clob, Dbclob,** or any **Long** value) will be placed. It must be a **Long** DMS table space and part of the same nodegroup as the table space that contains the base table. If not specified, the long values will be placed in the same table space as the base table.

- *next*—the size of the next extent in kilobytes. This value must be at least four times the minimum disk page size on your system.

- *dbspace*—the name of the dbspace where the table will be created.

- *first*—the size of the first extent for the table in kilobytes.

- *next*—the size of the next extent for the table in kilobytes.

- *seed*—the initial value for the **Identity** clause that provides a unique value for a column.

- *increment*—the value that will be added to the previous value of the **Identify** clause to create the new one.

- *segment*—the name of the segment where the table will be stored.

- *dbspace*—the name of the dbspace were the table will be created.

- *scopetable*—the name of a table that contains the scope of the column.

- *pctused*—the amount of space in a data block that must be used before another data block is allocated. There must be at least *pctused* space available in a block before a row can be inserted. If not specified, this value will default to 40 percent.

- *pctfree*—the amount of space in a data block that is reserved for future updates. Any insert that will result in less than *pctfree* space available will cause a new block to be created. If not specified, this value will default to 10 percent.

- *initrans*—specifies the initial number of transactions that might update a block. It can range from 1 to 255. If not specified, this value will default to 1.

- *maxtrans*—specifies the maximum number of transactions that might update a block. It can range from 1 to 255. If not specified, this value will default to 255.

- *lob*—a Large Object Block in the table.

- *pctversion*—the percentage full of the total LOB storage space that must be used before old storage is overlaid.

See Also   **Comment On** (statement), **Create Index** (statement), **Create Table** (statement), **Create View** (statement), **Drop Schema** (statement), **Grant** (statement)

Alter Tablespace

Syntax **IBM**

```
Alter Tablespace tablespacename
    {
    Add
        {
        Using ( containerstring [, containerstring ] . . . )
        [ On { Nodes | Node } ( nodenum [ To nodenum ] [, nodenum [ To nodenum ] . . . ) ]
        } . . . |
    Add
        {
        Using ( { File | Device } containerstring pages [,{ File | Device } containerstring
pages ] . . . )
        [ On { Nodes | Node } ( nodenum [ To nodenum ] [, nodenum [ To nodenum ] ] . . . ) ]
        } . . .
    }
    [ Prefetchsize prefetchpages ]
    [ Bufferpool bufferpool ]
    [ Overhead overheadtime ]
    [ Transferrate transfertime ]
```

Oracle

```
Alter Tablespace tablespace {
    Add Datafile filename [ Size size [ K | M ] ] [ Reuse ] [, filename [ Size size [ K | M
] ] [ Reuse ] . . . ] |
    Autoextend filename [ Size size [ K | M ] ] [ Reuse ] [, filename [ Size size [ K | M ]
] [ Reuse ] . . . ]
        [ On | Off ]
        [ Next next [ K | M ] ]
        [ Maxsiz [ Unlimited | maxsiz [ K | M ] ] ] |
    Rename Datafile filename [, filename ] . . . To filename [, filename ] . . . |
    Default Storage (
            [ Initial initial [ K | M ] ]
    [ Next next [ K | M ]
    [ Pctincrease increase ]
    [ Minextents minext ]
    [ Maxextents { maxext | Unlimited } ] ] |
        Minimum Extent extent [ K | M ] |
        { Read Only | Read Write } |
```

```
        { Online | Offline [ Normal | Temporary | Immediate ] } |
        [ Begin Backup | End Backup ] |
        [ Permanent | Temporary ] |
        [ Coalesce ] }
```

Usage The **Alter Tablespace** statement is used to add additional space or change various parameters in an existing table space.

You must have the **SYSCTRL** or **SYSADM** authority to define a table space.

Arguments
- *tablespacename*—the name of the table space.
- *nodenum*—a specific partition number. Node numbers are defined in the db2nodes.cfg file.
- *containerstring*—the name of the path where the table space will be stored on the system. It can contain an absolute path from the root directory or a relative path from the database directory. This value must be enclosed in single quotes (').
- *prefetchpages*—the number of 4k pages that will be read when prefetching data from the table space.
- *bufferpool*—the name of the buffer pool that will be used to hold pages in real memory.
- *overheadtime*—the average time required in milliseconds to position the disk to transfer data. This value will be used in the query optimizer to determine the cost of an I/O operation. This value includes the overhead in the controller, the average seek time, and the average latency time to perform a transfer. This value should be averaged when dealing with containers that span multiple types of disk drives. If omitted, this value will default to 24.1 milliseconds.
- *transfertime*—the average time required in milliseconds to transfer a single 4k page. This value will be used in the query optimizer to determine the cost of an I/O operation. This value should be averaged when dealing with containers that span multiple types of disk drives. If omitted, this value will default to 0.9 milliseconds.

Implementation Notes   IBM

When the table space was created you specified that it was either **Managed By System** or System Managed Space (SMS) and **Managed By Database** or Database Managed Space (DMS). These are two different ways to manage table spaces. While you can't change from one way to the other using the **Alter Tablespace** statement, you need to know how the table space was originally created, because the syntax of the **Alter Tablespace** statement varies depending on how the table space was created.

In SMS table spaces, the database uses the operating system's file system to create and manage disk space. A series of physical files, called containers, are created to hold the database pages. Any time there is a requirement for a new page, a new page is allocated to the end of the current container by the operating system. After an extent has been added to a container, the next container is selected. This distributes the table space pages evenly between all the containers.

Tip

You should use multiple containers when the size of your table space exceeds the largest file supported by the operating system. Thus, if the operating system imposes a two-gigabyte limitation on a file, you can create a ten-gigabyte table space by using five containers.

In a DMS table space, the database manages the space allocation itself. You can map the table space to either a disk drive (**Device**) or a file (**File**) that was created by the operating system. In either case, the total space in the container specified by *pages* is preallocated by the database. Once allocated, space can't be removed from a DMS table space. Also, because DMS spaces allocated on **Devices** don't use the normal file system procedures, you might need to increase the buffer pool space to account for the operating system's I/O buffering and caching. You can't specify a **Device** container on Windows 95, Windows NT, or OS/2.

Adding a new container to a table space will force the contents of the table space to be redistributed among all of the available containers. During this rebalancing process, the table space is unavailable for access.

You can also place each container on a specific node in a partitioned database by using the **On Node** clause. You can specify either a specific node number, a range of node numbers (using the **To** keyword), or a list of node numbers and node ranges.

Prefetchsize contains the number of pages that will be read from a table space when a prefetch operation is performed. Prefetching assists queries that are reading a table by attempting to eliminate I/O during the query processing.

Bufferpool specifies the name of the buffer pool that will be used for storing pages from the table space in memory.

Overhead specifies the average time required in milliseconds to position the disk to transfer data. This value will be used in the query optimizer to determine the cost of an I/O operation. This value includes the overhead in the controller, the average seek time, and the average latency time to perform a transfer. This value should be averaged when dealing with containers that span multiple types of disk drives. If omitted, this value will default to 24.1 milliseconds.

Transfer the average time required in milliseconds to transfer a single 4k page. This value will be used in the query optimizer to determine the cost of an I/O operation. This value should be averaged when dealing with containers spanning multiple types of disk drives. If omitted, this value will default to 0.9 milliseconds.

Oracle The **Alter Tablespace** statement lets you add more data files for storage using the **Add Datafile** clause. You can enable or disable the autoextend facility and manage its space allocation by using the **Autoextend** clause. You can rename data files using the **Rename Datafile** clause. You can also enable or disable any of the following options: **Read Write**, **Read Only**, **Online**, and **Offline**. You can also use the **Begin Backup** and **End Backup** to mark the database as available for a system backup. You can also mark the database as **Permanent** to store any type of Oracle database data or **Temporary** to only temporary segments. You can also use the **Coalesce** clause to combine neighboring free extents into larger free extents.

See Also **Create Tablespace** (statement), **Drop Tablespace** (statement)

Alter Trigger

STATEMENT

Oracle

Syntax
```
Alter Trigger [ user.]trigger
    { Enable | Disable | Compile [ Debug ] }
```

Usage The **Alter Trigger** statement allows you to enable, disable or compile a trigger. The **Debug** option allows you to capture debugging information when you recompile the trigger.

Arguments
- *user*—the name of user that created the trigger.
- *trigger*—the name of the trigger.

See Also **Create Trigger** (statement), **Drop Trigger** (statement)

Alter View

STATEMENT

Oracle

Syntax   `Alter View [ user.]view Compile`

Usage   The **Alter View** statement allows you compile a view to check for errors.

Arguments   ▪ *user*—the name of user that created the view.

            ▪ *trigger*—the name of the view.

See Also   **Create View** (statement), **Drop View** (statement)

Begin Declare Section

STATEMENT

ANSI • IBM

Syntax   `Begin Declare Section`

Usage   The **Begin Declare Section** statement begins a section where all host variables are declared using the normal syntax for the host programming language. The **End Declare Section** statement is placed after all of the host variables have been declared.

        All host variables must be defined in the declare section before they are used. Also, no SQL statements can be placed in the declare section or an error will occur.

See Also   **End Declare Section** (statement)

Begin Work

STATEMENT

Informix

Syntax   `Begin Work`

Usage   The **Begin Work** statement marks the beginning of a transaction that consists of multiple SQL statements. The transaction is ended with a **Commit** or **Rollback** statement.

See Also   **Commit** (statement), **Rollback** (statement)

Call

Syntax　Call { *procname* | :*hostvar* } [(:*hostvar* [, :*hostvar*])] | Using Descriptor *descriptor*

Usage　The **Call** statement runs a stored procedure that is executed in the database server and will return data to the client. Note that this statement can only be embedded in an application program.

You can specify the name of a procedure either explicitly as *procname* or by using a *hostvar*. The procedure name itself can take the form of *name, library!name,* or *absolutepath!name.* When you specify *name,* the database will look for the procedure called *name* in the library called *name.*

External libraries are found on a UNIX or NT system in the directories sqllib/ function or sqllib/function/unfenced. On an OS/2 system, the LIBPATH environment will be used to determine which directories should be searched for fenced functions. Unfenced functions are located in the sqllib/function/unfenced directory.

If the function is not found in any of the external libraries, then the SYSCAT.PROCEDURES table is searched for where PROCNAME matches *name* and PROCSCHEMA is one of the values in **Current Function Path**. The first procedure that has the same number of parameters as *name* will be used. An error will occur if the procedure is not found.

If the name of the procedure is in the form *proclib!procname,* the external libraries will be searched for a library named *proclib* with a procedure called *procname.* If the form *absolutepath!name* is specified, then the library specified by *absolutepath* will be searched for a procedure called *name.*

Parameters for the procedure are specified by a series of *hostvars.* The type of each parameter passed to the routine must agree with the definition of the procedure or an error will occur.

The **Using Descriptor** clause is used to identify an SQL Descriptor area that contains a list of host variables in a single entity. These host variables contain information that will be passed to and from the routine. Also included is a flag called SQLIND that can be set to -1 if the parameter is not used to transmit data to the server and -128 if information will not be returned from the server.

Arguments　▪ *procname*—the name of a procedure.

▪ *hostvar*—the name of a host variable in a programming language.

▪ *descriptor*—an SQL Descriptor consisting of a series of host variables.

See Also　**Define Function** (statement), **Define Procedure** (statement)

Close

ANSI • IBM • Informix • MS SQL Server • Oracle • Sybase

Syntax   Close *cursorname* [With Release]

Usage   The **Close** statement closes a cursor and releases its resources to the database server.
          The **With Release** clause is an IBM extension that releases any read locks that might
          have been held open with the cursor.

Argument ▪ *cursorname*—the name of an open cursor.

See Also   **Define Cursor** (statement)

Comment On

IBM • Oracle

Syntax   **All**

```
Comment On Column tablename.columnname Is comment
Comment On Table tablename Is comment
```

IBM DB2

```
Comment On Alias aliasname Is comment
Comment On Constraint tablename.constraintname Is comment
Comment On [ Distinct | Data ] Type typename Is comment
Comment On Function functionname [ ( datatype [, datatype] . . . ) ] Is comment
Comment On Index indexname Is comment
Comment On Nodegroup nodegroupname Is comment
Comment On Package packagename Is comment
Comment On Procedure procedurename [ ( datatype [, datatype] . . . ) ] Is comment
Comment On Schema schemaname Is comment
Comment On Specific Function specificfunctionname Is comment
Comment On Specific Procedure specificprocedurename Is comment
Comment On Tablespace tablespacename Is comment
Comment On Trigger triggername Is comment
Comment On tablename ( columnname Is comment [,columnname Is comment ] . . . )
```

Usage The **Comment On** statement allows you to add or replace comments about database objects.

You must include the types of parameters when commenting on a function or a procedure when you have created multiple functions or procedures that have the same name. If there is only one function or procedure with that name, you might omit the parameter list. You can't **Comment On** system functions and procedures.

Tip

*To remove a comment, simply use the **Comment On** statement and assign a **Null** value as the comment.*

Authorization You must have the **SYSADM** or **DBADM** authorization, be the owner of the object, have the **ALTERIN** privilege on the schema, or have the **CONTROL** or **ALTER** privilege on the object.

Arguments
- *aliasname*—the name of an alias.
- *columnname*—the name of a column in a table.
- *comment*—a string that contains the comments that are associated with the object. If comments already exist for the object, they will be replaced with the new value of *comment*.
- *constraintname*—the name of a constraint.
- *datatype*—the name of a valid data type.
- *functionname*—the name of a user-defined function.
- *indexname*—the name of an index.
- *nodegroup*—the name of a group of nodes in a partitioned database.
- *packagename*—the name of a package.
- *procedurename*—the name of a procedure.
- *specificfunctionname*—the name of a function.
- *specificprocedurename*—the name of a procedure.
- *tablename*—the name of a database table or view.
- *tablespacename*—the name of a tablespace.
- *triggername*—the name of a trigger.
- *typename*—the name of a distinct type.

Implementation Notes   Oracle   Only **Comment On Column** and **Comment On Table** statements are supported.

See Also   **Disconnect** (statement), **Set Connection** (statement)

Commit

STATEMENT

ANSI • IBM • Informix • MS SQL Server • Oracle • Sybase

Syntax   Commit [Work]

Usage   The **Commit** statement ends a logical transaction and posts all changes to the database. All open cursors are closed and all locks are released. To abandon all changes to the database, the **Rollback** statement should be used.

Implementation Notes   IBM DB2   Cursors defined **With Hold** are not closed and the cursor is moved to the next row of the result set.

Microsoft Access   The **Commit** statement is not available in Access. The **CommitTrans** method should be used in its place.

See Also   **Rollback** (statement)

Connect

STATEMENT

ANSI • IBM • Informix • Oracle • Sybase

Syntax   Connect To { Default | *connection* }
          [As *connectionname*]
          [In Share Mode | In Exclusive Mode [On Single Node]]
          [User *userid* [Using *password*]] }

Usage   The **Connect** statement establishes a connection to a database server.

> **Tip**
>
> *You should always begin your programs with a **Connect** statement.*

Arguments   ▪ *connection*—a string or host variable that contains information needed to connect to the database. This is usually the name of the server. A host variable must always be preceded by a colon (:).

▪ *userid*—a string or host variable that contains authorization information.

▪ *password*—a string or host variable that contains the password corresponding to the userid.

Implementation Notes	ANSI	The **Using** clause is not part of the ANSI standard.
	IBM DB2	Cursors defined **With Hold** are not closed and the cursor is moved to the next row of the result set.

The **In Share Mode** and **In Exclusive Mode** clauses are IBM extensions that regulate other users' access to the database. **In Share Mode** permits other users to perform concurrent operations, but denies any other users from requesting exclusive access. **In Exclusive Mode** denies any other users from accessing the database. The **On Single Node** clause restricts the exclusive access to a single partition in the database. All other partitions are accessed in share mode.

The **Using** clause allows you to specify a password for the user.

	Microsoft Access	This statement is not supported in Access. Instead, you should use the **Connect** property and the **OpenRecordset** method.
	Microsoft SQL Server	This statement is not supported in SQL server. Instead you should use the Data Access Objects.

Example

```
connect to sample user db2admin using ''

Database Connection Information

    Database product     = DB2/NT 5.0.0
    SQL authorization ID = DB2ADMIN
    Local database alias = SAMPLE
```

This example shows how to **Connect** to the Sample database using the userid Db2admin. Note that the password is specified as an empty string (") since I don't have a password on this userid. (Kids, don't do this at home. Always use a password on all database userids.)

See Also **Disconnect** (statement), **Set Connection** (statement)

Create Bufferpool

Syntax   Create Bufferpool *bufferpool*
       [All Nodes | Nodegroup *nodegroup* [, Nodegroup *nodegroup*] . . .]
       Size *numberpages*
       [Except On Node[s] (*nodenumber* [To *nodenumber*]) Size *numberpages*] . . .
       [[Not] Extended Storage]

Usage   Buffer pools are used by table spaces to hold data in main memory. This permits you to determine how much main memory to allocate to a particular tablespace. The **Create Bufferpool** statement creates a buffer pool definition on all nodes or just the specified node groups. It is also possible to change the number of buffers on a node-by-node basis using the **Except On Nodes** clause.

      The size of each buffer page is 4,096 bytes, and *numberpages* is the number of pages that will be allocated on for the server. In a partitioned database, this value reflects the number of pages on each node.

> ### Tip
>
> *Bufferpools are the way that real memory on the server is allocated for the database server. Therefore there should be sufficient real memory to handle all of the buffer pools, the database system, and the operating system. If there is not sufficient memory, then only the default buffer pool will be used. If there isn't sufficient space, then a minimal default buffer pool will be used.*

      The **Extended Storage** allows pages that are migrated from the buffer pool to be cached in extended storage (assuming that extended storage is available). **Not Extended Storage** means that the pages will not be cached.

Authorization   You must have the **SYSCTRL** or **SYSADM** authority to create buffer pool definitions.

Arguments   ▪ *bufferpool*—the name of the bufferpool to be created.

      ▪ *nodegroup*—specifies the name of a new nodegroup that will be added to the list of nodes using this bufferpool. The node groups IBMCATGROUP and IBMTEMPGROUP can't be specified.

      ▪ *numberpages*—the number of pages in the buffer pool.

See Also   **Alter Bufferpool** (statement)

Create Cluster

Syntax
```
Create Cluster [ user.]cluster
    ( column datatype [, column datatype ] . . . )
    {
        Pctused pctused |
        Pctfree pctfree |
        Size size [ K | M ] |
        Initrans initrans |
        Maxtrans maxtrans |
        Storage (
            [ Initial initial [ K | M ] ]
            [ Next next [ K | M ] ]
            [ Pctincrease increase ]
            [ Minextents minext ]
            [ Maxextents { maxext | Unlimited } ]
            [ Optimal { optimal [ K | M ] | Null } ]
            [ Freelists freelists ]
            [ Freelist Groups freelistgroup ]
        [ Tablespace tablespace ]
        [ Index | [ Hash is column ] Hashkeys hashkeys ]
        [ Nocache | Cache ]
    [ Parallel [ Degree degree ][ Instances instance ]
        | Noparallel ]
```

Usage   The **Create Cluster** statement is used to create a cluster that will be shared among
several tables. Each column in the cluster will be stored only once no matter how many
tables are included in the cluster. Use **Create Table**'s **Cluster** clause to specify this
cluster.

Arguments ▪ *user*—the name of the user creating the cluster.

▪ *cluster*—the name of the cluster.

▪ *column*—the name of a column to be included in the cluster.

▪ *datatype*—a valid data type associated with the *column*.

▪ *pctused*—the amount of space in a data block that must be used before another data
block is allocated. There must be at least *pctused* space available in a block before a row
can be inserted. If not specified, this value will default to 40 percent.

- *pctfree*—the amount of space in a data block that is reserved for future updates. Any insert that will result in less than *pctfree* space available will cause a new block to be created. If not specified, this value will default to 10 percent.

- *size*—this value should be the average amount of space to store all the rows in all the tables for a single cluster key. The physical block size should be evenly divisible by this value. Specifying too large a value might decrease the time to access the data, but can waste space.

- *initrans*—specifies the initial number of transactions that might update a block. It can range from 1 to 255. If not specified, this value will default to 1.

- *maxtrans*—specifies the maximum number of transactions that might update a block. It can range from 1 to 255. If not specified, this value will default to 255.

- *initial*—specifies the amount of storage in bytes for the first extent. **K** or **M** indicates that this value is in kilobytes or megabytes respectively. If not specified, this value will default to two data blocks.

- *next*—specifies the amount of storage in bytes for the rest of the extents. **K** or **M** indicates that this value is in kilobytes or megabytes respectively. If not specified, this value will default to five data blocks.

- *increase*—specifies the percentage increase that the next extent should be over the previous extent. If zero is specified, the next extent will be the same size as the previous extent. The default value is 50 percent.

- *minext*—specifies the minimum number of extents. If not specified this value defaults to 1.

- *maxext*—specifies the maximum number of extents or **Unlimited**.

- *optimal*—specifies the optimal size of a rollback segment in bytes. **K** or **M** indicates that this value is in kilobytes or megabytes respectively. **Null** indicates that the database doesn't deallocate any rollback extents.

- *freelists*—specifies the number of free lists for each free list group.

- *freelistgroups*- specifies the number of free list groups.

- *tablespace*—the name of the tablespace that will hold the cluster.

- *instance*—specifies the number of instances that should be used with the Parallel Query option.

- *degree*—specifies the number of parallel query servers to use.

See Also   **Alter Cluster** (statement)

Create Controlfile

Syntax
```
Create Controlfile
    [ Reuse ] [ Set ] Database database
    Logfile [ Group group ] filename
        [, [ Group group ] filename ] . . .
        { Resetlogs | Noresetlogs }
    Datafile filename [, filename ] . . .
    [ Maxlogfiles maxlogfiles ]
    [ Maxlogmembers maxlogmembers ]
    [ Maxloghistory maxloghistory ]
    [ Maxdatafiles maxdatafiles]
    [ Maxinstances maxinstances ]
    [ Archivelog | Noarchivelog ]
```

Usage The **Create Controlfile** statement is used to create a new control file for an existing database.

> ### Tip
>
> *Backup your database prior to using this statement, because it will overlay your database's existing control file.*

Arguments
- *database*—the name of the user creating the cluster.
- *group*—identifies the set of log files.
- *filename*—the name of a physical disk file. This name must be enclosed in single quotes (').
- *maxlogfiles*—the maximum number of redo log file groups that can exist.
- *maxlogmembers*—the maximum number of redo log files in any log file group.
- *maxloghistory*—the maximum number of archived redo log file groups for the Parallel Server option.
- *maxinstances*—the maximum number of database instances that can mount and open the database.

See Also **Create Database** (statement)

Create Database

Syntax **IBM**

```
Create Database [ DB ] database
    [ On [ path | drive ] ]
    [ Alias databasealias ]
    [ Using Codeset codeset Territory territory ]
    [ Collate Using [ System | Compatibility | Identity ] ]
    [ Numsegs numsegs ]
    [ DFT_EXTENT_SZ extentsize ]
    [ Catalog Tablespace
        { System Using ( containerstring [, containerstring ] . . . ) |
        Database Using ( { File | Device } containerstring pages [,{ File | Device }
    containerstring pages ] . . . ) }
        [ Extentsize extentpages ]
        [ Prefetchsize prefetchpages ]
        [ Bufferpool bufferpool ]
        [ Overhead overheadtime ]
        [ Transferrate transfertime ]
User Tablespace
        { System Using ( containerstring [, containerstring ] . . . ) |
        Database Using ( { File | Device } containerstring pages [,{ File | Device }
    containerstring pages ] . . . ) }
        [ Extentsize extentpages ]
        [ Prefetchsize prefetchpages ]
        [ Bufferpool bufferpool ]
        [ Overhead overheadtime ]
        Transferrate transfertime ]
[ Temporary Tablespace
        { System Using ( containerstring [, containerstring ] . . . ) |
        Database Using ( { File | Device } containerstring pages [,{ File | Device }
    containerstring pages ] . . . ) }
        [ Extentsize extentpages ]
        [ Prefetchsize prefetchpages ]
        [ Bufferpool bufferpool ]
        [ Overhead overheadtime ]
        [ Transferrate transfertime ]
    [ With commentstring ]
```

Informix

```
Create Database database
    [ In dbspace ]
    [
        With { [ Buffered ] Log ] |
        Log Mode Ansi
    ]
```

MS SQL Server

```
Create Database database
    [ On
        {
        Default [= dbsize ]|
        dbdevice [= dbsize ] [,dbdevice [= dbsize ] ] . . .
        }
    [ Log On dbdevice [= dbsize ] [,dbdevice [= dbsize ] ] . . . ]
    [ For Load ]
```

Oracle

```
Create Database database
    [ Controlfile Reuse ]
    Logfile [ Group group ] filename [ Size size [ K | M ]
        [, [ Group group ] filename [ Size size [ K | M ] ] . . .
        { Resetlogs | Noresetlogs }
    [ Maxlogfiles maxlogfiles ]
    [ Maxlogmembers maxlogmembers ]
    [ Maxloghistory maxloghistory ]
    [ Datafile filename [ Size size [ K | M ] [, filename [ Size size [ K | M ] ]
    ] . . . ]
    [ Autoextend filename [ Size size [ K | M ] [, filename [ Size size [ K | M ] ]
    ] . . . ]
        [ On | Off ]
        [ Next next [ K | M ] ]
        [ Maxsiz [ maxsiz [ K | M ] | Unlimited ] ] ]
    [ Maxdatafiles maxdatafiles]
    [ Maxinstances maxinstances ]
    [ Archivelog | Noarchivelog ]
    [ Exclusive ]
    [ Character Set charset ]
```

Usage   The **Create Database** statement is used to create a new database.

Arguments
- *database*—the name of the new database.
- *dbdevice*—the logical name of the database device where the database will be stored.
- *dbsize*—specifies the number of megabytes to be allocated on the *dbdevice*.
- *group*—identifies the set of log files.
- *filename*—the name of a physical disk file. This name must be enclosed in single quotes (').
- *size*—of the *filename* in bytes. If **K** is specified, then *size* is in kilobytes. If **M** is specified, then *size* is in megabytes.
- *maxlogfiles*—the maximum number of redo log file groups that can exist.
- *maxlogmembers*—the maximum number of redo log files in any log file group.
- *maxloghistory*—the maximum number of archived redo log file groups for the Parallel Server option.
- *next*—specifies the size that the data file will be expanded to when it runs out of space.
- *size*—the maximum size of a data file.
- *maxinstances*—the maximum number of database instances that can mount and open the database.

Implementation Notes

MS SQL Server	This statement is used to create storage for a new database. You can specify the size and location of the database files and the log files. Specifying **Default** will build the database on the default *dbdevice*.
	The **For Load** clause prevents anyone but the database owner from accessing the database until after the database has been loaded.
Oracle	Specifying **Controlfile Reuse** will reuse a control file if it already exists. **Logfile** is used to specify the physical file names associated with the redo log. **Resetlogs** means that any existing log files will be reused and erased, while **Noresetlogs** means that the any existing log files will not be erased before being reused.
	The **Datafile** clause specifies the names of the physical files that will contain the data for the database. You can specify multiple files and you can **Autoextend** those files when the become full.

Archivelog means that the contents of the redo logs are not overwritten and can be used to help recover the database in the event of a system problem. **Noarhivelog** means that the information contained in the redo log may be overwritten when the information is no longer needed.

Exclusive means that the database supports only one instance unless the **Alter Database Dismount** and **Alter Database Mount Parallel** statements are executed to enable parallel execution.

You can specify the character set used to store the data by using the **Character Set** clause.

See Also   **Alter Database** (statement), **Create Controlfile** (statement), **Drop Database** (statement)

Create Default

STATEMENT

MS SQL Server • Sybase

Syntax   `Create Default [ owner.]defaultname As expr`

Usage   The **Create Default** statement allows you to associate a name with a constant value. This value can be used anywhere you would use a normal expression.

Arguments   ▪ *owner*—the name of the user who created the default value.

▪ *defaultname*—the name of the default value.

▪ *expr*—an expression that contains only constant values.

See Also   **Drop Default** (statement)

Create Distinct Type

Syntax Create Distinct Type **[schema.]typename** As **datatype**
        [With Comparisons]

Usage The **Create Distinct Type** statement is used to create a new data type based on an existing data type. This allows stronger type checking, because the standard functions and operators do not automatically handle the new data type unless they are specifically written or the **With Comparisons** clause is used.

    Distinct type allows functions to be created with standard names such as **Length** or **Trim** but return different values than the standard function. This can be useful when you create an abstract data type that will hold non-standard information.

    The **With Comparisons** clause specifies that the system should generate comparison operators for the new data type. This clause should not be used when **Blob**, **Clob**, **Dbclob**, **Long Varchar**, or **Long Vargraphic** is specified for *datatype*.

Authorization You must have the **DBADM** or **SYSADM** authority, the **CREATIN** authority for an existing schema, or the **IMPLICIT_SCHEMA** authority for a new schema.

Arguments ▪ *schema*—the name of a schema. If the schema doesn't exist, it will automatically be created for you.

    ▪ *typename*—the name of the new data type. This can't be one of the following reserved words: **All**, **And**, **Any**, **Between**, **Exists**, **In**, **Like**, **Match**, **Not**, **Null**, **Or**, **Overlaps**, **Similar**, **Some**, or **Unique**.

    ▪ *datatype*—specifies an existing data type available in DB2.

See Also **Comment On** (statement), **Create Function** (statement), **Drop** (statement)

Create Event Monitor

Syntax
```
Create Event Monitor eventmonitor
    For event [, event ] . . .
    Write To { Pipe pipename | File path [ fileopt ] . . . }
    [ Autostart | Manualstart ]
    [ On Node nodenumber ]
    [ Local | Global ]
```

Usage
The **Create Event Monitor** statement specifies which events should be recorded for analysis. The events to be recorded are specified using the **For** clause. Where the event information will be written is specified with the **Write To** clause. **Autostart** means that the event monitor is automatically started each time the database is started, while **Manualstart** means that the event monitor will not be started until the **Set Event Monitor State** statement is executed. The event monitor can be restricted to a single node using the **On Node** clause. The **Global** clause can be used to report deadlocks for all nodes in the system. **Local** is used to monitor events that happen only on the local node.

Authorization
You must have the **DBADM** or **SYSADM** authority to create event monitors.

Arguments
■ *eventmonitor*—the name of the event monitor.

■ *event*—will record a record when one of the following events occurs. The syntax for an event is:

```
{ Database |
    Tables |
    Deadlocks |
    Bufferpools |
    Connections [ Where condition ] |
    Statements [ Where condition ] |
    Transactions [ Where condition ] }
```

■ A **Database** event will occur when the last application disconnects from the database. A **Table** event will occur for each table that has changed since the first connection to the database when the last application disconnects from the database. A **Deadlocks** event will occur whenever a deadlock occurs. A **Bufferpools** event will occur when the last application disconnects from the database. A **Connections** event will occur whenever an application disconnects from the server. A **Statements** event will occur whenever an SQL statement finishes. A **Transactions** event will occur when a transaction completes (i.e., **Commit** or **Rollback** statement is executed). The **Where** clause allows you to restrict the number of records retrieved by selecting only those records you want.

- *condition*—an expression that determines which events should be recorded. It has the following syntax:

  [Not] [( ] { Appl_id | Auth_id | Appl_name } { = | <> | > | < | >= | <= | Like | Not
      Like } *string* [ )] [{ And | Or } *condition*] . . .

- *condition* returns either **True** or **False** based on tests involving **Appl_id**, **Auth_id,** or **Appl_name** and a string constant.

- *pipe*—the name of the pipe where the event records will be written.

- *path*—the directory path where the event files will be written. Filenames have the form 00000000.evt, 00000001.evt, etc. Even though multiple files might be written, the data should be treated as a single large file. If the path begins with the root directory, an absolute path is assumed. Otherwise the path is assumed to be a relative path to the DB2EVENT directory.

- *fileopts*—zero or more of the following items described below:

  { **Maxfiles** { **None** | *numberfiles* } |
      Maxfilesize { **None** | *pages* } |
      Buffersize *bufpages* |
      [**Blocked** | **Unblocked**]
      [**Append** | **Replace**] }

- **Maxfiles** specifies the maximum number of files containing event information that can exist in the directory indicated by *path*. Once there are *numberfiles* in the event log directory, the event monitor will shut itself off. The keyword **None** means that there is no limit to the number of files. **Maxfilesize** contains the maximum size in 4k byte pages the file can reach before a new one is opened. Default for UNIX systems is 1000 4k pages, while the default for all other platforms is 200 4k pages. The keyword **None** means that the file can grow as large as needed and *numberfiles* should be set to 1. **Buffersize** specifies the size of each buffer in 4k pages. The default value is one page or two 4k pages. Because the maximum size of these buffers is limited by DBHEAP space, this value might need to be increased if you are using a large number of events. **Blocked** means that if both internal event buffers are full, the event agent will be blocked during the physical I/O to prevent any lost data. **Nonblocked** means that the agent will continue to collect data while the physical I/O is taking place. While there is a possibility of data loss, this option has less of an impact on the system. **Append** specifies that if an event log file exists from a previous session, any new data will be appended to the end of the file. **Replace** specifies that any existing event files will be erased and the event information will be recorded in the 00000000.evt file.

- *nodenumber*—the number of the node on which the events will be monitored.

See Also   **Set Event Monitor State** (statement)

Create Function

Syntax

IBM

```
Create Function function
    ( [ datatype [ As Locator ] [, datatype [ As Locator ] . . . ] )
    { Returns
        {
        { datatype [ As Locator ] | datatype Cast From datatype [ As Locator ] } |
        Table ( [ column datatype [ As Locator ] [, column datatype [ As Locator ] . . . ] )
    [ Specific specific ]
    External [ Name name ] Language { C | Java | OLE }
    Parameter Style { DB2SQL | DB2General }
    { Deterministic | Not Deterministic }
    [ Fenced | Not Fenced ]
    [ Not Null Call | Null Call ]
    No SQL
    { No External Action | External Action }
    [ No Scratchpad | Scratchpad ]
    [ No Final Call | Final Call ]
    [ Allow Parallel | Disallow Parallel ]
    [ No Dbinfo | Dbinfo ]
    [ Cardinality cardinality ]
```

Oracle

```
Create [ Or Replace ] Function [user].function [ ( arg [ In | In Out | Out ] datatype [, arg
    [ In | In Out | Out ] datatype ] . . . ) ] Return datatype [ As | Is ] sqlstatements
```

Usage   The **Create Function** is used to define a function in the database.

Authorization   On DB2, you must have the **DBADM** or **SYSADM** authority or **IMPLICIT_SCHEMA** authority on the database if the schema name does not exist or **CREATIN** privilege for the schema if the schema does exist. **Not Fenced** also requires the **CREATE_NOT_FENCED** authority on the database or the **DBADM** or **SYSADM** authority.

On Oracle, you must have either the **Create Procedure** or **Create Any Procedure** privilege.

Arguments   ■ *function*—the name of the function.

■ *datatype*—a valid data type.

- *specific*—an alternate name for the function. It can be used to source, drop, or comment on the function, but it can't be used to call the function.

Tip

Use this name to provide a unique name for the function. This is especially useful when you have multiple functions with the same name, but use different data types for arguments.

- *name*—the external name of the function.
- *user*—the name of the user who will be the owner of the function. If not specified, this will default to the user who created the function.
- *arg*—the name of the parameter.
- *sqlstatements*—a block of SQL statements.

Implementation Notes   IBM

The function name is followed by a list of data types enclosed in parentheses. Each data type corresponds to the data type of the parameter for the function. Even if the function has no parameters, the parentheses are required. The **As Locator** clause is used with large objects such as **Blobs**, **Clobs**, **Dbclobs**, and any **Long** data type to return a reference to the object rather than the object itself. This can reduce the number of bytes that need to be transferred between the server and the client, which could lead to improved performance.

For calls to scalar functions, the data type of the return value from the function is specified using the **Return** clause. You can also convert the data type of the return value from one type to another, compatible, data type by using the **Cast From** clause. This is useful when you wish to return a different value from an existing function.

If the function returns a table, the **Returns Table** clause is specified. It lists the *column* name and *datatype* of each column in the returned table.

The **Specific** clause is used to provide a unique name for the function that can be referenced with the **Drop** and **Comment** statements and the **Source** clause. This value can't be used for any other function. If this clause is not included, a specific name of the form SQLyymmddhhmmsshhn will be created for you.

The **External** clause is used to identify an external routine that will be called when the function is invoked. The **Language** clause is used to specify the type of programming language that the function was written in. Only **C**, **Java**, and **OLE** are legal values for this clause.

You can specify a value for *name* in the **Name** clause, which is the name of the external routine. This value must be enclosed in single quotes (' '). For functions written in **C** this value takes the form of *name*, *library!name,* or *absolutepath!name.* When you specify *name*, the database will look for the procedure called *name* in the library called *name.* If the **Name** clause is not used, *name* will be assumed to be the same as *function.*

External libraries are found on UNIX or NT systems in the directories sqllib/function or sqllib/function/unfenced. On an OS/2 system, the LIBPATH environment will be used to determine which directories should be searched for fenced functions. Unfenced functions are located in the sqllib/function/unfenced directory.

If the function is not found in any of the external libraries, then the SYSCAT.PROCEDURES table is searched for where PROCNAME matches *name* and PROCSCHEMA is one of the values in **Current Function Path**. The first procedure that has the same number of parameters as *name* will be used. An error will occur if the procedure is not found.

If the name of the procedure is in the form *proclib!procname,* the external libraries will be searched for a library named *proclib* with a procedure called *procname.* If the form *absolutepath!name* is specified, then the library specified by *absolutepath* will be searched for a procedure called *name.*

For functions written in **Java**, this value takes the form of *classid!methodid.* If *classid* is part of a package, then the complete package prefix must be included. The Java virtual machine will look in the appropriate directory.

Even through **OLE** isn't a real programming language, functions written to OLE specifications can be called. You can specify the function as either *progid!method* or *clsid!method; progid* and *clsid* identify the appropriate module, and *method* identifies an OLE method.

The **Parameter Style** clause specifies how the parameters are passed to the routine. **DB2SQL** is used when **Language** is either **C** or **OLE**, while **DB2General** is used when **Language Java** is specified.

The **Deterministic** clause is used to identify whether the function will always return the same results each time they are called in a transaction with a given set of parameters, while **Non Deterministic** can return different results. This information will be used by the query optimizer.

The **Not Fenced** clause is used to indicate that the routine can be safely run inside the database's address space. Specifying **Fenced** means that the function runs outside the database's address space. **Language OLE** routines must be run as **Fenced**.

Tip

*Use extreme caution when using **Not Fenced** functions, because a run-time error can corrupt the database's address space.*

You can specify **Not Null Call** to suppress calling the routine whenever at least one of the parameters passed to the function is **Null**. **Null Call** is default and means that the routine will always be called.

No SQL implies that the function can't make any SQL calls. This clause is mandatory.

No External Action implies that no changes outside of the database are made. This can be important because the optimizer might restructure an operation such that a function is called fewer times than was originally coded yet still performs the desired operation against the database. By specifying **External Action**, you can communicate to the optimizer that calling the function takes some action that involves something beyond the database server's control, such as creating or deleting a file or sending a message. This clause is mandatory.

Because user-defined functions should be reentrant, the **Scratchpad** clause exists to provide dedicated storage for the function that will be preserved from one call to the next. This storage is 100 bytes long and initialized to binary zeros for the first call. The storage will be reinitialized each time a new statement is processed. In a partitioned database, the storage will be allocated in each server if the **Allow Parallel** clause is also specified on the function definition.

Tip

*Use the option with **Final Call** when your function spends a lot of time initializing itself to preserve that information and save processing time on the next call. Use the **Final Call** to release any system resources such as memory after execution has been completed.*

An additional parameter can be included in the function call that describes whether the function is being called for the first time, an intermediate time, or the last time by specifying the **Final Call** clause. This means that the function could initialize **Scratchpad** storage on the first call or release a system resource on the last call. The first call is also a normal call, meaning the function should return a proper value. The final call need not return a proper value, because it is called either at the end of a statement or the end of a transaction. Specifying **No Final Call** means that the additional parameter will not be included and the routine will not be called one last time before processing has finished.

The **Allow Parallel** and **Disallow Parallel** clauses indicate to the optimizer whether the query can be broken down into smaller sub-tasks (**Allow Parallel**) that are processed concurrently. This would most likely happen in a partitioned database. Thus, if your function returns a value such as a counter where the value must be unique across all partitions, use **Disallow Parallel**. However, if your function merely loads static information that would be the same in all partitions, using **Allow Parallel** could speed up processing. The **Disallow Parallel** clause is required when returning a table.

Use the **Dbinfo** clause to pass the following information to the function: database name, application authorization id, code page, schema name, table name, column name, database version and release, platform, and table result column numbers (not included in scalar functions).

If the function returns a table, you can use the **Cardinality** clause to provide an estimate of the number of rows that will be returned. If not specified, a finite value will be assumed by the database server. If the function never returns an end of table condition (i.e., infinite cardinality), problems can occur during query processing when clauses such as **Group By** or **Order By** expect to receive an end of table condition.

Oracle

The **Create Function** statement defines or replaces a function in the database. You specify a list of arguments that can be passed to (**In**), returned from (**Out**), or passed to and returned from (**InOut**) the function. Each argument has an associated data type. Since this is a function, there is also a data type associated with the function itself. The block of statements can consist of any legal PL/SQL statement.

See Also   **Create Procedure** (statement), **Drop Function** (statement)

Create Index

IBM • Informix • MS Access • MS SQL Server • Oracle • Sybase

Syntax

IBM DB2

```
Create [ Unique ] Index indexname
    On tablename ( columnname [ Asc | Desc ] [,columnname [ Asc | Desc ] ] . . . )
```

Informix

```
Create [ Unique | Distinct ] [ Cluster ] Index indexname
    On tablename ( columnname [ Asc | Desc ] [,columnname ] . . . )
    [ Fillfactor fillfactor ]
    [ Enabled | Disabled | Filtering [ With Error | Without Error ] ]
```

Microsoft Access

```
Create [ Unique ] [ Clustered | Nonclustered ] Index indexname
    On tablename ( columnname [ Asc | Desc ] [,columnname [ Asc | Desc ] ] . . . )
    [ With [ { Primary | Disallow Null | Ignore Null } ]
```

Microsoft SQL Server

```
Create [ Unique ] [ Clustered | Nonclustered ] Index indexname
    On tablename ( columnname [,columnname ] . . . )
    [ With [ Pad_index ]
    [[,] Fillfactor = fillfactor ]
    [[,] Ignore_dup_key ]
    [[,]  Sorted_data | Sorted_data_reorg ]
    [[,] Ignore_dup_row | Allow_dup_row ]
    [ On segmentname ]
```

Oracle

```
Create [ Unique | Bitmap ] Index indexname
    On { tablename ( columnname [ Asc | Desc ] [,columnname [ Asc | Desc ] ] . . . ) |
    Cluster [ cluster ] }
    [
        Pctused pctused |
        Pctfree pctfree |
        Initrans initrans |
        Maxtrans maxtrans |
        Storage storage |
        { Logging | Nologging } |
        { Tablespace tablespace | Default } |
        { Nosort | Reverse }
    ] . . .
```

```
        [
            Global Partition By Range ( columnname [, columnname ] . . . ) ( Partition [
        partition ] Values Less Than [ ( valuelist ) ]
            [
                Pctused pctused |
                Pctfree pctfree |
                Initrans initrans |
                Maxtrans maxtrans |
                Storage (
                    [ Initial initial [ K | M ] ]
                    [ Next next [ K | M ]
                    [ Pctincrease increase ]
                    [ Minextents minext ]
                    [ Maxextents { maxext | Unlimited } ]
                    [ Optimal { optimal [ K | M ] | Null } ]
                    [ Freelists freelists ]
                    [ Freelist Groups freelistgroup
        { Logging | Nologging } |
            ] . . . |
            Local ( Partition [ partition ]
            [
                Pctused pctused |
                Pctfree pctfree |
                Initrans initrans |
                Maxtrans maxtrans |
                Storage (
                    [ Initial initial [ K | M ] ]
                    [ Next next [ K | M ]
                    [ Pctincrease increase ]
                    [ Minextents minext ]
                    [ Maxextents { maxext | Unlimited } ]
                    [ Optimal { optimal [ K | M ] | Null } ]
                    [ Freelists freelists ]
                [ Freelist Groups freelistgroup |
                { Logging | Nologging } |
                ] . . . ]
            [ Parallel [ Degree degree ][ Instances instance ] | Noparallel
        ]
```

Usage   The **Create Index** statement defines an index on a table to help improve performance.

Authorization   On DB2 you must have the **DBADM** or **SYSADM** authority, or **CONTROL** or **INDEX** privileges on the table plus either the **IMPLICIT_SCHEMA** authority on the database if the schema name doesn't exist or **CREATEIN** if the schema exists. On Oracle you must have the **INDEX** privilege on the table or the **CREATE ANY INDEX** privilege.

Arguments   ▪ *indexname*—the name of the index. This value might include any optional qualifiers.

▪ *tablename*—the name of the table.

▪ *columnname*—a name of a column in the table. A maximum of 16 columns might be included in the index.

▪ *fillfactor*—an integer value that specifies how full an index page must be before another index page is created.

▪ *segmentname*—specifies the name of the database segment in which the index will be created.

▪ *cluster*—the name of the cluster.

▪ *pctused*—the amount of space in a data block that must be used before another data block is allocated. There must be at least *pctused* space available in a block before a row can be inserted. If not specified, this value will default to 40 percent.

▪ *pctfree*—the amount of space in a data block that is reserved for future updates. Any insert that will result in less than *pctfree* space available will cause a new block to be created. If not specified, this value will default to 10 percent.

▪ *initrans*—specifies the initial number of transactions that might update a block. It can range from 1 to 255. If not specified, this value will default to 1.

▪ *maxtrans*—specifies the maximum number of transactions that might update a block. It can range from 1 to 255. If not specified, this value will default to 255.

▪ *initial*—specifies the amount of storage in bytes for the first extent. **K** or **M** indicates that this value is in kilobytes or megabytes respectively. If not specified, this value will default to two data blocks.

▪ *next*—specifies the amount of storage in bytes for the rest of the extents. **K** or **M** indicates that this value is in kilobytes or megabytes respectively. If not specified, this value will default to five data blocks.

▪ *increase*—specifies the percentage increase that the next extent should be over the previous extent. If zero is specified, the next extent will be the same size as the previous extent. The default value is 50 percent.

▪ *minext*—specifies the minimum number of extents. If not specified this value defaults to 1.

▪ *maxext*—specifies the maximum number of extents or **Unlimited**.

▪ *optimal*—specifies the optimal size of a rollback segment in bytes. **K** or **M** indicates that this value is in kilobytes or megabytes respectively. **Null** indicates that the database doesn't deallocate any rollback extents.

▪ *freelists*—specifies the number of free lists for each free list group.

▪ *freelistgroups*—specifies the number of free list groups.

▪ *instance*—specifies the number of instances that should be used with the Parallel Query option.

▪ *value*—specifies the amount of space to be kept when unused storage is deallocated.

- *degree*—specifies the number of parallel query servers to use.
- *tablespace*—the name of the tablespace where the index will reside.
- *partition*—the name of the partition where the index will reside on a parallel server.
- *valuelist*—the values used to determine in which partition the information should be stored. Each value in *valuelist* must correspond to the columns specified in the **Range** clause.

Implementation Notes	IBM DB2	If **Unique** is specified, then the table can't have two rows that have duplicate values for the index's columns. Note that **Null** is treated the same as any other column value. Thus, having an index on a single column means that only one row in the table can contain a **Null** value in that column.
	Informix	If **Unique** is specified, then the table can't have two rows that have duplicate values for the index's columns. **Distinct** is a synonym for **Unique**. Specifying the **Cluster** option will physically reorganize the table based on the index's key columns. Only one **Cluster** index is permitted per table.

The **Fillfactor** clause specifies how full an index node will be before a new node is created. The value can range from 1 to 100 and the default value is 90 percent. Specifying a higher value makes the index more efficient for applications that do not insert and update the rows in the table. Specifying a lower value reduces the number of times the node will need to be split, so applications that perform a lot of inserts and updates will be more efficient.

The **Disabled** clause disables the index so that inserts, updates, and deletes do not change the index. Because the index is disabled, its contents are not used during query optimization. The **Enabled** index means the index is updated after every insert, update, or delete and it is used during query optimization.

If you have a **Unique** index, you can also enable **Filtering**. **Filtering** writes any rows that have a duplicate key value created by an insert or update into a violations table associated with the base table. Diagnostic information about the operation is written into the diagnostic table associated with the base table. You can optionally instruct the database not to return an error code when the duplicate key error occurs by specifying **Without Error** after the **Filtering** keyword. Error codes can be returned with the **With Error** keyword.

Microsoft Access

Primary indicates that the index can be used to uniquely identify each row in the table. If you specify **Primary**, you don't need to specify **Unique**. **Disallow Null** means that the index's columns can't include any **Null** values. Rows that have **Null** values in the index columns can be excluded by specifying **Ignore Null**, so only those records without **Null** values will be included in the index.

Microsoft SQL Server

Clustered and **Nonclustered** apply to Microsoft SQL Server. **Clustered** indexes are used to maintain the physical order of the data in the table. **Nonclustered** indexes are default and simply provide another way to retrieve data in sorted order.

Allow_dup_row and **On**. **Pad_index** mean that the **Fillfactor** setting applies to the index pages as well as the data pages.

Ignore_dup_key will prevent a duplicate row from being added to a table. Use caution when this clause is used, because it is possible for an **Update** to change column values in such a way as to create a duplicate row; when the update fails, the original row is lost and can't be undone with a **Rollback**. **Sorted_data** instructs the database server that the data in the table is already in sorted order, while **Sorted_data_reorg** not only assumes that the data is sorted, but also reorganizes the data in the pages to use the value supplied by **Fillfactor**. **Ignore_dup_row** is used to eliminate duplicate rows in a clustered index. **Allow_dup_rows** allows you to keep duplicate rows in a clustered index.

See Also   **Alter Index** (statement), **Drop Index** (statement)

Create Nodegroup

STATEMENT

IBM

Syntax
```
Create Nodegroup nodegroup
    [
    On All Nodes |
    On { Nodes | Node } ( nodenum [ To nodenum ] [, nodenum [ To nodenum ] . . . )
```

Usage
The **Create Nodegroup** statement names a group of one or more nodes. You can specify a list of node numbers or a range of node numbers using the **To** keyword.

Authorization
You must have the **SYSCTRL** or **SYSADM** authority to define a node group.

Arguments
- *nodegroup*—the name of the nodegroup. This name can't be qualified.
- *nodenum*—a specific partition number. Node numbers are defined in the db2nodes.cfg file.

See Also
Alter Nodegroup (statement), **Drop Nodegroup** (statement)

Create Procedure

STATEMENT

IBM • Informix • MS SQL Server • Oracle

Syntax
IBM

```
Create Procedure procedure
    ( [ [ In | Out | Inout ] datatype [ As Locator ] [,[ In | Out | Inout ] datatype [ As
    Locator ] . . . ] )
    [ Specific specific ]
    [ Result Sets results ]
    External [ Name name ] Language { C | Java | OLE }
    Parameter Style { DB2SQL | DB2General }
    { Deterministic | Not Deterministic }
    [ Fenced | Not Fenced ]
    [ Null Call ]
```

Informix

```
Create [ DBA ] Procedure procedure
    [ ( arg { datatype [ Default value ] |
        Like table.column [ Default value ] |
        References { Byte | Text } [ Default Null ] [,] } . . . ) ]
    Returning { datatype | References { Byte | Text } [,] } . . . ;
    sqlstatement [; sqlstatement ] . . . End Procedure
    [ Document docinfo [, docinfo ] . . . ]
    [ With Listing In path ]
```

MS SQL Server

```
Create { Proc | Procedure } [owner.]procedure[;procnumber]
    [ ( @arg datatype [= default] [ Output] [,@arg datatype [= default] [ Output] ] . . . )
    ]
    [ For Replication |
        With Recompile |
        { With | , } Encryption ]
    As sqlstatement [; sqlstatement ] . . .
```

Oracle

```
Create Procedure [user.]procedure
    [ ( arg [ In | Out | In Out ] datatype [, arg [ In | Out | Inout ] datatype ] . . . ) ]
    { Is | As } block
```

Usage
Create Procedure is used to define a procedure in the database.

Authorization
On DB2, you must have the **DBADM** or **SYSADM** authority, **IMPLICIT_SCHEMA** authority on the database if the schema name does not exist, or **CREATIN** privilege for the schema if the schema does exist. **Not Fenced** also requires the **CREATE_NOT_FENCED** authority on the database or the **DBADM** or **SYSADM** authority.

Informix users must have the **Resource** privilege on the database to create a procedure.

If you want to create a procedure in an Oracle database, you need the **Create Procedure** or **Create Any Procedure** privilege.

Arguments
▪ *procedure*—the name of the procedure.

▪ *arg*—the name of an argument to the procedure.

▪ *datatype*—a valid data type.

▪ *block*—a list of one or more SQL statements that comprise the procedure.

- *specific*—an alternate name for the function. It can be used to source, drop, or comment on the function, but it can't be used to call the procedure.

> **Tip**
>
> *Use this name to provide a unique name for the procedure. This is especially useful when you have multiple procedures with the same name, but use different data types for arguments.*

- *name*—the external name of the procedure.
- *results*—the approximate upper limit of rows that will be returned as a result set by this procedure.
- *table*—the name of a table or a view.
- *column*—the name of a column in a table that will be used to determine the data type for a particular argument of the procedure.
- *value*—a constant that will be used if a value is not specified as part of the argument.
- *sqlstatement*—an SQL statement that will be executed as part of the procedure.
- *owner*—the userid that owns the procedure.
- *procnumber*—a number used to associate this procedure with other procedures.
- *default*—a default value that will be used if the argument is omitted when the procedure is called.
- *docinfo*—a string enclosed in single quotes (') that describes to someone how to use the procedure.
- *path*—the name of the path where the listing will be stored. This value must be enclosed in quotes.

Implementation Notes   IBM

The procedure name is followed by a list of data types enclosed in parentheses. Each data type corresponds to the data type of the parameter for the function. The data type can optionally be preceded by **In**, **Out**, or **Inout**, indicating that the parameter contains information that is only read by the procedure, only returned by the procedure, or read and returned by the procedure. If not specified, **In** is assumed.

Even if the procedure has no parameters, the parentheses are required. The **As Locator** clause is used with large objects such as **Blobs**, **Clobs**, **Dbclobs**, and any **Long** data type to return a reference to the object rather than to the object itself. This might reduce the number of bytes that need to be transferred between the server and the client, which could lead to improved performance.

The **Specific** clause is used to provide a unique name for the procedure that can be referenced with the **Drop** and **Comment** statements and the **Source** clause. This value can't be used for any other function. If this clause is not included, a specific name of the form SQLyymmddhhmmsshhn will be created for you.

Results specifies the approximate upper limit of rows that will be returned.

The **External** clause is used to identify an external routine that will be called when the procedure is invoked. The **Language** clause is used to specify the type of programming language that the procedure was written in. Only **C**, **Java**, and **OLE** are legal values for this clause.

You can specify a value for *name* in the **Name** clause, which is the name of the external routine. This value must be enclosed in single quotes ('). For functions written in **C** this value takes the form of *name, library!name,* or *absolutepath!name*. When you specify *name*, the database will look for the procedure called *name* in the library called *name*. If the **Name** clause is not used, *name* will be assumed to be the same as *function*.

External libraries are found on a UNIX or NT system in the directories sqllib/function or sqllib/function/ unfenced. On an OS/2 system, the LIBPATH environment will be used to determine which directories should be searched for fenced functions. Unfenced functions are located in the sqllib/function/unfenced directory.

If the function is not found in any of the external libraries, then the SYSCAT.PROCEDURES table is searched for where PROCNAME matches *name* and PROCSCHEMA is one of the values in **Current Function Path**. The first procedure that has the same number of parameters as *name* will be used. An error will occur if the procedure is not found.

If the name of the procedure is in the form *proclib!procname*, the external libraries will be searched for a library named *proclib* with a procedure called *procname*. If the form *absolutepath!name* is specified, then the library specified by *absolutepath* will be searched for a procedure called *name*.

For functions written in **Java** this value takes the form of *classid!methodid*. If *classid* is part of a package, then the complete package prefix must be included. The Java virtual machine will look in the appropriate directory.

Even through **OLE** isn't a real programming language, procedures written to OLE specifications can be called. You can specify the procedure as either *progid!method* or *clsid!method*; *progid* and *clsid* identify the appropriate module and *method* identifies an OLE method.

The **Parameter Style** clause specifies how the parameters are passed to the routine. **DB2SQL** is used when **Language** is either **C** or **OLE**, while **DB2General** is used when **Language Java** is specified.

The **Deterministic** clause is used to identify whether the procedure will always return the same results each time they are called in a transaction that has a given set of parameters, while **Non Deterministic** can return different results. This information will be used by the query optimizer.

The **Not Fenced** clause is used to indicate that the routine can be safely run inside the database's address space. Specifying **Fenced** means that the routine runs outside the database's address space. **Language OLE** routines must be run as **Fenced**.

Tip

*Use extreme caution when using **Not Fenced** functions, because a run-time error can corrupt the database's address space.*

You can specify **Not Null Call** to suppress calling the routine whenever at least one of the parameters passed to the procedure is **Null**. **Null Call** is default and means that the routine will always be called.

Informix

The **Create Procedure** statement defines a procedure in the database. The **DBA** clause marks that procedure as a privileged procedure. A list of arguments is specified with corresponding data types and optionally followed by default values. An argument can also be defined to be **Like** a column in a table or that **References Text** or **Byte** data. The procedure may return a set of rows, with each row containing the specified list of data types and **References**. A list of SQL statements to be executed are included next, followed by the **End Procedure** clause. Comments on how to use the procedure are optionally listed in the **Document** clause and the **With Listing In** clause specifies where to place the listing file that will contain any errors or warnings generated while compiling the procedure.

MS SQL Server

The **Create Procedure** statement defines a procedure in the database. You can specify a value for *procnum* that can be used to create a group of related procedures that can be dropped with a single drop statement. Each argument consists of an argument name (*arg*), its data type (*datatype*), and an optional default value that will be used when the argument is omitted when the procedure is called.

The **For Replication** clause is used to create a filter-stored procedure that will be executed by replication. The **Recompile** clause means that the procedure is recompiled each time it is used. Note that you can't specify both **For Replication** and **Recompile**. The **Encryption** clause encrypts the SQL statements when they are stored in the database.

Oracle

The **Create Procedure** statement defines or replaces a procedure in the database. You specify a list of arguments that can be passed to (**In**), returned (**Out**), or passed to and returned from (**InOut**) the function. Each argument has an associated data type. The block of statements can consist of any legal PL/SQL statement.

See Also
Call (statement), **Create Function** (statement), **Drop Procedure** (statement)

Create Rule

STATEMENT

MS SQL Server • Sybase

Syntax
Create Rule [*owner.*]*rulename* As *expr*

Usage
The **Create Rule** statement allows you to define a rule that can be used to determine if a column or user-defined data type value is acceptable.

Arguments
- *owner*—the name of the user who created the rule.
- *rulename*—the name of the rule.
- *expr*—an expression that evaluates to either **True** or **False**. This expression is essentially the same as the **Where** clause of a **Select** statement.

See Also
Drop Rule (statement)

Create Schema

Syntax
```
Create Schema
    {
    schema |
    Authorization authorizationname |
    schema Authorization authorizationname
    }
    [
    commenton |
    createindex |
    createtable |
    createview |
    grant
    ] . . .
```

Usage   The **Create Schema** statement defines a schema that holds a set of tables and related objects, and grants privileges to these resources. You can also specify the objects as part of the **Create Schema** statement or execute those statements separately and reference the schema's name. These objects include: the **Comment On** statement, the **Create Index** statement, the **Create Table** statement, the **Create View** statement, and the **Grant** statement. *schema* is an IBM extension that allows you to specify the name of the schema.

Authorization   You must have the **SYSCTRL** or **SYSADM** authority, plus the appropriate authority to use each of the statements included, to create a schema using any *schema* or *authorization* name. Without these capabilities, you can only create a schema where the *schema* and *authorization* match your user id.

Arguments   ▪ *schema*—the name of the schema that will contain the synonym.

        ▪ *authorizationname*—the name of the user id that will own the schema. If not specified, it will default to the user id of the person executing the **Create Schema** statement.

       ▪ *createindex*—a legal **Create Index** statement.

       ▪ *createtable*—a legal **Create Table** statement.

       ▪ *createview*—a legal **Create View** statement.

       ▪ *grant*—a legal **Grant** statement.

See Also   **Comment On** (statement), **Create Index** (statement), **Create Table** (statement), **Create View** (statement), **Drop Schema** (statement), **Grant** (statement)

Create Synonym

STATEMENT

IBM • Informix • Oracle

Syntax   Create [Public | Private] [Synonym | Alias] [{*schema* | *user*}.]*name* For *object* [**@***database_link*]

Usage   The **Create Synonym** statement defines an alternate name for a database object. **Public** is used by Oracle to make the synonym available to all users. **Alias** is an alternate word that means the same as **Synonym** and is available on IBM DB2 and Oracle systems.

Authorization   You must have the **SYSCTRL** or **SYSADM** authority, the **IMPLICIT_SCHEMA** authority on the database if the schema name doesn't exist, or **CREATEIN** if the schema exists, to create a synonym.

Arguments   ▪ *schema*—the name of the schema that will contain the synonym.

       ▪ *user*—the name of the user associated with the synonym.

       ▪ *name*—the name of the synonym.

       ▪ *object*—the name of the real object that the synonym will point to. This can be a table, a view, or another synonym.

       ▪ *database_link*—a link to a remote database in Oracle.

See Also   **Drop Synonym** (statement)

Create Table

Syntax   **IBM**

```
Create Table tablename (
    {
    column datatype
        [
        Not Null |
        [ With ] Default
            [
            constant |
            variable |
            castfunction ( { constant | variable } ) |
            Null
            ] |
        [ Logged | Not Logged ] [ Compact | Not Compact ] |
        [ Constraint constraint ]
            [
            Primary Key [ Clustered | Nonclustered ] |
            Unique |
            References reftable [ ( refcolumn [, refcolumn ] . . . ) ]
                [
                On Delete No Action |
                On Delete Restrict |
                On Delete Cascade |
                On Delete Set Null
                ]
                [
                On Update No Action |
                On Update Restrict
                ] |
            Check ( checkcondition )
                ]
            ] . . . |
        [ Constraint constraint ] { Unique | Primary Key } ( column [ , column ] . . . ) |
        [ Constraint constraint ] Foreign Key ( column [ , column ] . . . ) References
reftable [ ( refcolumn [, refcolumn ] . . . ) ]
            [
            On Delete No Action |
            On Delete Restrict |
            On Delete Cascade |
            On Delete Set Null
            ]
```

```
        [
        On Update No Action |
        On Update Restrict
        ] |
    [ Constraint constraint ] Check ( checkcondition ) ]
    [,] } . . .
    [ Data Capture None | Data Capture Changes ]
    [ In tablespace [ Index In indexspace ] [ Long In longspace ] ]
    [ Partitioning Key ( column [, column ] . . . ) [ Using Hashing ] ]
    [ Not Logged Initially ]
```

Informix

```
Create Table
    { column datatype
        [ Default {
            constant |
            variable |
            Null } }
        [ Not Null
            [ Constraint constraint [
            Disabled |
            Enabled |
            Filtered [ Without Error | With Error ] ] ]
        [ { Unique |
            Distinct |
            Primary Key |
            References table [ ( column [, column ] . . . ) ] [ On Delete Cascade ] |
            Check ( checkcondition ) } ]
            [ Constraint constraint [
            Disabled |
            Enabled |
            Filtered [ Without Error | With Error ] ] ] ] |
    {
        Unique ( column [, column ] . . . ) |
        Distinct ( column [, column ] . . . ) |
        Primary Key ( column [, column ] . . . ) |
        Foreign Key ( column [, column ] . . . ) References table [ ( column [, column ] . .
    . ) ] [ On Delete Cascade ] |
        Check ( checkcondition ) }
    [ Constraint constraint [
    Disabled |
    Enabled |
    Filtered [ Without Error | With Error ] ] ] ]
    [,] }
```

```
[ In dbspace ]
[ Extent Size first ] [ Next Size next ]
[ Lock Mode { Page | Row } ]
```

MS SQL Server

```
Create Table table (
    ( { column datatype
        [ Null | Not Null | Identity [ ( seed, increment ) ] ]
        [ Constraint constraint
            { { Primary Key | Unique } [ Clustered | Nonclustered ] ( column [, column ] . . .
) [ On segment ] |
            [ Foreign Key ( column, [, column ] . . . ) ] References table [ ( column [,
column ] . . . ) ] |
        Default { constant | variable | Null } |
        Check [ Not For Replication ] ( checkcondition ) ] [,] } . . . )
    [ On segment ]
```

Oracle

```
Create Table table
    ( {
        column datatype
            [ Default constant ]
            [ With Rowid ] [ Scope Is scopetable ]
            Constraint constraint {
                [ Not ] Null |
                { Unique | Primary Key }
                [ Using Index ]
                [ References table ( column ) ] [ On Delete Cascade ]
                [ Check ( checkcondition ) ]
                [ Exceptions Into table ]
                [ Disable ] } |
        Constraint Constraint constraint {
            [ Not ] Null |
            { Unique | Primary Key }
            [ Using Index ]
            [ References table ( column ) ] [ On Delete Cascade ]
            [ Check ( checkcondition ) ]
            [ Exceptions Into table ]
            [ Disable ] } |
        Ref ( column ) With Rowid |
        Scope For ( column ) Is table }
        } [,] . . . )
        { [ Organization { Heap | Index }
```

```
        | Pctthreshold [ Including column ] [ Overflow |
        [ Pctfree pctfree |
        Pctused pctused |
        Initrans initrans |
        Maxtrans maxtrans |
        Storage storage |
        Tablespace tablespace ] |
    [ Lob ( lob [, lob ] . . . ) Store As
        ( Tablespace tablespace |
        Storage storage |
        Chunk chunk |
        Pctversion pctversion |
        Cache |
        Nocache Logging |
        Nocache Nologging |
        Index [ lobindex ]
            [ ( Tablespace tablespace |
            Storage storage |
            Initrans initrans |
            Maxtrans maxtrans ) ]
    Nested Table nestedtable Store As storagetable |
    { Logging | Nologging } |
    Cluster cluster ( column [, column ] . . . ) |
    Parallel parallel
    Partition By Range ( column [, column ] . . . )
    Partition [ partition ] Values Less Than ( constant [, constant ] . . . ) |
    Enable |
    Disable ] . . .
    [ As selectstatement ]
```

Usage   The **Create Table** statement is used to create a table. Within the table, you can specify a series of columns that hold data and constraints that verify data and specify other table characteristics.

Each column in the table must be assigned a valid data type. Then **Not Null** can be specified to insure that the column always contains data. You can also specify a default value for the column to be used when a new row is inserted into the table and a value is not specified, or specified as **Default**. This is done by using the **With Default** clause. The default value can be **Null**, a standard constant, a system variable such as **Current Date** or **User**, or a function that will cast a value from one data type to another.

For large objects (LOB), such as **Blobs**, **Clobs**, **Dbclobs**, or any **Long** data type, you can choose not to log any changes to this column. While you can log changes up to one gigabyte in size, you probably shouldn't log changes any larger than 10 megabytes. **Not Logged** has no impact on normal **Rollback** or **Commit** operations; however, in the event you have to recover the database from a backup copy and try to roll forward with the database log, the information necessary to recover the LOBs will not be available. In this case, the large object will be assigned a value of zero.

You can also free any unused pages in the LOBs by specifying **Compact;** the disadvantage with specifying this option is that there might be a performance hit when you update a LOB with a larger size.

For each column, you can specify a constraint that will define the column as a **Primary Key**, insuring that the column has a **Unique** value in the table or that it acts as a value for a foreign key in another table using a **References** clause. This means that the value must exist in the other table before the new row can be inserted or the current row can be updated. Note that no LOBs can be included as part of the foreign key.

When a record is deleted in the referred table, you have the option either to take no action and not process any constraints (**On Delete No Action**), process all constraints and then take no action (**On Delete Restrict**), process all constraints and pass the delete onto any dependent tables (**On Delete Cascade**), or set each foreign key value in the dependent table to **Null** (**On Delete Set Null**). When a record is updated in the referred table, you have the option either to take no action and not process any constraints (**On Update No Action**) or process all constraints and then take no action (**On Update Restrict**).

The **Check** clause is used to verify the value of a column or the contents of a row any time the row is inserted or updated. If the *checkcondition* is included as part of a column definition, then it might only refer to that column. Otherwise, it might refer to any column in the table. You can't use subqueries, column functions, host variables, parameter markers, system variables, or user functions that return variants, use **External Action**, or use **Scratchpad**.

You can also specify **Constraints** that define a **Primary Key** for the table or define a particular column or set of columns to be **Unique**. Also, you can define a **Foreign Key** that means the value in the list of columns must exist in another table.

In situations where you plan to replicate data, you must specify **Data Capture Changes**. This means that the Capture program can get the information it needs to capture all changes needed for replication.

You can specify the name of the table space the table should reside in by using the **In** clause. The **Index In** and **Long In** clauses let you place index and long values in different table spaces, although these options apply only to table spaces that have the **Managed By Database** clause.

Tip

For the most part, you needn't worry about placing indexes and long values in different table spaces. However, if you need optimal performance from your database, consider creating your index in a table space on the fastest available disk drive. Conversely, if you don't need quick access to long values, place them in a table space that is on a slow disk drive.

The **Partitioning Key** defines the columns that will be used to physically partition the database. You can't use long values as part of the key. If this clause is not specified, the primary key will be used. If the primary key is not specified, then the first column that does not contain a long value will be used. Because **Using Hashing** is the only method available for partitioning, it will be assumed if you don't specify it.

If you specify **Not Logged Initially**, any **Insert, Update**, or **Delete** operations that follow the **Create Table** statement and are part of the same unit of work will not be logged. This clause is useful if you plan to initially load the table immediately after creating it.

In Informix database, you can specify either **Row** or **Page** level locking. Row level locking offers a higher degree of concurrency, but at a cost of more overhead and the potential of exceeding the maximum number of available locks. Page level locking is more efficient, but can lock rows that aren't related to the query.

Authorization   You must have the **SYSCTRL** or **SYSADM** authority, plus the appropriate authority to use each of the statements included to create a schema using any *schema* or *authorization* name. Without these capabilities, you can only create a schema where the *schema* and *authorization* match your user id.

Arguments ▪ *tablename*—the name of the table. It must not already exist in the database. This name can be qualified with either a schema name or a user id followed by a period and the name of the table.

▪ *column*—refers to the name of a column in the table.

▪ *datatype*—a valid data type.

▪ *constant*—a literal.

▪ *variable*—one of the following system variables: **Current Date, Current Time, Current Timestamp**, or **User**. Note that the *column* must be of the same data type as the variable.

▪ *castfunction*—a function that is used to convert a value to the same data type as *column*.

▪ *constraint*—the name of the constraint. This value must not duplicate the name of any constraint already defined. If not specified, a name will be generated by the system.

▪ *reftable*—the name of a base table that holds the foreign key's columns.

▪ *refcolumn*—the name of a column in *reftable* that will be used as part of the foreign key.

▪ *checkcondition*—an expression that verifies the contents of the column any time a row is inserted or updated. If the *checkcondition* is included as part of a column definition, then it can only refer to that column. Otherwise, it can refer to any column in the table. You can't use subqueries, column functions, host variables, parameter markers, system variables, or user functions that return variants, use **External Action**, or use **Scratchpad**.

- *tablespace*—the name of the table space where the table will be placed. If not specified, this value will default to the **IBMDEFAULTGROUP** table space. If **IBMDEFAULTGROUP** table space does not exist, then the database will place it in the user's table space or the **USERSPACE1** table space. If none of these table spaces exist, an error will be returned. Also, unless otherwise specified, this table space will be used to store all long values (**Blob**, **Clob**, **Dbclob,** or any **Long** value) and any indexes.

- *indexspace*—the name of the table space where any indexes will be placed. It must be a **Regular** Database Managed Space (DMS) table space and part of the same nodegroup as the table space that contains the base table. If not specified, the indexes will be placed in the same table space as the base table.

- *longspace*—the name of the table space where long values (**Blob**, **Clob**, **Dbclob,** or any **Long** value) will be placed. It must be a **Long** DMS table space and part of the same nodegroup as the table space that contains the base table. If not specified, the long values will be placed in the same table space as the base table.

- *dbspace*—the name of the dbspace where the table will be created.

- *first*—the size of the first extent for the table in kilobytes.

- *next*—the size of the next extent for the table in kilobytes.

- *seed*—the initial value for the **Identity** clause that provides a unique value for a column.

- *increment*—the value that will be added to the previous value of the **Identify** clause to create the new one.

- *segment*—the name of the segment where the table will be stored.

- *scopetable*—the name of a table that contains the scope of the column.

- *pctused*—the amount of space in a data block that must be used before another data block is allocated. There must be at least *pctused* space available in a block before a row can be inserted. If not specified, this value will default to 40 percent.

- *pctfree*—the amount of space in a data block that is reserved for future updates. Any insert that will result in less than *pctfree* space available will cause a new block to be created. If not specified, this value will default to 10 percent.

- *initrans*—specifies the initial number of transactions that might update a block. It can range from 1 to 255. If not specified, this value will default to 1.

- *maxtrans*—specifies the maximum number of transactions that might update a block. It can range from 1 to 255. If not specified, this value will default to 255.

- *lob*—a Large Object Block in the table.

- *chunk*—specifies the size of the unit of storage used to store an LOB.

* *pctversion*—the percentage full of the total LOB storage space that must be used before old storage is overlaid.

* *lobindex*—the name of the LOB index.

* *nestedtable*—the name of the nested table in this table.

* *storagetable*—the name of the "real" table that will hold the data for the nested table.

* *selectstatement*—generates the initial data for this table.

See Also **Comment On** (statement), **Create Index** (statement), **Create Table** (statement), **Create View** (statement), **Drop Schema** (statement), **Grant** (statement)

Create Tablespace

STATEMENT

IBM

Syntax IBM

```
Create [ Regular | Long | Temporary ] Tablespace tablespacename
    [ In [ Nodegroup ] nodegroup ]
    {
    Managed By System
        {
        Using ( containerstring [, containerstring ] . . . )
        [ On { Nodes | Node } ( nodenum [ To nodenum ] [, nodenum [ To nodenum ] . . . ) ]
        } . . . |
    Managed By Database
        {
        Using ( { File | Device } containerstring pages [,{ File | Device } containerstring
    pages ] . . . )
        [ On { Nodes | Node } ( nodenum [ To nodenum ] [, nodenum [ To nodenum ] . . . ) ]
        } . . .
    }
    [ Extentsize extentpages ]
    [ Prefetchsize prefetchpages ]
    [ Bufferpool bufferpool ]
    [ Overhead overheadtime ]
    [ Transferrate transfertime ]
```

```
Oracle
```

```
Create Tablespace tablespacename
    Datafile filename [ Size size [ K | M ] [ Reuse ] [, filename [ Size size [ K | M ] ] [
    Reuse ] ] . . . ]
    [ Autoextend filename [ Size size [ K | M ] [ Reuse ] [, filename [ Size size [ K | M ]
    [ Reuse ] ] ] . . . ]
        [ On | Off ]
        [ Next next [ K | M ] ]
    [ Maxsiz [ maxsiz [ K | M ] | Unlimited ] ]
    [ Minimum Extent minext [ K | M ] ]
        [ Default Storage (
            [ Initial initial [ K | M ] ]
            [ Next next [ K | M ]
            [ Pctincrease increase ]
            [ Minextents minext ]
            [ Maxextents { maxext | Unlimited } ]
            [ Optimal { optimal [ K | M ] | Null } ]
            [ Freelists freelists ]
            [ Freelist Groups freelistgroup ]
    [ Online | Offline ]
    [ Permanent | Temporary ]
```

Usage   The **Create Tablespace** statement creates a table space in the database.

Authorization   You must have the **SYSCTRL** or **SYSADM** authority to define a table space.

Arguments
- *tablespacename*—the name of the table space.
- *nodegroup*—the name of the nodegroup where the table space will be stored.
- *nodenum*—a specific partition number. Node numbers are defined in the db2nodes.cfg file.
- *containerstring*—the name of the path where the table space will be stored on the system. It can contain an absolute path from the root directory or a relative path from the database directory. This value must be enclosed in single quotes (').
- *extentpages*—the number of 4k pages that will be written to a container before switching to the next container.
- *prefetchpages*—the number of 4k pages that will be read when prefetching data from the table space.

- *bufferpool*—the name of the buffer pool that will be used to hold pages in real memory.
- *overheadtime*—the average time required in milliseconds to position the disk to transfer data. This value will be used in the query optimizer to determine the cost of an I/O operation. This value includes the overhead in the controller, the average seek time, and the average latency time to perform a transfer. This value should be averaged when dealing with containers that span multiple types of disk drives. If omitted, this value will default to 24.1 milliseconds.
- *transfertime*—the average time in milliseconds to transfer a single 4k page. This value will be used in the query optimizer to determine the cost of an I/O operation. This value should be averaged when dealing with containers that span multiple types of disk drives. If omitted, this value will default to 0.9 milliseconds.
- *filename*—the name of the disk file that will contain the table space. This name must be enclosed in single quotes (').
- *size*—specifies the total size of the file in bytes. **K** or **M** indicates that this value is in kilobytes or megabytes respectively.
- *next*—specifies the amount of storage in bytes for the rest of the extents. **K** or **M** indicates that this value is in kilobytes or megabytes respectively. If not specified, this value will default to five data blocks.
- *initial*—specifies the amount of storage in bytes for the first extent. **K** or **M** indicates that this value is in kilobytes or megabytes respectively. If not specified, this value will default to two data blocks.
- *maxsiz*—specifies the maximum size of the file in bytes. **K** or **M** indicates that this value is in kilobytes or megabytes respectively. If not specified, this value will default to five data blocks.
- *increase*—specifies the percentage increase that the next extent should be over the previous extent. If zero is specified, the next extent will be the same size as the previous extent. The default value is 50 percent.
- *minext*—specifies the minimum number of extents. If not specified this value defaults to 1.
- *maxext*—specifies the maximum number of extents or **Unlimited**.
- *optimal*—specifies the optimal size of a rollback segment in bytes. **K** or **M** indicates that this value is in kilobytes or megabytes respectively. **Null** indicates that the database doesn't deallocate any rollback extents.
- *freelists*—specifies the number of free lists for each free list group.
- *freelistgroups*—specifies the number of free list groups.

Implementation Notes   IBM

Regular tablespaces can contain any type of data. A **Long** table space can contain **Blobs**, **Clobs**, and **Dbclobs**. **Long** table spaces are valid only with table spaces that are **Managed By Database**. **Temporary** table spaces contain temporary tables that hold intermediate results from sorts and joins.

Tip

*Every database needs at least one **Temporary** table space. More than one, however, isn't necessary and could have a negative impact on the database, because a temporary table must be wholly contained in a single table space. Thus it is better to have one large table space than two smaller ones.*

You can specify which *nodegroup* should contain the table space in a partitioned database. If your database is not partitioned, this clause isn't necessary.

Managed By System or System Managed Space (SMS) and **Managed By Database** or Database Managed Space (DMS) are two different ways to manage table spaces. In SMS table spaces, the database uses the operating system's file system to create and manage disk space. A series of physical files, called containers, are created to hold the database pages. Any time there is a requirement for a new page, a new page is allocated to the end of the current container by the operating system. After *extentpages* have been added to a container, the next container is selected. This distributes the table space pages evenly among all the containers.

Tip

You should use multiple containers when the size of your table space exceeds the largest file supported by the operating system. Thus, if the operating system imposes a two-gigabyte limitation on a file, you can create a 10-gigabyte table space by using five containers.

In a DMS table space, the database manages the space allocation itself. You can map the table space to either a disk drive (**Device**) or a file (**File**) that was created by the operating system. In either case, the total space in the container specified by *pages* is preallocated by the database. Once allocated, space can't be removed from a

DMS table space. Also, because DMS spaces allocated on **Devices** don't use the normal file system procedures, you might need to increase the buffer pool space to account for the operating system's I/O buffering and caching. You can't specify a **Device** container on Windows 95, Windows NT, or OS/2.

Tip

In general you should use SMS rather than DMS. Under the proper conditions, DMS can offer significantly better performance, but at a cost of flexibility.

You can also place each container on a specific node in a partitioned database by using the **On Node** clause. You can specify either a specific node number, a range of node numbers (using the **To** keyword), or a list of node numbers and node ranges.

Extentsize contains the number of pages that should be allocated in a container before switching to a new container.

Prefetchsize contains the number of pages that will be read from a table space when a prefetch operation is performed. Prefetching assists queries that are reading a table by attempting to eliminate I/O during the query processing.

Bufferpool specifies the name of the buffer pool that will be used for storing pages from the table space in memory.

Overhead specifies the average time in milliseconds to position the disk to transfer data. This value will be used in the query optimizer to determine the cost of an I/O operation. This value includes the overhead in the controller, the average seek time, and the average latency time to perform a transfer. This value should be averaged when dealing with containers that span multiple types of disk drives. If omitted, this value will default to 24.1 milliseconds.

Transfer is the average time in milliseconds to transfer a single 4k page. This value is used in the query optimizer to determine the cost of an I/O operation. This value should be averaged when dealing with containers that span multiple types of disk drives. If omitted, this value will default to 0.9 milliseconds.

Oracle

The **Datafile** clause specifies the files that will provide the actual disk storage for the tablespace. Specifying **Size** and **Reuse** means that if the file already exists, it will be erased and reused. Specifying **Size** without **Reuse** means that the file must not exist. If **Size** is not specified, the file must already exist and be empty.

Autoextend will increase the data files automatically if needed, but only if the **On** clause is specified. The **Next** clause specifies the size of the extent.

Maxsiz is used to limit the maximum size of the data file. By default, the size of the data file is **Unlimited**.

Online means that the tablespace is avilable for immediate use by the database, while **Offline** means that the storage is allocated to the tablespace and only needs to be brought online by the **Alter Tablespace** command.

See Also   **Alter Tablespace** (statement), **Drop Tablespace** (statement)

Create Trigger
STATEMENT

IBM

Syntax   **IBM**

```
Create Trigger trigger
    { No Cascade Before | After }
    { Insert | Delete | Update [ Of column [, column ] . . . ] }
    On table
    [ Referencing
        {
        Old [ As ] correlation [,] |
        New [ As ] correlation [,] |
        Old_table [ As ] identifier [,] |
        New_table [ As ] identifier [,]
        } . . .
    ]
    { For Each Row | For Each Statement }
    Mode Db2sql
    [ When ( condition ) ]
    { statement | Begin Atomic { statement ; } . . . End }
```

Informix

```
Create Trigger trigger
    { Insert | Delete | Update [ Of column [, column ] . . . ] }
        On table
        [ Referencing
            [ Old [ As ] correlation [,] ]
            [ New [ As ] correlation [,] ] ]
        [ Before [ When ( condition ) ] ( statement [, statement ] . . . ) ]
        [ For Each Row [ When ( condition ) ] ( statement [, statement ] . . . ) ]
        [ After [ When ( condition ) ] ( statement [, statement ] . . . ) ]
    [ Enabled | Disabled ]
```

MS SQL Server

```
Create Trigger trigger
    On table
    For { Insert | Delete | Update }
    [ With Encryption ]
    [ Referencing
    As
        [ If Update ( column ) [ { And | Or } Update ( column ) . . . ]
        { sqlstatement |
        Begin sqlstatement [; sqlstatement ] . . . End
```

Oracle

```
Create [ Or Replace ] Trigger trigger
    { Before | After | Instead Of }
    { Insert | Delete | Update [ Of column [, column ] . . . ] }
    On table
    [ Referencing
        [ Old [ As ] correlation [,] ]
        [ New [ As ] correlation [,] ] ]
    [ For Each Row ]
    [ When ( condition ) ]
    statement [; statement ] . . .
```

Usage   The **Create Trigger** statement describes an action that is taken when a row is inserted, deleted or updated in a table.

You must have the **SYSCTRL** or **SYSADM** authority, the **ALTER** authority on the specified table, and **IMPLICIT_SCHEMA** on the database if the schema name doesn't exist or **CREATEIN** if the schema exists. Also, you must have the appropriate authority to execute the *statements*, plus the **SELECT** privilege on any table involved in the trigger.

Arguments
- *trigger*—the name of the trigger.
- *column*—the name of a column in *table*.
- *table*—the name of the table.
- *correlation*—an alternate name for *table* that is used to identify the row that triggered the trigger.
- *identifier*—an alternate name for *table* that is used to identify the set of rows that triggered the trigger.
- *condition*—a condition when **True** means that the *statement* will be executed and when **False** means that the *statement* will not be executed.
- *statement*—a SQL statement that will be executed when the trigger is triggered.

Implementation Notes   IBM

The **Create Trigger** statement describes an action that is taken when a row is inserted, deleted, or updated in a table.

No Cascade Before is an IBM extension that indicates that the trigger will be fired before any changes are made to the table and insures that any actions caused by the trigger will not fire any other triggers. **After** means that the trigger will be fired after the changes are made to the table.

Insert, **Delete**, and **Update** indicate which SQL statement will fire the trigger. A list of *columns* can also be specified with the **Update** statement, so that the **Trigger** will only be fired when one of the specified *columns* is updated.

The **On** clause indicates the name of the table that is associated with the trigger. The **Referencing** clause provides alternate names for the current row that is being affected with a before image (**Old**) or after image (**New**). You can also specify **Old_table** or **New_table** to reference all the affected rows before the rows were changed and after the rows were changed, plus the rows changed by triggers in *table* that included **No Cascade Before**. This information is used in *statement*. You can only specify each of the clauses once and each name can't duplicate any other name.

Specify **For Each Row** if you want the trigger's actions to be applied to each row of the table. Specify **For Each Statement** if you want to limit the action of the trigger to executing only once during the execution of a statement. This clause is not compatible with the **No Cascade Before** clause.

The **Begin Atomic** clause is an IBM extension that permits you to combine multiple SQL statements into one large statement that is treated as one large complex statement.

Mode Db2sql is an IBM extension that is used to specify the mode of the trigger. This is the only available mode in DB2. Use the **When** clause to specify a *condition* that determines if the triggered routine will be executed. Finally you must specify either a single *statement* or a series of *statements* (using the **Begin Atomic** clause) that will be executed when the trigger is fired.

Informix

The **Create Trigger** statement allows you to define actions that take place when an **Insert**, **Update** or **Delete** is performed against the specified table.

Triggers can be created for **Insert** and **Delete** statements. **Update** statements are also supported and you have the ability to define a trigger on only the columns that are being updated.

You can define actions that will be taken **Before** the triggering statement is executed, **After** the triggering statement is executed and **For Each Row** that is directly affected by the triggering statement.

The **When** clause is used to determine if any action should be taken. The *condition* is exactly the same as the **Where** clause of a **Select** statement and returns **True** if the action is to be taken or **False** if no action is to be taken.

Each action consists of one or more SQL statements selected from the following list: **Delete**, **Execute**, **Insert** and **Update**.

You can use the **Enable** or **Disable** triggers for the table. While by default the trigger is enabled, you can change the mode at any time by using the **Set** statement.

MS SQL Server

The **Create Trigger** statement defines the actions taken when an **Insert**, **Update** or **Delete** statement is executed.

In addition to any **Update** statement, you can activate the trigger based on the actual updates to each column by using the **If Update** clause.

Oracle

The **Create Trigger** statement allows you to define the actions taken when an **Insert**, **Update** or **Delete** is executed on a specific table. You can also specify a list of columns for the **Update** trigger.

You can define actions that will be taken **Before** the triggering statement is executed, **After** the triggering statement is executed or **Instead Of** the triggering statement.

The **Referencing** clause allows you to define correlation references so you can access the old and new values in the **When** clause and the SQL statements.

The **For Each Row** clause indicates that the trigger operates for each row affected by the triggering statement. Only when *condition* in the **When** clause is **True**, the SQL statements will be executed.

See Also   **Create Table** (statement), **Delete** (statement), **Drop Trigger** (statement), **Insert** (statement), **Select** (statement), **Update** (statement)

Create View

STATEMENT

IBM • Informix • MS SQL Server • Oracle • Sybase

Syntax

```
Create [ Or Replace ] [ Force | Noforce ] View viewname [ ( column [, column ] . . . ) ] [
    With Encryption ] As
    [ With tableexpr [, tableexpr ] . . . ] selectstatement
    [ With [ Cascaded | Local ] Check Option | Read Only ]
```

Usage

The **Create View** statement defines a different way to look at a table or collection of tables. The *viewname* can be optionally followed by a list of *columns*. There must be a one-to-one match between the number of columns in this list and the number of columns returned by *selectstatement*.

The **Or Replace** clause is an Oracle extension that automatically drops the old view if it exists before creating the new view.

The **Force** clause is an Oracle extension that permits a view to be created without checking to see if the underlying base tables exist. **Noforce** means that the base tables must exist for the view to be created.

The **With Encryption** is a Microsoft SQL Server extension that encrypts the actual **Select** statement used to create the view in the database catalog.

The **With** *tablexpr* clause is an IBM extension is used to create one or more temporary views that exist only inside the new view. These temporary views can then be used in *selectstatement*.

The **With Check Option** is used with updateable views to insure that any rows inserted or updated conform to the view's definition. If this clause is omitted, it is possible to insert rows into the view that might not be visible to the viewer. This clause can't be used with read-only views, or an error will be generated. Specifying **Local** means that the checking is restricted to the information in *selectstatement*. **Cascaded** means that checking is done through every intermediate view until the base tables are reached. (**Local** and **Cascaded** are IBM extensions to this clause).

The **Read Only** clause is used by Oracle to indicate that the view can't be updated.

Authorization
You must have the **SYSCTRL** or **SYSADM** authority or the **CONTROL** or **SELECT** privilege on the specified table or view. You must also have **IMPLICIT_SCHEMA** on the database if the schema name doesn't exist or **CREATEIN** if the schema exists.

Arguments
- *viewname*—the name of the view.
- *column*—the name of a column in the *view*.
- *tableexpr*—is used to create a temporary view and takes the form of:

  `tablename [ ( column [, column] . . . ) ] As ( selectstatement )`

- where *tablename* is the name of the temporary view, *column* is the name of the columns that will be returned by the view, and *selectstatement* is a **Select** statement that is used to create the rows for the view.
- *selectstatement*—a **Select** statement that returns the rows in the view.

See Also
Create Table (statement), **Select** (statement)

Declare Cursor

STATEMENT

ANSI • IBM • Informix • MS SQL Server • Oracle • Sybase

Syntax
`Declare cursorname Cursor [ With Hold ] For { selectstatement | statementname }`

Usage
The **Declare Cursor** statement defines a cursor that allows your program to move through the results of a query.

The **With Hold** clause will keep the cursor open after a **Commit** and position it at the next row, but free all locks other than those associated with the new row position. A **Rollback** will close all open cursors even if the **With Hold** clause is specified.

Arguments
- *cursorname*—the name of the cursor.
- *selectstatement*—any valid select statement, without the **Into** clause.
- *statementname*—the name of a prepared **Select** statement.

Implementation Notes ANSI
The **With Hold** clause is expected to be part of the new SQL3 standard.

See Also
Prepare (statement), **Select** (statement)

Delete

IBM • Informix • MS Access • MS SQL Server • Oracle • Sybase

Syntax
```
Delete From { table | view }
    [ [ As ] correlation ] Where searchcondition | Where Current Of cursor
    ]
```

Usage   The **Delete** statement is used to delete one or more rows from a table or view. After the
Delete statement has been completed, use the **Commit** statement to post the changes to
the database or the **Rollback** statement to abandon the changes. If you do not specify
either the **Where** or **Where Current Of** clause, all of the rows in the table will be
deleted.

Arguments   ▪ *table*—the name of a base table. This name can be qualified as *schema.table*. If *schema* is
not specified, it defaults to the current user id.

▪ *view*—the name of a view. This name can be qualified as *schema.view*. If *schema* is not
specified, it defaults to the current user id.

▪ *correlation*—an alternate name for *table* or *view*.

▪ *searchcondition*—the same as the *searchcondition* from the **Where** clause of the **Select**
statement. This clause is used to select the rows to be updated.

▪ *cursor*—an open cursor. This points to the row to be deleted.

See Also   **Commit** (statement), **Create Table** (statement), **Insert** (statement), **Rollback** (statement), **Select** (statement), **Update** (statement)

Describe

IBM • Oracle

Syntax   `Describe statement Into descriptor`

Usage   The **Describe** statement extracts information about a prepared SQL statement and
saves the results in the SQLDA. This statement can only be used from within an
application program.

Arguments ▪ *statement*—the name of a prepared statement.

▪ *descriptor*—the name of a prepared statement.

See Also **Execute** (statement), **Prepare** (statement)

Disconnect

STATEMENT

ANSI • IBM • Informix • MS SQL Server • Oracle • Sybase

Syntax   Disconnect { Default | Current | All [SQL] | *connection* }

Usage   The **Disconnect** statement terminates a connection to a database. The **Default** keyword
indicates that the default connection to the database should be closed. The **Current**
keyword indicates that the current connection to the database should be closed. **All**
implies that all connections to the database should be closed. *Connection* specifies the
name of the database connection that should be closed. A *hostvar* can also be used to
provide the name of the connection to be closed.

Argument ▪ *connection*—a literal or host variable that contains the name of the connection to the
database. This can be the name of the server or other connection information supplied
in the **As** clause of the **Connect** statement. A host variable must always be preceded by
a colon (:).

Implementation Notes		
	ANSI	The **SQL** keyword is an IBM extension that is not part of the standard.
	IBM DB2	The **SQL** keyword is supplied to be compatible with the **Release** statement. The **Default** keyword is not supported.
	Microsoft Access	This statement is not supported in Access. Instead, you should use the **Close** method.
	Oracle	The **Disconnect** statement has no parameters and can be abbreviated as **Disc**.

See Also **Connect** (statement), **Set Connection** (statement)

Drop Bufferpool

Syntax   Drop Bufferpool *bufferpool*

Usage   The **Drop Bufferpool** statement deletes a buffer pool from the database server. An error will occur if any table spaces are currently using the buffer pool. The storage held by the buffer pool will not be reclaimed until after the database server has been restarted.

Argument   ▪ *bufferpool*—the name of the buffer pool to be deleted. This buffer pool must already exist in the catalog.

See Also   **Alter Bufferpool** (statement), **Create Bufferpool** (statement)

Drop Cluster

Syntax   Drop Cluster [*user.*]*cluster*
              [Including Tables [Cascade Constraints]

Usage   The **Drop Cluster** statement deletes a cluster from the database. The **Including Tables** clause specifies that all tables in the cluster should also be deleted. Without this clause you can only delete an empty cluster. The **Cascade Constraints** clause drops all constraints that refer to the cluster.

Arguments ▪ *user*—the name of the user who created the cluster.
           ▪ *cluster*—the name of the cluster to be dropped.

See Also   **Alter Cluster** (statement), **Create Cluster** (statement)

Drop Database

STATEMENT

IBM • Informix • MS SQL Server • Oracle

Syntax Drop Database *database* [, *database*] . . .

Usage The **Drop Database** statement deletes a database from the server. All references, objects, and storage related to the database are also deleted.

Argument ▪ *database*—the name of a database.

Implementation Notes Informix Informix permits you to delete only one database at a time.

See Also **Alter Database** (statement), **Create Database** (statement)

Drop Default

STATEMENT

MS SQL Server • Sybase

Syntax Drop Default [*owner.*]*defaultname*

Usage The **Drop Default** statement deletes the default value from the database.

Arguments ▪ *owner*—the name of user that created the default value.
  ▪ *defaultname*—the name of the default value.

See Also **Create Default** (statement)

Drop Distinct Type

STATEMENT

IBM

Syntax   Drop Distinct Type **typename**

Usage   The **Drop Distinct Type** statement deletes a distinct type from the database. Any functions that include the type as a parameter or return value will also be dropped from the database.

Argument   ▪ *typename*—the name of a distinct type.

See Also   **Create Distinct Type** (statement), **Drop Function** (statement)

Drop Event Monitor

STATEMENT

IBM

Syntax   Drop Event Monitor **eventmonitor**

Usage   The **Drop Distinct Type** statement deletes an event monitor from the database. An error will occur if you attempt to drop the monitor while it is active. Any files created by the event monitor will not be deleted by this statement.

Argument   ▪ *eventmonitor*—the name of an event monitor.

See Also   **Create Event Monitor** (statement)

Drop Function

STATEMENT

IBM • Oracle

Syntax   Drop Function *function* [(*datatype* [, *datatype*] . . .)]

Usage   The **Drop Function** statement deletes a function from the database. If more than one
          function with the name *function* exists in the database, the list of *datatypes* must be
          specified to identify the desired function. The sizes of the data type can be omitted;
          however, if they are specified, they must match exactly those from the function
          definition.

Argument ▪ *function*—the name of a function.

See Also **CreateFunction** (statement)

Drop Index

STATEMENT

IBM • Informix • MS Access • MS SQL Server • Oracle • Sybase

Syntax   Drop Index *indexname*

Usage   The **Drop Index** statement deletes an index from the database. The index for a primary
          key on a table can't be dropped as well as indexes used to support unique constraints.
          Any packages that have a dependency on this index will be invalidated.

Argument ▪ *index*—the name of an index.

See Also **Create Index** (statement)

Drop Nodegroup

Syntax   Drop Nodegroup *nodegroup*

Usage   The **Drop Nodegroup** statement deletes a nodegroup. This will in turn drop all table spaces in the nodegroup and all tables, packages, constraints, views, triggers, and so forth will be dropped or invalidated, as appropriate.

Argument   ▪ *nodegroup*—the name of a nodegroup.

See Also   **Alter Nodegroup** (statement), **Create Nodegroup** (statement)

Drop Package

Syntax   Drop Package *package*

Usage   The **Drop Package** statement deletes a package from the database.

Argument   ▪ *package*—the name of a package.

See Also   **Create Package** (statement)

Drop Procedure

IBM • Informix • MS SQL Server • Oracle • Sybase

Syntax   Drop Procedure *procedure* [(*datatype* [, *datatype*] . . .)]

Usage   The **Drop Procedure** statement deletes a procedure from the database. If more than one procedure with the name *procedure* exists in the database, the list of *datatypes* must be specified to identify the desired procedure. The sizes of the data type can be omitted; however, if they are specified, they must match exactly those from the procedure definition.

Argument   ▪ *procedure*—the name of a procedure.

See Also   **Create Procedure** (statement)

Drop Rule

MS SQL Server • Sybase

Syntax   Drop Rule *[owner.]rulename*

Usage   The **Drop Rule** statement allows you to drop a rule from the database.

Arguments   ▪ *owner*—the name of the user who created the rule.
         ▪ *rulename*—the name of the rule.

See Also   **Create Rule** (statement)

Drop Schema

Syntax Drop Schema *schema* [Restrict]

Usage   The **Drop Schema** statement deletes a schema from the server. The **Restrict** keyword allows you to insure that no objects remain in the schema before it is deleted.

Argument ▪ *schema*—the name of a schema.

See Also **Create Schema** (statement)

Drop Synonym

Syntax Drop { Synonym | Alias } *synonym*

Usage   The **Drop Synonym** statement deletes a synonym from the database and makes all tables, views, and triggers that reference it inoperative. **Alias** is an alternate name for **Synonym** on IBM DB2 databases.

Argument ▪ *synonym*—the name of a synonym.

See Also **Alter Domain** (statement), **Create Domain** (statement), **Rename Table** (statement)

Drop Table

STATEMENT

IBM • Informix • MS Access • MS SQL Server • Oracle • Sybase

Syntax Drop Table *tablename* [Cascade Constraints]

Usage The **Drop Table** statement deletes a table from the database. All indexes, primary keys, foreign keys, views, and triggers will be dropped or made inoperative as necessary.

The **Cascade Constraints** is an Oracle extension that drops all related constraints that refer to this table.

Argument ▪ *tablename*—the name of a table.

See Also **Alter Table** (statement), **Create Table** (statement)

Drop Tablespace

STATEMENT

IBM • Oracle

Syntax Drop Tablespace *tablespacename* [Including Contents]

Usage The **Drop Tablespace** statement deletes a table space from the database. All objects that are wholly contained within the table space will also be dropped. An error will be returned if there are any objects in the table space that have part of their data in another table space.

The **Including Contents** is an Oracle extension that is not specified. It prevents you from dropping a table space that is not empty.

Argument ▪ *tablespacename*—the name of a table space.

See Also **Alter Tablespace** (statement), **Create Tablespace** (statement)

Drop Trigger

IBM • Informix • MS SQL Server • Oracle • Sybase

Syntax   Drop Trigger *trigger*

Usage   The **Drop Trigger** statement deletes a trigger from the database. Dropping a trigger will invalidate any package that references the trigger.

Argument ▪ *trigger*—the name of a trigger.

See Also **Create Trigger** (statement)

Drop View

IBM • Informix • MS SQL Server • Oracle • Sybase

Syntax   Drop View *viewname*

Usage   The **Drop View** statement deletes a view from the database. Dropping a view will invalidate any trigger or view that references *viewname*.

Argument ▪ *viewname*—the name of a view.

See Also **Alter Table** (statement), **Create Table** (statement)

End Declare Section

ANSI • IBM

Syntax   End Declare Section

Usage   The **End Declare Section** statement begins a section where all host variables are declared using the normal syntax for the host programming language. The **Begin Declare Section** statement is placed before any host variables are declared.

All host variables must be defined in the declare section before they are used. Also, no SQL statements can be placed in the declare section, or an error will occur.

See Also **Begin Declare Section** (statement)

Execute

IBM • Informix • MS SQL Server • Oracle • Sybase

Syntax   Execute
          { *preparedstatement* [Using
            [Descriptor :*descriptor*] |
            :*hostvar*, [:*hostvar*] . . .
            ] |
          Immediate :*statement*
          }

Usage   The **Execute** statement allows a program to execute a previously prepared SQL
          statement or to prepare and execute an SQL statement on the fly . The *descriptor* or list
          of host variables can supply a list of values that will be substituted for question marks
          (?) that were included in *preparedstatement*.

          The **Immediate** clause will prepare and execute selected SQL statements on the fly.
          These statements include: **Comment On, Commit, Delete, Grant, Insert, Lock, Table,
          Revoke, Rollback, Set Constraints, Set Current Explain Mode, Set Current Explain
          Snapshot, Set Current Function Path, Set Current Query Optimization, Set Event
          Monitor State, Signal Sqlstate**, and **Update**, plus any **Alter** or **Create** statement.
          Unlike the normal **Execute** statement, the **Execute Immediate** statement doesn't
          support question marks (?) and parameter substitution.

Arguments ▪ *preparedstatement*—the name of a prepared statement. Note that if a **Select** statement is
           used, an error will occur.

           ▪ *descriptor*—the name of an SQL descriptor area that contains zero or more host variables.

           ▪ *hostvar*—the name of the host variable.

           ▪ *statement*—the name of a host variable that contains an SQL statement.

See Also   **Prepare** (statement)

Execute Procedure

Syntax   Execute Procedure ***preparedstatement***
          (*arg* [, *arg*] . . .)
          [Into :*hostvar*, [:*hostvar*] . . .]

Usage   The **Execute Procedure** statement executes a stored procedure.

Arguments   ▪ *preparedstatement*—the name of a prepared statement.

   ▪ *argr*—takes the form:

   [*parameter* =] { *expr* | *singlevalueselect* }

   ▪ where *parameter* is the name of a parameter of the stored procedure from the **Create Procedure** statement *expr*, is an expression of the proper type for the parameter, and *singlevalueselect* is a **Select** statement that retrieves a single value that is used as the value for the parameter in the stored procedure.

   ▪ *hostvar*—the name of the host variable.

See Also   **Create Procedure** (statement), **Prepare** (statement), **Select** (statement)

Fetch

Syntax   Fetch **cursor**
          {
          Into :**hostvar** [, :**hostvar**] . . . |
          Using Descriptor :**descriptor**
          }
                  Informix   Fetch
              [
              Next |
              Previous |
              Prior |
              First |
              Last |
              Current |
              Relative [+ | –] ***position*** |

```
        Absolute position
        ]
    cursor
        {
        Into :hostvar [, :hostvar ] . . . |
        Using Descriptor desc |
        Descriptor sqlda
        }
```

Usage   The **Fetch** statement moves the cursor to the next row and copies the values from the columns into the specified list of host variables. **Sqlcode** will be set to +100 when the last row is reached or you attempt to move the cursor beyond the last row. Otherwise **Sqlcode** will be set to zero.

Arguments   ▪ *cursor*—the name of an open cursor.

▪ *hostvar*—the name of the host variable that will receive the contents of a column.

▪ *descriptor*—the name of an SQL descriptor area that contains zero or more host variables.

▪ *position*—for a relative position this value contains the number of rows from the current row. The next row is 1, the previous row is -1 and the current row is 0. For an absolute position this value contains the absolute row number. A value of 1 is the first row in the table, 2 is the second row, and so forth.

▪ *desc*—a string containing the name of the system descriptor area.

▪ *sqlda*—a reference to an sqlda structure containing the type and location of the values that correspond to the question mark ('?') in a prepared statement.

See Also   **Declare Cursor** (statement), **Describe** (statement), **Open Cursor** (statement)

Flush

Syntax   Flush { **cursor** | **:hostvar** }

Usage   The **Flush** statement forces the rows that a **Put** statement buffered to the database.

Arguments   ▪ *cursor*—an open cursor id.

▪ *hostvar*—a host variable containing a open cursor id.

See Also   **Put** (statement)

Free

Syntax   Free { *object* | *:hostvar* }

Usage   The **Free** statement releases the resources associated with the specified database object.

Arguments ■ *object*—a cursor id or a statement id.
           ■ *hostvar*—a host variable containing a cursor id or a statement id.

See Also   **Fetch** (statement), **Prepare** (statement), **Select** (statement)

Free Locator

Syntax   Free Locator *variable* [, *variable*] . . .

Usage   The **Free Locator** statement releases one or more locator variables that reside in the database server.

Argument   ■ *variable*—the name locator variable that resides in the database server.

See Also   **Fetch** (statement), **Select** (statement)

Grant

Syntax   Grant *priv* [, *priv*] On [*object*] [*objectname*] To { Public | [Group | User]
          authorizationname } [,{ Public | [Group | User] *authorizationname* }] . . . [With
          Grant Option]

Usage   The **Grant** statement is used to give a user or users various security privileges on a
          database. Privileges are based on *objects*, such as **Database, Index, Package, Schema**, or
          Table. Giving privileges to **Public** means that all users in the database have that level
          of access.

Because the **Database** object encompasses the entire database, there are no specific *objectnames* associated with the privileges for the **Database** object. Note that the **With Grant Option** does not apply to the **Database** object. The list of privileges for the **Database** object are:

- **BINDADD**—required to create packages.
- **CONNECT**—required to access the database.
- **CREATETAB**—required to create tables in the database. This privilege automatically grants the **CONTROL** privilege on any table that is created.
- **CREATE_NOT_FENCED**—required to define functions and procedures as **Not Fenced**.
- **DBADM**—grants the user the database administrator authority, so the user can access any object in the database and can also grant the **BINDADD**, **CONNECT**, **CREATETAB**, **CREATE_NOT_FENCED**, and **IMPLICIT_SCHEMA** authorities to other users.
- **IMPLICIT_SCHEMA**—permits user to implicitly create schemas by using statements like **Create Table** and **Create View** without using the **Create Schema** statement.

Privileges associated with an **Index** object are based on the actual name of the index, which is specified in *objectname*. Note that the **With Grant Option** does not apply to the **Index** object. These privileges are:

- **CONTROL**—required to **Drop** an index.

Privileges associated with a **Package** object are based on the actual name of the package, which is specified in *objectname*. Note that the **With Grant Option** does not apply to the **Package** object. These privileges are:

- **BIND**—required to rebind a package. (The **BINDADD** privilege on the **Database** is required to create the package.) Also, the appropriate privileges that are part of the package are required for each table. This privilege is automatically granted when the user has the **CONTROL** privilege.
- **CONTROL**—required to rebind, **Drop**, or execute a package. This privilege is automatically granted to the user who creates the package.
- **EXECUTE**—required to execute a package. This privilege is automatically granted when the user has the **CONTROL** privilege.

Privileges associated with a **Schema** object are based on the actual name of the schema, which is specified in *objectname*. You can also specify **With Grant Option** if you want the users to be able to **Grant** these privileges to other users. These privileges are:

- **ALTERIN**—required to **Alter** or **Comment On** any object in the schema.
- **CREATEIN**—required to create new objects in the schema. Note that other privileges might be required to actually create the objects.
- **DROPIN**—required to drop an object in the schema.

Privileges associated with a **Table** object are based on the actual name of the table or view, which is specified in *objectname*. (Note that the *object* keyword **Table** is optional and can be omitted.) You can also specify **With Grant Option** if you want the users to be able to **Grant** these privileges to other users. These privileges are:

- **ALL**—the same as **ALL PRIVILEGES**.

- **ALL PRIVILEGES**—grants all privileges on the table or view, except for **CONTROL**, to the users.

- **ALTER**—required to use the **Alter Table** statement, the **Create Trigger**, or the **Comment On** statement. This privilege is not available for views.

- **CONTROL**—grants the **CONTROL, DELETE, INSERT, SELECT,** and **UPDATE** for views and tables, plus **ALTER, INDEX,** and **REFERENCES** for tables. Also includes the **With Grant Option**. Note that unless you also have the **SYSADM** or **DBADM** authority, you can't **Grant** the **CONTROL** authority to another user.

- **DELETE**—required to **Delete** one or more rows from a table.

- **INDEX**—required to use the **Create Index** statement on a table. Note that the creator of an index is automatically granted the **CONTROL** privilege to use the **Drop Index** statement. This privilege is not available for views.

- **INSERT**—required to **Insert** one or more rows into the table.

- **REFERENCES**—required to use the **Create Table** and **Alter Table** statements to create and drop foreign keys, using all of the columns in the specified table as the parent.

- **REFERENCES** (*column* [, *column*] . . .)—required to use the **Create Table** and **Alter Table** statements to create and drop foreign keys, using the specified list of columns in the table. This privilege is not available for views.

- **SELECT**—required to read rows from the table, to create views, and to run the Export utility program.

- **UPDATE**—required to **Update** one or more rows in the table.

Arguments   ▪ *priv*—the name of a security privilege.

▪ *object*—the name of a security object: **Database, Index, Package, Schema,** or **Table**. If omitted, **Table** will be assumed.

▪ *authorizationname*—the name of either a user or group of users that will be granted the privileges.

See Also   **Alter Table** (statement), **Create Schema** (statement), **Create Table** (statement), **Create View** (statement), **Drop Schema** (statement), **Drop Table** (statement), **Revoke** (statement)

Include

STATEMENT

IBM

Syntax   Include { SQLCA | SQLDA | *name* }

Usage   The **Include** statement copies a block of code into your application program. This block of code can be the SQL Communications Area (**SQLCA**), which contains the **SQLSTATE** and **SQLCODE** variables along with other variables needed to use SQL from your program; the SQL Descriptor Area (**SQLDA**), which contains the variables that will hold the output of the **Describe** statement and *name*, which is the name of an external file that will be embedded in your program.

Argument ▪ *name*—the name of an external file.

See Also   **Begin Declare Section** (statement), **Call** (statement), **Describe** (statement), **End Declare Statement** (statement), **Execute** (statement), **Fetch** (statement), **Open** (statement), **Prepare** (statement)

Info

STATEMENT

Informix

Syntax   Info
           {
           Tables |
           Columns *table* |
           Indexes *table* |
           Access *table* |
           Privileges *table* |
           References *table* |
           Status *table*
           }

Usage   The **Info** statement displays information about the tables in a database or information about the columns, indexes, user access privileges, reference privileges, other privileges, and general status about a specific table.

Argument ▪ *table*—the name of a table in the database.

See Also   **Alter Table** (statement), **Create Table** (statement), **Drop Table** (statement)

Insert

Syntax

```
Insert Into { table | view } [ ( column [, column ]. . . ) ]
    {
VValues
    rowvalues [, rowvalues ] . . . |
    [ With tableexpr [, tableexpr ] . . . ] selectstatement |
    Default Values |
    Execute Procedure proc [ ( arg [, arg ] . . . ) ]
    }
```

Usage
The **Insert** statement adds new rows into the specified *table* or *view*. There are two basic forms of the statement. The first form inserts a series of values into the table. The second form inserts rows extracted from a query. All rows inserted into the table must pass all **Constraints** and all **Check** conditions. After the **Update** statement has been completed, use the **Commit** statement to post the changes to the database or the **Rollback** statement to abandon the changes.

The **Execute Procedure** clause is an Informix extension that allows you to use a stored procedure that will generate information to be loaded into the table with the **Select** statement.

The **With** clause is an IBM extension that is used to create one or more temporary views that exist only for the duration of the **Insert** statement.

The **Default Values** clause is a Microsoft SQL Server extension that will load default values into a row. If one of the columns is of type **Identity**, then the next available value will be loaded. If any column does not have a default value and doesn't permit **Null** values, an error will occur when the statement is executed.

Arguments
- *table*—the name of a base table. This name can be qualified as *schema.table*. If *schema* is not specified, it defaults to the current user id.

- *view*—the name of a view. This name can be qualified as *schema.view*. If *schema* is not specified, it defaults to the current user id.

- *column*—the name of a column in the table or view.

Tip

*If you are using the **Insert** statement from a program, you should take the time to specify the name of each column.*

- *rowvalues*—a list of one or more values to be inserted into a new row in the table or view. If more than one value is listed, the values that correspond to a single row must be enclosed in parentheses, as in the following syntax listing:

```
{ value | ( value [, value] . . . ) }
```

Each *value* can be **Null**, **Default**, a host variable reference (*:hostvar*), or an expression. If an expression is specified, it can be a simple literal like 123.45 or 'Christopher J. Freeze,' a database variable like **User** or **Current Time**, or a more complex expression involving functions, arithmetic, and so forth, so long as the result is the same data type as the column.

The order of each *value* corresponds to the order of the *columns* following the name of the table or view. If the list of *columns* isn't specified, then the list of values must be in the same order as listed in the table or view.

Multiple rows of *rowvalues* can be inserted in a single statement, separated by commas.

- *tableexpr*—is used to create a temporary view and takes the form of:

```
tablename [ ( column [, column] . . . ) ] As ( selectstatement )
```

- where *tablename* is the name of the temporary view, *column* is the name of the columns that will be returned by the view, and *selectstatement* is a **Select** statement that is used to create the rows for the view.

- *selectstatement*—a **Select** statement that will retrieve rows and insert them into the specified *table* or *view*.

Examples
```
insert into Employees values
       (1001, 'James', 'Christopher', 00, 125000.00),
       (1002, 'Ashley', 'Samantha', 00, 100000.00),
       (1003, 'Heyer', 'Jill', 10, 100000.00),
       (1004, 'Bucky', 'Raymond', 10, 90000.00)
```

This example shows how to use the **Insert** statement to add multiple rows into the Employees table.

See Also   **Commit** (statement), **Create Table** (statement), **Delete** (statement), **Rollback** (statement), **Select** (statement), **Update** (statement)

Load From

Syntax   Load From *filename* [Delimiter *delim*]
        Insert Into *table* [(*column* [, *column*] . . .)]

Usage   The **Load From** statement inserts each row in a file into the specified table. The first field in the file will be loaded into the first column of the table. The second field will be loaded into the second column and so forth. You can specify a list of columns as part of the **Load** statement and the fields in the file will be loaded into the columns in that order.

Arguments   ▪ *filename*—the name of the file to be loaded into the database. This name must be enclosed in single quotes (').

        ▪ *delim*—a single character enclosed in single quotes (') that is used to separate each column in the file. If not specified, it will default to the vertical var (' | ').

        ▪ *table*—the name of a table or insertable view in the database.

        ▪ *column*—the name of a column in *table*.

See Also   **Alter Table** (statement), **Create Table** (statement), **Drop Table** (statement), **Unlock Table** (statement)

Lock Table

Syntax   Lock Table *tablename* In { Share | Exclusive | Row Share | Row Exclusive | Share Update | Share Row Exclusive } Mode [Nowait]

Usage   The **Lock Table** statement prevents concurrent updates when *tablename* is locked in **Share Mode** and prevents concurrent reads or updates when *tablename* is locked in **Exclusive Mode**. **Row Share** and **Share Update** mean the same thing and exist to prevent other users from locking the entire table, but does permit concurrent updates. **Row Exclusive** permits only one user to access the table. **Nowait** prevents the lock request from waiting until it can be completed.

Argument   ▪ *tablename*—the name of a base table.

Implementation Notes	IBM DB2	Unlock the table by using a **Commit** or **Rollback** statement. Only the **Share** and **Exclusive** clauses are available. **Nowait** is also not available.
	Informix	Unlock the table by using the **Unlock** statement. Only the **Share** and **Exclusive** clauses are available. **Nowait** is also not available.
	Oracle	Unlock the table by using a **Commit** or **Rollback** statement.

See Also   **Alter Table** (statement), **Create Table** (statement), **Drop Table** (statement), **Unlock Table** (statement)

Open

STATEMENT

IBM • Informix • Oracle • Sybase

Syntax
```
Open cursor
    [
    Using :hostvar [, :hostvar ] . . . |
    Using Descriptor :descriptor
    ] [ With Reoptimization ]
```

Usage   The **Open** statement opens a cursor for use with the **Fetch** statement. The cursor must be closed when this statement is opened, or an error will occur. The **With Reoptimization** clause available on Informix database servers automatically re-**Prepares** a query before the cursor is opened.

The list of host variables (*hostvar*) or the **Descriptor** supply information that can be substituted into the **Select** statement that was defined with the **Declare Cursor** statement.

Arguments   ▪ *cursor*—the name of the cursor to be opened.

▪ *hostvar*—the name of the host variable whose contents will be substituted into the **Declare Cursor**'s **Select** statement.

▪ *descriptor*—the name of an SQL descriptor area that contains zero or more host variables that will be substituted into the **Declare Cursor**'s **Select** statement.

See Also   **Declare Cursor** (statement), **Describe** (statement), **Fetch** (statement), **Select** (statement)

Output

Syntax   Output { *filename* | Pipe *program* } [Without Headings] *selectstatement*

Usage   The **Output** statement is used to send the output of a **Select** statement to a disk file or a program. You can use the **Without Headings** clause to prevent the query's headings from being sent.

Arguments ▪ *filename*—the name of the program where the output from the query will be stored.
           ▪ *program*—the name of the program where the output from the query will be sent.
           ▪ *selectstatement*—a valid **Select** statement.

See Also   **Select** (statement)

Prepare

Syntax   Prepare statement
              [Into :descriptor]
              From :hostvar

Usage   The **Prepare** statement is used to dynamically prepare a statement for execution. The statement is stored in *hostvar*. If the **Intro** clause is specified and the statement was successfully prepared, information about the statement is placed into *descriptor*.
         The **Prepare** statement supports the following statements: **Comment On, Commit, Delete, Drop, Grant, Insert, Lock, Table, Revoke, Rollback, Set Constraints, Set Current Explain Mode, Set Current Explain Snapshot, Set Current Function Path, Set Current Query Optimization, Set Event Monitor State, Signal Sqlstate, Update**, plus any **Alter** or **Create** statement.

Arguments ▪ *statement*—the name of the statement to be prepared.
           ▪ *descriptor*—the name of an SQL descriptor area (SQLDA) that will contain information about the newly prepared statement.
           ▪ *hostvar*—the name of the host variable that contains the statement to be prepared.

See Also   **Declare Cursor** (statement), **Describe** (statement), **Fetch** (statement), **Select** (statement)

Put

Syntax
```
Put cursor
    [
    From variable [ :indvar | $indvar | Indicator indvar ] [,variable [ :indvar | $indvar |
    Indicator indvar ]  ] |
    Using
        { Sql Descriptor descriptor |
        Descriptor sqlda
        }
```

Usage   The **Put** statement saves information in a row buffer that will later be written to the
database using the **Flush** statement.

Arguments ▪ *cursor*—a cursor id or a host variable containing a reference to a cursor.

▪ *variable*—a host variable whose contents replace the question mark ('?') in a prepared
statement.

▪ *indvar*—a host variable that will receive a return code.

▪ *descriptor*—a string containing the name of the system descriptor area.

▪ *sqlda*—a reference to an sqlda structure containing the type and location of the values
that correspond to the question mark ('?') in a prepared statement.

See Also   **Flush** (statement)

Raiserror

Syntax   Raiserror { ***msgid*** | ***msgstr*** }, ***severity, state*** [, ***arg*** [, ***arg***] . . .]) [With Log]

Usage   The **Raiserror** statement is to return a user defined error message. The **With Log** clause
records the error in the server error log and the event log.

Arguments ▪ *msgid*—a user defined message in the SYSMESSAGES table.

▪ *msgstr*—a string containing a user defined message up to 255 characters long. Arguments may be substituted using a C style Printf format.

▪ *severity*—a user specified severity in the range of 0 to 18. Fatal error with severity in the
range of 19 to 25 may be used by the system administrator with the **With Log** clause.
These errors will terminate the user's connection.

- *state*—an **Integer** value from 1 to 127 containing the state of the error.
- *arg*—an **Int, Char, Varchar, Binary** or **Varbinary** value that will be substituted into the *msgstr*. A maximum of 20 values may be specified.

See Also   **Declare** (statement)

Recover

STATEMENT

Oracle

Syntax
```
Recover [ Automatic ] [ From location ]
    [ { [
        [ Standby ] Database ] [
            Until Cancel |
            Until Time datetime |
            Until Change changenum |
            Using Backup Controlfile ] . . . |
        Tablespace tablespace [, tablespace ] . . . |
        Database databasefile [, databasefile ] . . . |
        Logfile logfile |
        Continue [ Default ] |
        Cancel
        } ]
    [ Parallel [ Degree degree ][ Instances instance ]
        | Noparallel ]
```

Usage   The **Recover** statement recovers a database from a logfile group. The **Automatic** clause allows the recovery process to automatically be generated during the recovery process. The **From** clause specifies the location of the redo logfile group. Unless the **Tablespace** clause is specified the entire database is recovered. The recovery process can be terminated at the end of the log files, or until a specified *changenum* or *datetime* is specified.

Arguments
- *location*—specifies the location of the redo logfile group to be recovered.
- *datetime*—specifies the last date and time that should be recovered.
- *changenum*—specifies the last system change number to be recovered.
- *tablespace*—the name of the tablespace to be used.
- *databasefiles*—specifies the name of the database files to be used.
- *logfile*—specifies the name of the redo log file to be used.

■ *instance*—specifies the number of instances that should be used with the Parallel Query option.

■ *degree*—specifies the number of parallel query servers to use.

See Also   **Alter Database** (statement)

Release

Syntax   `Release { server | :hostvar | Current | All [ SQL ] }`

Usage   The **Release** statement puts the specified connection or all connections in a release pending state. You can specify the name of the server explicitly or by using a host variable. You can also specify **Current** to release the current connection or **All** to release all connections. (The **SQL** parameter is optional and has no effect).

Arguments ■ *server*—the name of a database server.

■ *hostvar*—the name of a host variable that contains the name of a database server.

See Also   **Connect** (statement)

Rename Column

Syntax   `Rename Column tablename.column To newcolumn`

Usage   The **Rename Column** statement changes the name of a column in a table. Existing constraints will be updated if it appears as part of a correlation name inside the **For Each Row** clause of a trigger, in the **Into** clause of an **Execute Procedure**, or when it is the trigger column in the **Update** clause.

Arguments ■ *tablename*—the name of a table.

■ *column*—the name of a column in *tablename*.

■ *newcolumn*—the name of the new column.

See Also   **Alter Table** (statement), **Create Table** (statement), **Drop Table** (statement)

Rename Database

STATEMENT

Informix

Syntax   Rename Database *database* To *newdatabase*

Usage   The **Rename Database** statement changes the name of a database.

Arguments   ▪ *database*—the name of a database.
▪ *newdatabase*—the name of the new database.

See Also   **Alter Database** (statement), **Create Database** (statement)

Rename Table

STATEMENT

IBM • Informix

Syntax   Rename Table *tablename* To *newtable*

Usage   The **Rename Table** statement changes the name of a table. The current table can't be used in a view, be referenced in a trigger, have any check constraints, or be a parent or a dependent table in a referential integrity constraint.

Arguments   ▪ *tablename*—the name of a table. This name can be fully qualified with the schema name.
▪ *newtable*—the name of the new table. This name can not be qualified.

See Also   **Alter Table** (statement), **Create Table** (statement), **Drop Table** (statement)

Revoke

IBM • Informix • Oracle • Sybase

Syntax   Revoke *priv* [, *priv*] On [*object*] [*objectname*] From { Public | [Group | User]
           authorizationname } [,{ Public | [Group | User] *authorizationname* }] . . . [Cascade
           Constraints]

Usage   The **Revoke** statement is used to remove various security privileges from a user or
           group of users on a database. Privileges are based on *objects* such as **Database**, **Index**,
           Package, **Schema**, or **Table**. Removing privileges from **Public** means that a privilege
           that was available to all users in the database will need to be explicitly granted to each
           user that needs that level of access. The **Cascade Constraints** clause can be used in
           Oracle to delete any constraints that were granted by the user with the **References**
           privilege.

           Because the **Database** object encompasses the entire database, there are no specific
           objectnames associated with the privileges for the **Database** object. The privileges for the
           Database object are:

- **BINDADD**—required to create packages.

- **CONNECT**—required to access the database.

- **CREATETAB**—required to create tables in the database. This privilege automatically grants the **CONTROL** privilege on any table that is created.

- **CREATE_NOT_FENCED**—required to define functions and procedures as **Not Fenced**.

- **DBADM**—grants the user the database administrator authority, so the user can access any object in the database and can also grant the **BINDADD**, **CONNECT**, **CREATETAB**, **CREATE_NOT_FENCED**, and **IMPLICIT_SCHEMA** authorities to other users.

- **IMPLICIT_SCHEMA**—permits user to implicitly create schemas by using statements like **Create Table** and **Create View** without using the **Create Schema** statement.

Privileges associated with an **Index** object are based on the actual name of the index, which is specified in *objectname*. These privileges are:

- **CONTROL**—required to **Drop** an index.

Privileges associated with a **Package** object are based on the actual name of the package, which is specified in *objectname*. These privileges are:

- **BIND**—required to rebind a package. (The **BINDADD** privilege on the **Database** is required to create the package.) Also, the appropriate privileges that are part of the package are required for each table. This privilege is automatically granted when the user has the **CONTROL** privilege.

- **CONTROL**—required to rebind, **Drop**, or execute a package. This privilege is automatically granted to the user who creates the package.

- **EXECUTE**—required to execute a package. This privilege is automatically granted when the user has the **CONTROL** privilege.

Privileges associated with a **Schema** object are based on the actual name of the schema, which is specified in *objectname*. These privileges are:

- **ALTERIN**—required to **Alter** or **Comment On** any object in the schema.

- **CREATEIN**—required to create new objects in the schema. Note that other privileges might be required to actually create the objects.

- **DROPIN**—required to execute drop an object in the schema.

Privileges associated with a **Table** object are based on the actual name of the table or view, which is specified in *objectname*. (Note that the *object* keyword **Table** is optional and can be omitted.) The list of these privileges are:

- **ALL**—the same as **ALL PRIVILEGES**.

- **ALL PRIVILEGES**—grants all privileges on the table or view except for **CONTROL** to the users.

- **ALTER**—required to use the **Alter Table** statement, the **Create Trigger** statement, or the **Comment On** statement. This privilege is not available for views.

- **CONTROL**—grants the **CONTROL**, **DELETE**, **INSERT**, **SELECT**, and **UPDATE** for views and tables, plus **ALTER**, **INDEX**, and **REFERENCES** for tables. Also includes the **With Grant Option**. Note that unless you also have the **SYSADM** or **DBADM** authority, you can't **Grant** the **CONTROL** authority to another user.

- **DELETE**—required to **Delete** one or more rows from a table.

- **INDEX**—required to use the **Create Index** statement on a table. Note that the creator of an index is automatically granted the **CONTROL** privilege to use the **Drop Index** statement. This privilege is not available for views.

- **INSERT**—required to **Insert** one or more rows into the table.

- **REFERENCES**—required to use the **Create Table** and **Alter Table** statements to create and drop foreign keys, using all of the columns in the specified table as the parent.
- **REFERENCES** (*column* [, *column*] . . .)—required to use the **Create Table** and **Alter Table** statements to create and drop foreign keys, using the specified list of columns in the table. This privilege is not available for views.
- **SELECT**—required to read rows from the table, to create views, and to run the Export utility program.
- **UPDATE**—required to **Update** one or more rows in the table.

Arguments ▪ *priv*—the name of a security privilege.

▪ *object*—the name of a security object: **Database**, **Index**, **Package**, **Schema**, or **Table**. If not specified, **Table** will be assumed.

▪ *authorizationname*—the name of either a user or group of users who will be granted the privileges.

See Also **Alter Table** (statement), **Create Schema** (statement), **Create Table** (statement), **Create View** (statement), **Drop Schema** (statement), **Drop Table** (statement), **Revoke** (statement)

Rollback

STATEMENT

ANSI • IBM • Informix • Oracle • Sybase

Syntax `Rollback [ Work ]`

Usage The **Rollback** statement ends a logical transaction by discarding all changes to the database. All open cursors are closed, and all locks are released. To save all of the changes to the database, the **Commit** statement should be used.

Implementation Notes Microsoft Access The **Rollback** statement is not available in Access. The **Rollback** method should be used instead.

See Also **Commit** (statement)

Select

ANSI • IBM • Informix • MS Access • MS SQL Server • Oracle • Sybase

Syntax

Simple Select

```
Select [ All | Distinct ] columnexpr [, columnexpr ] . . .
[ Into :hostvar [, :hostvar ] . . . ]
From tablename correlation [,tablename correlation ] . . .
Where whereexpr
[ Order By orderkey [ Asc | Desc ] [, orderkey [ Asc | Desc ] ] . . . [ For Read Only | For
    Fetch Only ]
[ Group By
    {
    groupexpr [, groupexpr ] . . . |
    Grouping Sets ( groupexpr [, groupexpr ] . . . ) |
    Rollup ( groupexpr [, groupexpr ] . . . ) |
    Cube ( groupexpr [, groupexpr ] . . . )
    } . . .
[ Having havingexpr ]
[ For Read Only | For Fetch Only ]
[ For Update [ Of column [, column ] ] ]
[ Optimize For numrows { Rows | Row } ]
```

Complex Select

```
{ simpleselect | ( complexselect ) | valueclause }
[ Union [ All ] | Except [ All ] | Intersect [ All ] { simpleselect | ( complexselect ) |
    valueclause } ]
```

Usage

The **Select** statement has two forms: simple and complex. The simple **Select** statement is the most common and is used to perform a single query. The complex **Select** statement takes multiple **Select** statements and **Value** statements and combines their results.

The simple **Select** statement retrieves one or more rows of information from the database. The **All** keyword means that all qualifying rows from the database will be selected. The **Distinct** keyword means that only unique rows will be retrieved. If not specified, **All** is assumed.

Next is a list of *columnexprs* that correspond to the columns that will be returned. *Columnexpr* has the following syntax:

```
{ [schemaname.]tablename.columnname | tabledesignator.columnname |
    columnname |
    expr }
```

where *schemaname* refers to the name of the schema that owns the table or the view that includes the specified *columnname*. If not specified, this value will default to your default schema. *Tablename* refers to the name of the table or view that contains the column. If not specified, the database system will determine the appropriate name of the table or view based on the information supplied in the **From** clause.

Correlation also comes from the **From** clause, and it provides an alternate way to reference the table or view. If *columnname* by itself is specified, then the appropriate table or view name will be determined from the **From** clause.

You can also specify an expression for *expr* that will return a single value. This can be as simple as a constant or a complex expression that involves several different columns.

Finally, you can use an asterisk (*) anywhere *columnname* is specified. This special character means that all columns associated with the table or view will be returned.

Tip

While using an asterisk to retrieve all columns in a table can be very useful while working with interactive queries, you should list each column you want to access from your program.

The **Into** clause contains a list of host variables where the information from a single row is retrieved. Each hostvar is preceded by a colon. This clause is available only when using SQL from within a program, using the Exec SQL statement.

The **From** clause contains a list of tables and views that will be used to satisfy the query and has the following syntax:

[*schemaname.*]

where *schemaname* refers to the name of the schema that owns the table or view. If *schemaname* is not specified, then the default schema will be used. *Tablename* refers to the name of the table or view that will be used to help satisfy the query. The table designator is used to provide an alternate name for the table in the query.

Tip

Use tabledesignators when you have a complex query, such as a nested query in which the same table is referenced in more than one way.

The **Where** clause contains an expression that when **True** means that the row will be returned.

The **Order By** clause contains a list of column names or numbers that will be used to sort the results of the query. You can also indicate whether the information in that particular column should be sorted in ascending (**Asc**) or descending (**Desc**) order.

Specifying a number for *orderkey* refers to the relative position of *columexpr* in the **Select** statement. If the **Order By** clause is not specified, then the rows will be returned unordered.

The **Group By** clause contains a series of specifications that describe how to summarize the selected rows. To use the **Group By** clause, you need to specify a list of columns as part of the **Select** statement that you want to aggregate, plus one or more expressions, such as **Count** or **Max**, that perform data aggregation. Then, in the **Group By** clause you specify the same list of columns that you want to aggregate. The **Select** statement will then sort the data in the order listed in the **Group By** clause and return a summary row for each unique combination of values.

Groupexpr consists of a column name listed in the **Select** clause or a series of column names enclosed in parentheses. The **Grouping Sets** clause allows you to specify multiple levels of grouping. **Grouping Sets** ((a,b)) is equivalent to **Group By** a,b. The **Rollup** clause allows you to specify a list of columns, and the rows will be grouped from right to left. **Rollup**(a,b) is equivalent to **Grouping Sets** ((a,b), (a), ()). **Cube** creates a summary table with all possible combinations of the specified columns. Thus,

Cube(a,b)

is equivalent to **Grouping Sets** ((a,b), (a),(b),()). Note that *groupexpr* can be a pair of empty parentheses () to represent the grand total when used as part of the **Grouping Sets**, **Rollup**, or **Cube** clauses.

The **Having** clause contains an expression that determines whether results of an aggregation should be returned. Typically it is used to determine if the intermediate grouping of a **Group By** clause should be returned. If the **Group By** clause is not specified, the results will be returned for the entire **Select** statement. *havingexpr* must include an aggregation function referencing a grouping column.

The **For Read Only** and **For Fetch Only** clauses mean the same thing. You can use a cursor positioned **Delete** or **Update** against the results of a select where either clause is specified. This might help to improve performance, because the database manager doesn't need to perform exclusive locks.

The **Optimize For** clause specifies the expected number of rows that will be retrieved. If not specified, the query optimizer will assume that every row in the table or view will be retrieved. Specifying a smaller number of rows might improve performance significantly. If the number of rows exceeds this value, the query will continue to run; however, performance might be significantly degraded.

The **For Update** clause identifies the columns that can be updated in the selected rows. If no columns are specified, then all updateable columns are assumed. This information will be used by the query optimizer to improve performance.

Implementation Notes	IBM DB2	The length attribute of an *orderkey* can't be greater than 254 characters for a **Char** or **Varchar** column or greater than 127 characters for a **Graphic** or **Vargraphic** column.

MS SQL Server	You can't specify the length of a **Bit** array. Also, a column defined as a **Bit** can't be assigned a **Null** value and can't be used as part of an index. The **Binary** data type in MS SQL Server is more like the ANSI **Bit** data type than the MS SQL Server **Bit** data type.
Sybase SQL Server	You can't specify the length of a **Bit** array. Also, a column defined as a **Bit** can't be assigned a **Null** value and can't be used as part of an index. The **Binary** data type in Sybase SQL Server is more like the ANSI **Bit** data type than the Sybase SQL Server **Bit** data type.

Arguments
- *columnexpr*—a column expression that corresponds to a single column and has the following syntax:

```
{ [schemaname.]tablename.columnname | tabledesignator.columnname |
   columnname |
   expr [ [ As ] newcolumn ] }
```

- where *schemaname* refers to the name of the schema that owns the table or view that includes the specified *columnname*. If not specified, this value will default to your default schema. *Tablename* refers to the name of the table or view that contains the column. If not specified, the database system will determine the appropriate name of the table or view based on the information supplied in the **From** clause. All columns in a table can be specified by using an asterisk (*) in place of *columnname*. The **As** *newcolumn* clause can be used to provide a column name to an expression.

- *hostvar*—a variable in an application program.

- *tablename*—the name of a table or view.

- *correlation*—an alternate name for *table*.

- *whereexpr*—an expression that when **True** means that the row will be selected.

- *orderkey*—is either the name of a column, an integer value that indicates the relative position of a column in the row (1 is the first column, 2 is the second and so fourth), or an expression that returns a single value.

- *groupexpr*—consists of a column name listed in the **Select** clause or a series of column names enclosed in parentheses. The **Grouping Sets** clause allows you to specify multiple levels of grouping. **Grouping Sets** ((a,b)) is equivalent to **Group By** a,b. The **Rollup** clause allows you to specify a list of columns, and the rows will be grouped from right to left. **Rollup**(a,b) is equivalent to **Grouping Sets** ((a,b), (a), ()). **Cube** creates a summary table with all possible combinations of the specified columns. Thus,

  Cube(a,b)

- is equivalent to **Grouping Sets** ((a,b), (a),(b),()). Note that *groupexpr* might be a pair of empty parentheses () to represent the grand total when used as part of the **Grouping Sets**, **Rollup**, or **Cube** clauses.

- *havingexpr*—an expression used when **True** means that the aggregation will be returned.
- *Numrows*—the number of rows that you expect the query to return. If not specified, this value will default to the total number of rows in the table. Exceeding this value might impose a performance penalty; however, in the case where you expect to retrieve relatively few rows, you might significantly improve performance.

Examples
```
select *
  from departments;
```

```
DEPTNO DEPTNAME                                MANAGER
------ --------------------------------------- ------
    0. Headquarters                            1001.
   10. Sales                                   1003.
   20. Shipping                                1005.
   30. Research and Development                1007.
   40. Maintenance                             1010.
   50. Assembly                                1012.
   60. Accounting                              1017.
```

```
  7 record(s) selected.
```

This example shows how to select all of the columns and all of the rows in a table.

```
select deptno, manager, deptname
  from departments
```

```
DEPTNO MANAGER DEPTNAME
------ ------- ---------------------------------------
    0.  1001. Headquarters
   10.  1003. Sales
   20.  1005. Shipping
   30.  1007. Research and Development
   40.  1010. Maintenance
   50.  1012. Assembly
   60.  1017. Accounting
```

```
  7 record(s) selected.
```

This example is similar to the example above, but each column is individually listed in the **Select** statement. Note that the columns in the result are the same as in the **Select** statement.

```
select deptname, lname
    from departments, employees
    where manager = empno
```

DEPTNAME	LNAME
Headquarters	James
Sales	Heyer
Shipping	Williams
Research and Development	Freeze
Maintenance	Osborne
Assembly	Kelly
Accounting	Wyler

   7 record(s) selected.

This example shows how to join the contents of two tables together. Only the rows where Manager and EmpNo are the same will be retrieved.

```
select deptname, lname
    from departments, employees
    where departments.manager = employees.empno
```

DEPTNAME	LNAME
Headquarters	James
Sales	Heyer
Shipping	Williams
Research and Development	Freeze
Maintenance	Osborne
Assembly	Kelly
Accounting	Wyler

   7 record(s) selected.

This example shows how table names can be used with columns to identify a column. This technique is important when you have the same name for a column in both tables.

```
select deptname, lname
    from departments d, employees e
    where d.manager = e.empno
```

DEPTNAME	LNAME
Headquarters	James
Sales	Heyer
Shipping	Williams
Research and Development	Freeze
Maintenance	Osborne
Assembly	Kelly
Accounting	Wyler

  7 record(s) selected.

This example shows how to use correlation names in the **Where** clause to qualify the column names.

```
select name
    from customers
    order by name
```

NAME

Barbara's OnDisplays
Barbie's House of Laptops
Becky's Kids Place
Bucky's Country Roundup
Goose's Kitty Katt Kitchen
Jennifer's Collectible Wheels
Jill's Just Plane Crazy
Joan's Technology Shop
Marie's Onsite Mainframes
Peter's Puppet Boutique
Randy's Universal Import-Export
Rosie's Garden Shop
Sargent Scott's Seafood and Steakhouse
Terry's Catnip Farm
Tracy's Treehouse
Waldo's Antique Computers and Stuff

  16 record(s) selected.

This example shows how to use the **Order By** clause to sort the results of a query.

```
select deptno, count(empno)
    from employees
    group by deptno
```

DEPTNO 2
```
------ ----------
   0.         2
  10.         2
  20.         2
  30.         3
  40.         2
  50.         5
  60.         2
```

7 record(s) selected.

This example shows how to use the **Count** function with the **Group By** clause to count the number of employees in each department.

```
select deptname, count(empno) As "Count"
    from employees e, departments d
    where e.deptno = d.deptno
    group by deptname, d.deptno
```

DEPTNAME	Count
Headquarters	2
Sales	2
Shipping	2
Research and Development	3
Maintenance	2
Assembly	5
Accounting	2

7 record(s) selected.

This example improves on the previous example by adding a join and using the **As** clause to name the column created by the **Count** function.

```
select deptname, count(empno) As "Count"
    from employees e, departments d
    where e.deptno = d.deptno
    group by deptname, d.deptno
    having count(empno) > 2
```

```
DEPTNAME                                      Count
------------------------------------------    ----------
Research and Development                           3
Assembly                                           5
```

```
 2 record(s) selected.
```

This example shows how to add the **Having** clause to the previous example to select only those departments having more than two employees.

See Also   **Create View** (statement), **Declare Cursor** (statement), **Insert** (statement)

Set Connection
STATEMENT

ANSI • IBM • Informix

Syntax   `Set Connection { Default | connection }`

Usage   The **Set Connection** statement permits you to change the current connection from one open connection to another.

> **Tip**
>
> *This statement is useful when you need to access multiple databases. Simply switch the database connection each time you need to access a different database.*

Argument   ▪ *connection*—a literal or host variable that contains the name of the connection to the database. This might be the name of the server or other connection information supplied in the **As** clause of the **Connect** statement. A host variable must always be preceded by a colon (:).

Implementation Notes   IBM DB2   The **Default** clause is not available in DB2.

See Also   **Connect** (statement), **Disconnect** (statement)

Setuser

MS SQL Server • Sybase

Syntax   Setuser [*user* [Noreset]]

Usage   The **Setuser** statement allows the database owner or system administrator to temporarily assume the userid of another user. Specifying **Noreset** prevents **Setuser** without specifying a userid from resuming the database owner's or system administrator's userid. In this case, you need to log off and sign back on as the database owner.

Argument   ▪ *user*—a valid userid enclosed in single quotes ('), If not specified, the userid of the database owner or system administrator will be resumed, unless **Noreset** was specified.

See Also   **Grant** (statement), **Revoke** (statement), **Use** (statement)

Shutdown

MS SQL Server • Sybase

Syntax   Shutdown [With Nowait]

Usage   The **Shutdown** statement stops the database server. Use care when specifying **With Nowait**. While the database stops quickly, there is a possibility that some transactions may not be properly completed.

See Also   **Start Violations Table** (statement)

Signal Sqlstate

STATEMENT

IBM

Syntax Signal Sqlstate *sqlstate* (*diagnostic*)

Usage The **Signal Sqlstate** statement returns an error condition.

A valid SQL state is constructed from the set of characters '0' to '9' and 'A' to 'Z.' SQL states consist of two parts. The first part is two characters long and the second part is three characters long. When the first part begins with the characters '0' to '6' or 'A' to 'H,' the second part must begin with the characters 'I' to 'Z.'

Note that SQL states that begin with '00,' '01,' and '02' are not error conditions, they can't be used as a value for *sqlstate*.

Arguments ▪ *sqlstate*—a valid SQL state.

▪ *diagnostic*—a **Char** or **Varchar** value that contains up to 70 characters of text information that describes the error.

See Also **Create Trigger** (statement)

Start Violations Table

STATEMENT

Informix

Syntax Start Violations Table For *table* Using [*violations, diagnostics*] [Max Rows *rows*]

Usage The **Start Violations Table** creates an association between *table* and a violations and diagnostic table. As violations occur, an entry will be created in the violations table..

Arguments ▪ *table*—the name of a base table.

▪ *violations*—the name of the violations table. If not specified, then a table name of *table* followed by '_vio' will be created.

▪ *diagnostics*—the name of the diagnostics table. If not specified then a table name of *table* followed by '_dia' will be created.

▪ *rows*—the maximum number of rows that will be inserted into the diagnostics table on a single **Insert** statement. The default value is unlimited.

See Also **Stop Violations Table** (statement)

Stop Violations Table

Syntax   `Stop Violations Table For` *`table`*

Usage   The **Stop Violations Table** statement breaks the association between *table* and its violations and diagnostic table. The violations and diagnostic table continues to exist after this statement is executed, but are no longer updated.

Argument   ▪ *table*—the name of a base table.

See Also   **Start Violations Table** (statement)

Truncate Table

Syntax   `Truncate Table` *`table`*

Usage   The **Truncate Table** statement deletes all of the rows from a specified table. This statement is faster than the equivalent **Delete** statement because the individual rows are not written to the log file. Hence you can't **Rollback** this statement.

Argument   ▪ *table*—the name of a base table.

See Also   **Delete** (statement)

Unlock Table

Syntax   Unlock Table *table*

Usage   The **Unlock Table** statement unlocks a table that was locked with the **Lock Table** statement.

Argument   ▪ *table*—the name of a base table.

See Also   **Create Trigger** (statement)

Update

Syntax   Update { *table* | *view* }
          [[As] *correlation*]
          Set
            {
            column = *value* [, *column* = *value*] . . . |
            (*columnlist*) = ({ *valuelist* | *singlerowselect* }) [,(*columnlist*) = (*valuelist* |
          singlerowselect })] . . .
            }
          { Where *searchcondition* | Where Current Of *cursor*
          }

Usage   The **Update** statement is used to change the values of one or more columns in one or more rows in a table or view. All rows that were changed in the table must pass all **Constraints** and all **Check** conditions. After the **Update** statement has been completed, use the **Commit** statement to post the changes to the database or the **Rollback** statement to abandon the changes.

Arguments   ▪ *table*—the name of a base table. This name can be qualified as *schema.table*. If *schema* is not specified, it defaults to the current user id. Oracle users may specify *@dblink* after the table name to specify a database link.

- *view*—the name of a view. This name can be qualified as *schema.view*. If *schema* is not specified, it defaults to the current user id. Oracle users may specify *@dblink* after the view name to specify a database link.

- *correlation*—an alternate name for *table* or *view* that can be used only when **Where** *searchcondition* has been specified.

- *column*—the name of a column from *table* or *view*.

- *value*—can be **Null**, **Default**, a host variable (*:hostvar*), or an expression. If an expression is specified, it can be a simple literal like 123.45 or 'Samantha A. Freeze,' a database variable like **User** or **Current Time,** or a more complex expression involving functions, arithmetic, and so forth, so long as the result is the same data type as the column.

- *columnlist*—a list of one or more *columns,* separated by commas, from the specified *table* or *view*.

- *valuelist*—a list of *values,* separated by commas, that correspond to the *columns* in *columnlist*. Each *value* can be **Null**, **Default**, a host variable (*:hostvar*), or an expression. If an expression is specified, it can be a simple literal like 123.45 or 'Jill T. Freeze,' a database variable like **User** or **Current Time,** or a more complex expression involving functions, arithmetic, and so forth, so long as the result is the same data type as the column.

- *singlerowselect*—a **Select** statement that returns a single row. Each returned column corresponds to the columns in *columnlist*. An error will occur if more than one row is returned. If no rows are returned, then **Null** will be assigned to each column in *columnlist*.

- *searchcondition*—the same as the *searchcondition* from the **Where** clause. This clause is used to select the rows to be updated.

- *cursor*—an open cursor. This points to the row to be updated.

Implementation Notes   MS Access   The **Where Current Of** clause isn't available in Access.

Example
```
select lname, salary
     from employees
     where salary < 23000;


  LNAME             SALARY
  ----------------  ------------
  Osborne             20000.00
  Smith               15000.00
  Brigham             21000.00


   3 record(s) selected.
```

```
update employees
   set salary = salary * 1.05;
```

```
DB20000I  The SQL command completed successfully.
```

```
select lname, salary
   from employees
   where salary < 23000;
```

LNAME	SALARY
Osborne	21000.00
Smith	15750.00
Brigham	22050.00

```
3 record(s) selected.
```

This example shows the salary for three employees who make less than 23,000. Then the **Update** statement is used to give them a five percent raise. The results of this statement are shown by the last **Select** statement.

See Also **Commit** (statement), **Create Table** (statement), **Delete** (statement), **Insert** (statement), **Rollback** (statement), **Select** (statement)

Update Statistics

STATEMENT

Informix • MS SQL Server • Sybase

Syntax **Informix**

```
Update Statistics
   {
   For Procedure proc |
   [ Low ] [ For Table table [ ( column [, column ] . . .) ] ] [ Drop Distributions ] |
   [ Medium ] [ For Table table [ ( column [, column ] . . .) ] ] [ Resolution resolution ]
   [ conf ] [ Distributions Only ] |
   [ High ] [ For Table table [ ( column [, column ] . . .) ] ] [ Resolution resolution ]
   [ Distributions Only ]
```

MS SQL Server

```
Update Statistics table [ index ]
```

Usage   The **Update Statistics** statement refreshes the statistical information used by the query optimizer to determine the most efficient way to solve a query.

> **Tip**
>
> *Using this statement whenever the number of records has changed significantly can really affect the performance of your database.*

Arguments   ▪ *proc*—the name of a stored procedure for which you wish to recalculate statistics.

▪ *table*—the name of a base table.

column—the name of a column in *table* for which you wish to recalculate statistics.
resolution—determines how small of an interval is used to track statistical information. For **Medium** this value will default to 3.5 percent. For **High** this value will default to 0.5 percent.
conf—specifies the confidence level that the statistics from **Medium** resolution will match those generated by specifying **High**.

Implementation Notes   Informix

There are three levels of statistics: **Low, Medium** and **High**. Each level processes more information to help the query optimizer build better queries, but at a cost of more time to collect and process the information. **High** will process every row in the table, while **Medium** uses statistical sampling to determine the same results.

See Also   **Create Index** (statement), **Create Table** (statement)

Use

STATEMENT

MS SQL Server • Sybase

Syntax   Use *database*

Usage   The **Use** statement switches to the new *database* from the current one.

Argument   ▪ *database*—the name of a database.

See Also   **Setuser** (statement)

Values

Syntax
```
Values { expr | ( expr [, expr ] . . . ) } Into { :hostvar | ( :hostvar [, :hostvar ] . . .
     ) }

Values { expr | ( expr [, expr ] . . . ) } [,{ expr | ( expr [, expr ] . . . ) } ] . . .
```

Usage   The **Values** statement is used to move a list of expressions into a series of host variables or to display a list of expressions in an interactive query session.

Arguments ▪ *expr*—an arbitrary expression that can be a column name, a parameter from a stored procedure, a variable, a numeric literal, a function that returns a numeric value, an expression enclosed by parentheses, or a table expression that returns a single numeric expression.

▪ *function*—the name of a routine to be called.

▪ *hostvar*—the name of a host variable containing a value for the return code.

See Also   **Select** (statement)

Whenever

Syntax
```
Whenever { Not Found | Sqlerror | Sqlwarning }
       {
           Continue |
           { Go To | Goto } [ : ] label |
           Stop |
           Call function
           Do function
           Exit [ Success | Failure | value | hostvar }
```

Usage   The **Whenever** statement is used in an application program to specify the action to be taken when a row is not found or an error or warning occurs. **Continue** means to ignore the error and continue processing. **Goto** means that control is transferred to the specified *label* in the program. **Stop** forces the program to stop execution immediately. **Call** means that *function* will be called each time an error is encountered. **Exit** forces the program to stop immediately and return either **Success**, **Failure**, or the specified return code.

Arguments   ▪ *label*—the name of a label in the host program.

▪ *function*—the name of a routine to be called.

▪ *value*—a constant that will be used as a return code.

▪ *hostvar*—the name of host variable containing a value for the return code.

Implementation Notes   IBM DB2   The **Stop**, **Call**, **Do** and **Exit** clauses are not supported.

Informix   The **Exit** and **Do** clauses are not supported.

Oracle   The **Goto**, **Stop**, and **Call** clauses are not supported.

See Also   **Execute** (statement), **Fetch** (statement)

Appendices

IV

Appendix A
About the Companion CD-ROM

The Companion CD-ROM included with your copy *The SQL Programmer's Reference* contains the entire book in hypertext format.

To Navigate the CD-ROM

To navigate the CD-ROM, please open the README.HTM file in your favorite browser. You will see a small menu with links to the chapters in the book.

Limits of Liability & Disclaimer of Warranty

The author and publisher of this book have used their best efforts in preparing the CD-ROM and the programs contained in it. These efforts include the development, research, and testing of the theories and programs to determine their effectiveness. The author and publisher make no warranty of any kind expressed or implied, with regard to these programs or the documentation contained in this book.

The author and publisher shall not be liable in the event of incidental or consequential damages in connection with, or arising out of, the furnishing, performance, or use of the programs, associated instructions, and/or claims of productivity gains.

Appendix B
Creating the Sample Database

The following SQL statements were used to create the sample tables used in the examples in this book. You can simply copy these statements from the Companion CD-ROM and paste them into your favorite database's interactive SQL query tool.

```
drop table Departments;

create table Departments (DeptNo Decimal(2), DeptName Char(40), Manager Decimal(4));

insert into Departments values
    (00, 'Headquarters', 1001),
    (10, 'Sales', 1003),
    (20, 'Shipping', 1005),
    (30, 'Research and Development', 1007),
    (40, 'Maintenance', 1010),
    (50, 'Assembly', 1012),
    (60, 'Accounting', 1017);

drop table Employees;

create table Employees (EmpNo Decimal(4), LName Char(16), FName Char(12), DeptNo
    Decimal(2), Salary Decimal(10,2));
```

```
insert into Employees values
    (1001, 'James', 'Christopher', 00, 125000.00),
    (1002, 'Ashley', 'Samantha', 00, 100000.00),

    (1003, 'Heyer', 'Jill', 10, 100000.00),
    (1004, 'Bucky', 'Raymond', 10, 90000.00),

    (1005, 'Williams', 'Wanda', 20, 35000.00),
    (1006, 'Applegate', 'Susan', 20, 25000.00),

    (1007, 'Freeze', 'Wayne', 30, 90000.00),
    (1008, 'Fleming', 'Shaun', 30, 80000.00),
    (1009, 'Blumgart', 'Ian', 30, 70000.00),

    (1010, 'Osborne', 'Chris', 40, 20000.00),
    (1011, 'Smith', 'Walter', 40, 15000.00),

    (1012, 'Kelly', 'Robert', 50, 30000.00),
    (1013, 'Tigger', 'Elwyn', 50, 27000.00),
    (1014, 'Dudley', 'Richard', 50, 25000.00),
    (1015, 'Jean', 'Bonnie', 50, 23000.00),
    (1016, 'Brigham', 'Linda', 50, 21000.00),

    (1017, 'Wyler', 'Robert', 60, 65000.00),
    (1018, 'Dau', 'Veronica', 60, 60000.00);

drop table Customers;

create table Customers (CustNo Decimal(4), Name Char(40), Address Char(32));

insert into Customers values
    (2001, 'Bucky''s Country Roundup', 'Davis, South Dakota'),
    (2002, 'Jill''s Just Plane Crazy', 'Beltsville, Maryland'),
    (2003, 'Marie''s Onsite Mainframes', 'Parkville, Maryland'),
    (2004, 'Waldo''s Antique Computers and Stuff', 'Baltimore, Maryland'),
    (2005, 'Barbara''s OnDisplays', 'Parkton, Maryland'),
    (2006, 'Terry''s Catnip Farm', 'College Park, Maryland'),
    (2007, 'Sargent Scott''s Seafood and Steakhouse', 'Laurel, Maryland'),
    (2008, 'Becky''s Kids Place', 'Tulsa, Oklahoma'),
    (2009, 'Tracy''s Treehouse', 'Duluth, Minnesota'),
    (2010, 'Peter''s Puppet Boutique', 'Scaggsville, Maryland'),
    (2011, 'Joan''s Technology Shop', 'Dallas, Texas'),
    (2012, 'Barbie''s House of Laptops', 'Bowie, Maryland'),
    (2013, 'Rosie''s Garden Shop', 'Richmond, Virginia'),
```

```
    (2014, 'Goose''s Kitty Katt Kitchen', 'Marion, South Dakota'),
    (2015, 'Jennifer''s Collectible Wheels', 'El Segundo, California'),
    (2016, 'Randy''s Universal Import-Export', 'Clarksville, Maryland');

drop table Items;

create table Items (ItemNo Decimal(4), ItemName Char(40), Cost Decimal(8,2));

insert into Items values
    (3001, 'The Big Comfy Laptop', 5000.00),
    (3002, 'The Tower Computer of Babel', 4000.00),
    (3003, 'The Desktop Daemon', 3000.00),
    (3004, 'The Big Bad Unix Workstation', 12000.00),
    (3005, 'The Itsy Bitsy Teenie Weenie Palmtop', 1000.00),
    (3006, 'The Monster Mainframe', 250000.00),
    (3007, 'The Modemraker', 250.00),
    (3008, 'The Backup to the Future Tape Drive', 750.00),
    (3009, 'The Smokey and the Disk Drive', 1100.00);

drop table Orders;

create table Orders (OrderNo Decimal(4), CustNo Decimal(4), SalesRep Decimal(4), Date
    Date);

insert into Orders values
    (9001, 2001, 1003, '10-1-1997'),
    (9002, 2002, 1004, '10-1-1997'),
    (9003, 2003, 1003, '10-2-1997'),
    (9004, 2004, 1004, '10-2-1997'),
    (9005, 2002, 1004, '10-2-1997'),
    (9006, 2005, 1004, '10-2-1997'),
    (9007, 2006, 1004, '10-3-1997'),
    (9008, 2001, 1003, '10-6-1997'),
    (9009, 2003, 1003, '10-7-1997'),
    (9010, 2004, 1004, '10-8-1997'),
    (9011, 2002, 1003, '10-8-1997'),
    (9012, 2007, 1003, '10-10-1997'),
    (9013, 2005, 1003, '10-13-1997'),
    (9014, 2008, 1004, '10-13-1997'),
    (9015, 2002, 1003, '10-13-1997'),
    (9016, 2009, 1004, '10-13-1997'),
    (9017, 2001, 1003, '10-14-1997'),
    (9018, 2003, 1003, '10-15-1997'),
    (9019, 2006, 1004, '10-15-1997'),
```

```
        (9020, 2010, 1003, '10-15-1997'),
        (9021, 2005, 1004, '10-17-1997'),
        (9022, 2001, 1003, '10-17-1997'),
        (9023, 2002, 1004, '10-20-1997'),
        (9024, 2004, 1003, '10-20-1997'),
        (9025, 2007, 1004, '10-20-1997'),
        (9026, 2009, 1003, '10-20-1997'),
        (9027, 2010, 1004, '10-21-1997'),
        (9028, 2011, 1004, '10-21-1997'),
        (9029, 2008, 1003, '10-22-1997'),
        (9030, 2001, 1003, '10-23-1997'),
        (9031, 2009, 1004, '10-24-1997'),
        (9032, 2011, 1004, '10-24-1997'),
        (9033, 2007, 1003, '10-24-1997'),
        (9034, 2012, 1003, '10-27-1997'),
        (9035, 2008, 1004, '10-27-1997'),
        (9036, 2013, 1003, '10-27-1997'),
        (9037, 2003, 1003, '10-27-1997'),
        (9038, 2014, 1003, '10-28-1997'),
        (9039, 2010, 1004, '10-28-1997'),
        (9040, 2004, 1004, '10-28-1997'),
        (9041, 2006, 1004, '10-28-1997'),
        (9042, 2009, 1003, '10-28-1997'),
        (9043, 2011, 1004, '10-28-1997'),
        (9044, 2001, 1003, '10-28-1997'),
        (9045, 2012, 1003, '10-28-1997'),
        (9046, 2015, 1004, '10-28-1997'),
        (9047, 2012, 1004, '10-28-1997'),
        (9048, 2002, 1004, '10-29-1997'),
        (9049, 2015, 1004, '10-30-1997'),
        (9050, 2016, 1003, '10-31-1997');

drop table OrderItems;

create table OrderItems (OrderNo Decimal(4), ItemNo Decimal(4), Quantity Decimal(4));

insert into OrderItems values
        (9001, 3001, 3),
        (9001, 3002, 3),
        (9001, 3003, 3),
        (9001, 3004, 3),
        (9001, 3005, 3),
        (9001, 3006, 2),
        (9002, 3005, 1),
        (9003, 3004, 4),
        (9004, 3008, 2),
```

```
(9005, 3001, 2),
(9005, 3002, 2),
(9006, 3003, 3),
(9007, 3007, 4),
(9007, 3008, 4),
(9007, 3009, 4),
(9008, 3003, 1),
(9009, 3007, 4),
(9009, 3008, 2),
(9009, 3009, 3),
(9010, 3001, 3),
(9010, 3003, 3),
(9011, 3004, 2),
(9012, 3005, 2),
(9013, 3005, 2),
(9014, 3001, 2),
(9014, 3002, 2),
(9014, 3003, 2),
(9014, 3004, 2),
(9014, 3005, 2),
(9015, 3001, 11),
(9016, 3003, 1),
(9017, 3007, 3),
(9017, 3008, 3),
(9017, 3009, 3),
(9018, 3001, 2),
(9018, 3002, 2),
(9019, 3001, 2),
(9019, 3002, 2),
(9020, 3003, 6),
(9020, 3004, 6),
(9021, 3003, 5),
(9021, 3004, 5),
(9022, 3005, 9),
(9023, 3004, 4),
(9025, 3001, 4),
(9025, 3002, 4),
(9025, 3003, 4),
(9025, 3004, 4),
(9026, 3007, 2),
(9026, 3008, 2),
(9026, 3009, 2),
(9027, 3002, 3),
(9028, 3001, 4),
(9029, 3005, 1),
```

```
(9030, 3006, 1),
(9031, 3005, 10),
(9032, 3004, 2),
(9032, 3005, 2),
(9033, 3002, 2),
(9033, 3004, 4),
(9034, 3001, 1),
(9034, 3002, 1),
(9035, 3003, 6),
(9035, 3009, 25),
(9036, 3001, 3),
(9036, 3002, 3),
(9036, 3003, 3),
(9037, 3006, 1),
(9038, 3002, 2),
(9038, 3004, 2),
(9038, 3007, 10),
(9038, 3008, 10),
(9038, 3009, 10),
(9039, 3001, 1),
(9040, 3001, 5),
(9040, 3002, 5),
(9041, 3005, 2),
(9042, 3002, 2),
(9042, 3003, 3),
(9043, 3001, 10),
(9043, 3002, 10),
(9044, 3006, 2),
(9045, 3003, 12),
(9045, 3004, 12),
(9045, 3005, 12),
(9046, 3002, 2),
(9046, 3003, 3),
(9047, 3001, 2),
(9047, 3002, 2),
(9048, 3002, 8),
(9049, 3001, 1),
(9050, 3001, 25),
(9050, 3002, 25),
```

```
     (9050, 3003, 25),
     (9050, 3004, 25),
     (9050, 3005, 25),
     (9050, 3006, 5),
     (9050, 3007, 25),
     (9050, 3008, 25),
     (9050, 3009, 25);

Select * from Departments;

Select * from Employees;

Select * from Customers;

Select * from Items;

Select * from Orders;

Select * from OrderItems;
```